Inside British Rail

Inside British Rail

Challenges and Progress on the Nationalised Railway 1970s–90s

Stephen Poole

The History Press

First published 2018

The History Press
The Mill, Brimscombe Port
Stroud, Gloucestershire, GL5 2QG
www.thehistorypress.co.uk

British Library Cataloguing in Publication Data.
A catalogue record for this book is available from the British Library.

ISBN 978 0 7509 8556 7

Typesetting and origination by The History Press
Printed and bound in Great Britain by TJ International Ltd

Contents

The Author

Stephen Poole was born in Norwich. In the 1960s he travelled to school in Hampshire behind steam engines and has been hooked on railways ever since.

Over a period of twenty years he worked for the Southern, London Midland and Western Regions of BR as well as for the Railfreight, InterCity and Network SouthEast business sectors, never staying long enough in any one job to become a true 'insider'. This gave him an insight not only into the internal complexities of the nationalised railway in its last two decades but also into the context in which the railway operated in terms of social, industrial, financial and political change.

After being made redundant as privatisation loomed, he worked for Eurotunnel and then as HM Inspector of Railways for the Health & Safety Executive and the Office of Rail Regulation. He now works independently, giving advice and guidance on railway safety and logistics as well as representing freight interests on the European Railway Traffic Management System project.

He now lives in York, having moved on average every six of his sixty-three years. When not visiting his daughter and granddaughter in Wales or his son in Leeds, he can often be seen in places all over the UK in the company of his real ale drinking friends. He now aspires to be a novelist and to live near the sea.

Stephen Poole appears in *The Nation's Railway: The Golden Age of British Rail* (BBC4 *Timeshift* series).

Author's Note

Seventy years ago the 'Big Four' British railway companies were taken into state ownership and then around fifty years later the nationalised British Rail was fragmented into more than ninety-five private companies. Both occasions, the second more politically motivated than the first, had lasting repercussions for users and for the working lives of railway people.

And twenty years on from privatisation the railway industry, its users and its staff still suffer from political, organisational and financial upheaval and controversy. The nationalisation *versus* privatisation argument rages on. The franchising concept causes problems for investment and attracts criticism of short-term profiteering at the public expense. Costs of major projects such as Great Western electrification and HS2 are soaring and require teams of experts, lawyers and consultants to establish and then manage the aspirations, responsibilities and liabilities of the multitude of separate companies involved. Some franchisees still run the dreadful 'Pacer' units, which BR had introduced as a temporary expedient in the 1980s, while others 'sweat the assets' of trains built by BR in the 1970s. Journey times on some routes are greater than they were under BR and fares are sometimes punitively high despite the substantial and creditable growth in passenger numbers.

Bold improvements such as London Overground and the Borders Railway have been public sector initiatives. By contrast the private-sector companies show little or no interest in providing a range of BR's former activities such as parcels, Motorail, mail on passenger trains, wagonload freight, out-of-gauge loads, cross-country sleeper trains and overnight seating trains, as well as shipping, hovercraft and hotels.

So it may be opportune to take a look back at how things really were in the days of state ownership. This book is a revision of *Behind the Crumbling*

Edge, my 2002 book, which was enthusiastically endorsed by the former Chairman of BR, the late Sir Peter Parker. In it I give an insight into a great variety of BR activities, told mainly from my personal experience as a railwayman from 1973 onwards.

My 2002 text remains unchanged, other than for a few minor corrections, updates and explanatory notes. So the book is essentially still my take on the railway industry as it was in the immediate post-privatisation era, but put into a 2018 context.

Stephen Poole

Introduction

One word sums up what was happening on BR in the 1970s, 1980s and 1990s: 'reorganisation'. This was the inescapable word for anyone who worked for the railway in the last decades of BR and one that eventually culminated in the breaking up of the nationalised network just short of its fiftieth anniversary into twenty-five passenger train companies, a track authority and more than seventy other companies to look after freight, engineering, catering, research, etc. I was greeted with the word even at my first interview for a railway job, back in 1973. The Field Organisation Report, devised by McKinsey and Co. Inc. on behalf of the British Railways Board, was due to be adopted with the consequent abolition of the South Eastern Divisional Manager's Office at Beckenham in south-east London. I was being offered a job there as a clerical officer and at my interview it was made clear that, as the last one in, I would be the first one out in the new, slimmer organisation.

I took the risk, I took the job. I survived and hung on through many reorganisations, with their consequent displacements and relocations. From this apparent misfortune I was able to experience the enormous diversity of railway activities described in this book – freight, passenger, parcels, sales, sleeping cars, track maintenance, traction control, etc. But much of that was only after the momentum for real change had actually been established, which was not until the 1980s. I quickly learned in the early days, by contrast, that while the railway management of the 1970s could talk *ad infinitum* about reorganisation, they were thwarted in its actual implementation because the railway was hampered with so many departments and tiers that all needed to be consulted about everything. It was also bogged down in a quicksand of trade union negotiation procedures that ensured any initiative was either stifled or was out of date before it could be implemented. So it was that the very things that most needed to be changed were the very things that stopped change from happening. But I don't think the railway was alone in this and neither was it necessarily a sign of an ailing, monolithic nationalised industry. It was part of British corporate life at the time.

Endless rounds of correspondence between the numerous departments; meetings up and down the unwieldy hierarchical and cross-functional tiers; and negotiations with trade union representatives at three or more levels all simply resulted in ideas going round and round until they were submerged in a quagmire of complexity and meaninglessness. Indeed, the Field Organisation itself, with its eight 'Territories' (to replace five Regions and twenty Divisions), foundered in the morass and was eventually put to rest in 1976. In that way the Divisional Manager's Office at Beckenham was saved – and managed, in fact, to hang on for another eleven years after I was told it was about to go. On the stairs of Euston House one day in 1974, when the Field Organisation was still thought likely to take over, John Palette was pointed out to me by my boss as 'Territorial Director, North-West (Designate)'. Years later, when I next saw him, he was presiding over the largely unreformed Southern Region from the wood-panelled general manager's office at Waterloo, much as if Sir Herbert Walker's Southern Railway of the 1930s and '40s still existed. Indeed, the Regions contrived, right up to 1991, to cling to the railway grouping heritage of 1923 that Field was supposed to have abolished and which nationalisation, or so one might have thought, was meant at the very least to have undermined. No wonder that Dr Michael Bonavia described the Regions as 'immortal' in his November 1976 *Modern Railways* article on the subject.

'Field' epitomised the railway organisational debate, which is as relevant now in the privatised era as it was then: should the railway be run on geographical principles, such as McKinsey's proposed Territories and the actually implemented Areas? Or should it be run on the basis of the historic lines of route, such as the South Eastern Division of the 1970s (and again of the early '90s) and the revived Great Western of InterCity and of First Group under privatisation? Or should it be run on functional lines, as with the separated businesses of Railfreight, InterCity, Red Star, etc. and now of Network Rail and the Train Operating Companies? Or, finally, should there be a combination of two or more of these systems? All have been tried, with varying degrees of success as the emphasis, largely politically led, has changed.

'The politicians could never make up their minds about railway organisation,' wrote Sir John Elliot in his Foreword to A.J. Pearson's *Man of the Rail*.

That was in 1967 but it holds true just as much today. The decisive Parliamentary victories of 1945 and 1979, one Labour and the other Conservative, each resulted in fundamental changes in the social, industrial and financial climate of Britain. How could the railway industry, dependent as it was upon Treasury largesse, hope to escape the effects of this? Of course, it couldn't – and now, as we enter a new millennium, we have the effects of another landslide victory for Labour, with its tighter regulatory stance and the advent of the Strategic Rail Authority.* And so the story continues.

Although the railway of the 1970s was impeded in changing itself in the ways I have described, things did change eventually. And the pace of change accelerated with the years, affecting each and every person who worked in the industry as management faintheartedness and political whim were gradually transformed into management brutality and political dictatorship. Very many things changed: some discreetly and some with all the subtlety of battlefield surgery. Political shifts, modernisation, rationalisation, accountability, the retail culture and staff productivity were just some of the broad headings of change. As an indication of the scale of change, over the last twenty or so years of BR, the annual turnover more than quadrupled to just over £4,500 million, despite the disposal of so many subsidiaries, while staff numbers declined by around 50 per cent. Passenger miles increased by 8 per cent to nearly 20,000 million per year while freight tonnage decreased by 30 per cent to under 140 million tonnes per year, but with a decline in the number of wagons to just 20,000 – a reduction of 92 per cent. First Railfreight and later InterCity freed themselves from the need for Government subsidy and BR ended up requiring a grant of £1,617 million for other passenger services in its last year, a figure increased to the £1,813 million paid by the Government to its private sector successors in 1996/7. Even InterCity's successors received

* 2018 update: The Strategic Rail Authority was very short-lived. The Labour Government lasted longer but did not reverse any of the privatisation measures.

more than £300 million of taxpayers' money that same year – in other words £300 million more than BR had required.

To achieve this scale of change, the railway reshaped itself, or was reshaped, sometimes with breathtaking arrogance, sometimes with all the loose hilarity of a TV sitcom and sometimes with a whimper, almost unnoticed. Decay and improvement, stringency and extravagance, despair and hope: they all ran alongside, amongst, above and beneath each other, strands of each fluttering in the wind and, occasionally, falling off at the fringes. In February 1977 the Chairman of the British Railways Board, Mr (later Sir) Peter Parker told the Government's Select Committee on Nationalised Industries of the 'crumbling edge of standards' on the railway. In this book I look not only at the 'crumbling edge' but also at the day-to-day realities of the writhing body behind it that struggled at times just to carry on.

Ever since being told in 1973 that my position on the railway was insecure I sat on the fence, dodged from department to department (sixteen jobs in twenty years) and observed what was going on, never quite feeling that I was a lasting part of it. This book is a fairly informal look at how things actually were and at how the concepts appeared to an 'outsider' on the inside. It is not meant to be a comprehensive account of any one or more aspects of the railway, but I hope it gives an idea of what was really going on day by day and night by night far from (but still, inevitably, touched by) the ideology, dogma and aspirations of the politicians, media and image makers. I hope it also shows that the railway was, and to some extent still is, far more diverse and complex than those same people could possibly imagine.

In giving this insight, I do not attempt to exhaust one subject at a time or, indeed, at all and nor do I stick to a chronological account of events. The reason for this is at the essence of what I am trying to show, which is that no one topic is capable of being isolated from others. In a complicated, vast and multi-functional industry things cropped up at different times, in different places and in different contexts, each time giving a different slant on interweaving arguments, both old and new.

Acknowledgements

I gratefully acknowledge the help of the following: The librarians at the Chartered Institute of Transport Library, Ashford Railway Library and University of Kent Library; John Bateson and Mike Denny of Roundel Design; 'High Speed Jim' Evans; Allan Barter; Brian Garvin; Bob Fridd and others who have helped with information and encouragement.

1

Computers, Engines and Ivory Towers

In the early 1970s BR had bought and installed, at a cost of around £10 million, a computerised vehicle management system developed by the USA's Southern Pacific Railroad. TOPS (Total Operations Processing System) was a fairly crude, punchcard system that the SP had found difficult to implement because they had so many handover points to and from other operators who either used different control systems or had none at all. In 1979 I visited the Freight Office of the SP in Austin, Texas, and found that they were still using TOPS as it had been when sold to BR several years earlier. Indeed, I was able to load the 'consist' for a train to Llano into their machine without difficulty.

Britain's railway system, having only the Harwich and Dover trainferries as outlets at the time, was better suited to TOPS and huge developments in its scope were made over the years. The Western Region had a further advantage in this respect: it had a busy freight network with only one outlet, this being the West of England line beyond Exeter. This was therefore an ideal proving ground for TOPS and, as a first step towards eventual national use, all freight movements in this area were put on to the new system. In 1975, at the time TOPS was extended to cover locomotive control and maintenance, I was working as an Assistant Traction Controller at Western Region HQ, Paddington. Our system of colour-coded tickets (one for each 'nag', as we called them at the time), upon which we recorded by hand every locomotive movement and the hours taken, as well as faults and other peculiarities, was supplemented and eventually replaced by TOPS. On the night shift for a couple of weeks we were accompanied by the TOPS Implementation Team, who showed us how to use the new system and invited us to devise our own TOPS enquiries and procedures to make the system work better for us. Broadly speaking, the implementation of TOPS led to the conclusion that the Western Region had been over-maintaining lots of its locomotives because we had been putting too many hours' use on the tickets. Traction maintenance on the WR was based on hours in traffic. Over-maintenance, extravagance and slow realisation of cost-saving possibilities will be a recurring theme in this book.

Locomotive control on BR in the 1970s was a very chaotic affair, with the five Regions having different systems, different fleets and huge jealousies – and all this a mere twenty-five years after nationalisation. Amongst loco controllers, the Eastern Region had the best reputation for actually knowing where all its engines were, but against this they had a strange system of giving them 'A' exams (known on the WR as the 'tickle brush') every three days, almost regardless of how much or how little work each machine had done. Owning Regions had the power to insist that their locomotives be stopped for examination when due, whether on or off the home Region. On one occasion the Eastern Region Traction Controller at York instructed me to ensure that one of his Class 45 locos, which had been standing at Bristol Bath Road for two days, be given an 'A' exam before being used again. Since its previous exam it had only run from Newcastle to Bristol. Of course, one may well ask why an expensive machine had been standing idle for two days.

Over-maintenance and over-provision kept a whole range of small depots in existence, some at relatively obscure places such as Worcester and Newton Abbot. The resulting amount of locomotive 'downtime' was phenomenal, especially on a railway such as the Western with no electrification and therefore needing fuelling time for its fleet as well as maintenance time. For years the Western resisted all pressure to electrify and even now the only wires are for the BAA-operated Heathrow Express and the Eurostar depot.* The Great Western itself remained for years as resolutely 'diesel only' as it wanted to be in 1954 when, in assessing the requirements for modernisation, all the Regions expressed 'a distinct preference for electric traction instead

* 2018 update: The Eurostar depot is now at Temple Mills in east London and GWR electrification is making limited and costly progress westwards.

of diesel, with the exception of the Western ...' (A.J. Pearson, *Man of the Rail*). The Western somehow carried the day, though, with the 1955 Modernisation Plan being mainly based on diesel traction. In capital terms diesel was, of course, the cheaper option.

The implications of lasting Regional independence and self-assertion were numerous and largely counter-productive. We had our fair share as Traction Controllers. The Western had persisted with the installation of GWR Automatic Warning System (AWS), which was not the same as the BR AWS being introduced on the rest of the railway. This meant that many Western diesels were route-restricted. In particular, the GWR AWS equipment fitted under the engines played havoc with the fourth-rail return feed on lines shared with London Transport. These locomotives were slowly being refitted with standard equipment and the GWR AWS magnets on the track were all removed by late 1975. By how long and at what cost the national implementation of this vital safety equipment was delayed by the Western's early intransigence is a matter of debate. Nevertheless, credit is due to the GWR for starting the implementation of AWS even if the particular form caused problems. Their system had its origins before the First World War while, in contrast, the Southern Region of BR had no form of AWS until the 1970s.

We guarded our own Regional locomotive fleets jealously, even though most machines could in fact travel anywhere on the railway. A favourite trick when traction was short was to send a type of locomotive on an inter-Regional working that could not be driven by the receiving Region's crews. In that way the traction always came back home and the other Region had to find power for the next leg of the working. Accordingly, we would put the diesel-hydraulic Class 52 'Westerns', which could only be driven by Western crews, on services to Birmingham while the London Midland would send Class 20s in pairs to Severn Tunnel Junction or would let the cumbersome sixteen-wheeled Class 40s come creeping in on overnight freights via Craven Arms, in the knowledge that Western crews were not trained to drive them.

When it came to the nightly inter-Regional locomotive balance, which was struck between all Regions' Traction Controllers and the BRB representative at 0600hrs each morning, we had to include in our favour all these locomotives that were of no use to us. In dire circumstances of imbalance we would be instructed by the Board to redress matters by double-heading trains out of the Region, but if in reality the imbalance consisted in part of engines we couldn't use, the result was the cancellation of internal services. Thus the words 'CAPE, no power', meaning cancelled, would reverberate through the telephone and teleprinter lines of a Region that, on paper, had a surplus of power. The balance was struck not only in terms of numbers but also of types. So, for instance, in the case of the unusable Class 20s arriving at Severn Tunnel Junction, the Western would be shown as having two Type 1s when it should have had none. The balance would therefore be shown as +2.

The problems caused by the inter-Regional balancing mechanism were numerous. On one occasion while I was at Paddington the day shifts had failed to rectify a locomotive imbalance between ourselves and the London Midland Region, resulting in the Board intervening and instructing us to send the LMR the requisite number of engines before the end of our night shift. The LMR, being bigger and better organised than the WR, could generally wield more clout in these matters. In this case the only way to fulfil the instruction was by using freight services from South Wales, even though the surplus was in fact at the London end of the Region. So we had to decimate our internal night freight services at the same time as double-heading freights to the LMR. No one was in a position to take a strategic view of the benefits or otherwise of this upheaval as the Board's representative on nights was only a recorder – a clerical officer employed to initiate pre-determined procedures rather than to make decisions in his own right. The next day what was by then an internal imbalance between South Wales and London was put right by double-heading passenger trains from Paddington, which should have happened the previous day. Whether the shortage of traction on the LMR would have led to a greater loss of revenue than did our internal cancellations was not considered. Operating at that time was distinctly separate from commercial considerations, the two only meeting reluctantly and at arms' length when timetable and resource changes were made.

Western traction of the mid 1970s consisted of Type 2 (Classes 25 and 31), Type 3 (Class 37) and Type 4 (such as Classes 46, 47, 50 and 52). Additionally, there were some lingering oddments: the experimental 1961 Brush locomotive D0280 *Falcon* was seeing out its days as a merry-go-round pilot on the coal circuit at Barry Docks, for example. Amidst this diverse plethora of ageing machines, the prototype Advanced Passenger Train and

the High Speed Diesel Train were be
HSDT had established a new wor
141mph and was well on its way to
on the Western Region in 1976,
Preparations were being made at
Controller, the 'D' having mysteri
having been no more than yet a
electrification' policy. The 125,
symbolise British success in ter
impact and survives today wit
than just a nose cone: the 125 was a comp
speed improvements and innovations in passenger coach design a
In its first two years on the Bristol and South Wales routes, business rose by 33 per cent. In the meantime, though, our express passenger services struggled on with Class 47 and Class 50 engines, limited to 95mph and 100mph respectively, helped out, of course, by our exclusive fleet of Class 52 diesel-hydraulics and a few Class 46s. Classes from other Regions worked on to the Western as well: not only the LMR 20s and 40s already mentioned but also most notably 33s from the Southern and 45s from the Eastern.

The HST (InterCity 125) is a lasting testament to British design and engineering, as well as to BR's ability to run national projects in a way barely feasible nowadays. In its original livery, a set waits at Plymouth. (Photo: Caley Photographic)

[illegible] Welsh coal, steel and chemical industries were still [illegible] there was a huge tonnage of traffic each night trickling [illegible]eight-only valley lines and then trundling over the Regional [illegible]d Supervisors, through their Freight Controllers, were forever [illegible]pecials to clear surplus traffic and in those days, as well as one or [illegible]gines being needed for each train, a Driver, Secondman and Guard [illegible]also required – a far cry from today's single manning. Many engines [illegible]ld not run in multiple with each other and so if double-heading was [illegible]eeded, two crews were necessary and the engines had to run in tandem, both being driven separately. Of the entire fleet of Class 47 locomotives, in effect the BR standard engine of the day, only two were fitted for multiple working at that time. These two, based on the Eastern Region, were known unofficially as Tweedledee and Tweedledum. How frequently they were at the same place at the same time when double-heading was actually needed I wouldn't like to say.

Until the virtual abolition of coal mining in the 1980s, huge tonnages of coal made their way down the numerous Welsh Valley lines for onward movement to many parts of the country. Here 37279 leads a coal train through Taffs Well. (Photo: Adrian Brennan)

In addition to these heavy traction and crew costs, the main freight route from South Wales was via Bromsgrove, where banking engines were needed for the notorious and spectacular 1 in 39 Lickey incline. Even sleeper trains needed assistance here, although most other passenger trains could manage the bank unaided. Two Class 37s from Cardiff Canton were employed at Bromsgrove on each shift as bankers – another expensive operation, at which no one apparently batted an eyelid.

About the only fully brake-fitted freight trains in the mid 1970s were the company block trains and merry-go-round coal trains. Most other freight trains were a mixture of unfitted or vacuum-fitted wagons, needing a brakevan at the rear. Some passenger trains were still vacuum braked as well and some were still steam heated. So as well as a multitude of classes of locomotives there was a great diversity of characteristics and staffing needs. A steam-heated passenger train needed the Secondman to operate the steam boiler. Many engines were stripped of their boilers, or never had them, the resulting space sometimes being occupied by blocks of concrete to aid traction. Others could provide vacuum braking or air braking only, some were permanently speed-limited and others would have one or more traction motors out of use, with varying degrees of permanency. So allocating and controlling these fleets was a complex affair, made even more confusing by the fact that proper class numbering was only just coming in.

The old numbering system gave little indication of type or capability – you simply had to know which loco was which and of what it was capable. Mistakes were made, perhaps inevitably, from time to time. Most mistakes resulted in cancellation or delay to services, while some meant that passenger trains ran without heat or at reduced speed, or that freight trains ran with reduced loads. Occasionally, though, a mistake would lead to unsafe working. On 2 June 1976 a passenger train had become derailed at Reading West Junction as a result of locomotive 50019 having a loose metal tyre, which had come adrift and had jammed in a set of points. After this, special attention was given to the examination of the fitting, profile and wear of tyres. One victim of this was 47257 of Cardiff Canton depot, which was limited to 40mph until its wheels could be refitted. Despite the restriction being shown in the Driver's book in the cab and on our locomotive control ticket, 47257 was put on to a Swansea–Paddington express one day, the mistake only coming to light when the loco number was passed to Reading Control. The train was stopped on signals somewhere near Didcot and proceeded at caution to Reading for a traction change. An internal enquiry ensued from which I, as Assistant Traction Controller on the South Wales panel that day, did not emerge with credit. I had entered the detail of the trip to London on the locomotive ticket without query, despite it having the coloured tab attached to it to signify the restricted working conditions. Full implementation of TOPS, with the generation of automatic warnings, would have stopped this sort of thing. But that was still to come.

As Traction Controllers we soon realised that the new TOPS locomotive control screens could be used for more than they were intended. The freeform message facility, known as 'ZZ', could be used to send messages from and to any screen or printer and, once this had been discovered, it was widely misused, especially on nights. Being a novice to the system (as we all were, of course), one of our Maintenance Controllers, known as Pal, was rather laboriously working through a screenful of information one night, updating the records as he went along when his screen was suddenly wiped clear and the message 'PAL FOR THE TWO O'CLOCK BREW' flashed up instead. The night air of Bayswater was shattered by the cry of 'Which *bastard* did that?' So we learned that ZZ messages wiped off anything you already had on your screen. Perhaps a quarter of a century later it really wouldn't hurt me to say, 'Sorry, Pal!'

All these activities took place in the attic of the Western Region HQ alongside Platform 1 at Paddington, although we overlooked Eastbourne Terrace rather than the station. The room was a disgrace in terms of decoration and maintenance: the walls were streaked with yellow–brown smears from the combined efforts of nicotine stains and a leaking roof, the window frames were rotten and out in the corridor there were pigeons nesting above the holes in the ceiling. Very strangely for a Region so proud of its past and of its independence this same dingy, inaccessible and dead-end corridor served as a gallery for framed photographs of past general managers, whose stern moustached faces peered out in the gloom at the surrounding dereliction.

Our telephone consoles at Paddington Control, into which we plugged our individual head or hand sets, were decrepit in the extreme. It was rumoured that they had been bought from the Ministry of Defence at the end of the Second World War for scrap value, being clapped out even then. Incoming calls were indicated by small flashing lights of different colours and not by any sort of sound. By no means all of the Western Region was yet covered by BR Extension Trunk Dialling and it was sometimes necessary to go through two operators before you could be switched through to the person with whom you wanted to speak. Sometimes it was simpler to use outside lines. What a contrast this was from the Southern Region, which had installed its first proper switchboard as far back as 1925 and had direct dialling to all locations within its boundaries. But then, as I have said, the Southern had no AWS. The ways in which I found different parts of the system to have developed in different ways and at different speeds as I moved around over the years was always a cause of fascination to me, the more so as I had fondly imagined when I joined that BR was one railway.

When not required on the Traction desk, I was often asked to cover the Assistant Freight Controller's job at Paddington. This post was unique as it was the only Milk Controller in the country and I think I was the last person to be trained in this role. To do the 'milk' you sat at a desk with a three-part slotted board in front of you, with a ticket for each milk tank wagon, rather like the traction control tickets. Colour codes indicated the ownership of the tanks and, although they could all be used as a common pool, the Controller would try to get the right company's tanks to the right place at the right time to meet the producers' stated demands. This avoided the payment of user fees from one company to another.

Milk trips ran from various dairies to the yards and the main trunk train ran up from St Erth to Acton Yard each evening, combining at Swindon with the South Wales trunk train from Whitland. In the early hours the trunk train was split at Acton and further trips took the wagons to the private sidings at the London distribution dairies such as Cricklewood, Vauxhall, Morden South, Ilford and Wood Lane – all now closed to rail freight. It would have been interesting to have assessed the ratio of train crew numbers to gallons of milk for these trips, but cost in those days did not seem to be a priority.

In the hot summer of 1975 there was a glut of milk in the West Country. We were able to make extra revenue by running surplus milk to Swindon and Carlisle on specials. Things became so bad (or, for us, so good) that the producers booked specials some days just to make space in the dairies. So we would send a Class 25 and crew to Chard Junction, for instance, take out the loaded tanks and return them, still loaded, later in the day. Eventually, of course, the milk went off, so then we were booked up to run specials to the creameries, one of which was miles along a freight-only line up in the hills beyond Carmarthen at Felin Fach. This was good for revenue and excellent for job satisfaction in that it took a lot of arranging. At that time, before anyone had worked out how much it really cost and before the words 'resource attribution' had been coined, there was still a great deal of flexibility in the system just waiting to be exploited in circumstances such as these.

The milk tanks, though, were outdated in comparison with the smart, chilled delivery vehicles of the road operators and when the decision had to be made as to whether or not to renew the fleet, the investment could not be justified by the Milk Marketing Board and the traffic was progressively lost to road. The milk-only branches such as Felin Fach and Hemyock disappeared and the regular milk contract ran out in October 1980. However, to bring the story more up to date, trial loads of milk tanks ran from Penrith to Cricklewood in around 2001, operated by Direct Rail Services. The advantage this time was that the milk was moved in piggyback trailers, which could then go to the London dairies without the need for the lightly loaded trip workings that made our operation both cumbersome and expensive, in terms of traction and crew resources as well as of infrastructure costs at the dairies.

Some of the 'freight-only' lines were sometimes used for weekend passenger train diversions when the main lines were being renewed. The long, straggling Vale of Glamorgan route, for instance, would be used if the main line between Bridgend and Cardiff was blocked, while a complicated move into the hills at Tondu would be made if the line towards Port Talbot was closed.* The winding, largely derelict and now closed route via Honeybourne to Stratford-upon-Avon would occasionally even be pressed into service if the line via Bromsgrove was out for engineering work. In the days before business sectorisation all these lines were seen simply as Western Region lines, for use as the Western saw fit, rather than being charged to the freight or passenger businesses. Overall business aspirations were subordinate to Regional interests in those days and, indeed, the Regions were the businesses, just as if there had never been such a thing as nationalisation.

* 2018 update: These two lines now both have regular passenger services again, but it is doubtful if this would have happened if they had not been retained for freight use in the meantime.

Distribution logistics made the Western Region Milk Controller's job interesting, but the grubby, unrefrigerated tank wagons were no match for the smart, chilled road competition. D1070 *Western Gauntlet* works a milk train through Plymouth. (Photo: Adrian Brennan)

The alternative routes existed mainly because of the heavy coal and steel traffic that originated at that time in various parts of Britain and which formed the mainstay of the railway freight system and, arguably, of the system as a whole. The severe contraction of the steel industry and the virtual elimination of the coal industry since then has resulted in the abolition of hundreds of route miles of railway, including many that were used for passenger diversions.

Apart from the milk, the other Western Region freight 'institution' was the Perishables, which also ran up from Cornwall to London daily, carrying produce from the mild climate of the Scilly Isles and the Penzance area for the London markets. The Assistant Freight Controller helped the Freight Controller in arranging the running of this train as well as the multitude of general and block services. Handwritten records were kept of loadings and timekeeping, of surplus traffic left behind, of specials arranged, of cancellations and of other information required from time to time by the daytime freight office. A 'yard state' of traffic on hand at each yard was recorded at the end of each shift so that priorities for the next shift could be established. At that time every railway Controller had his 'sheets', to be filled in during the turn of duty. Teams of Clerical Officers would then pore over these in the day, analysing loading patterns, creating timekeeping statistics and passing on intelligence to various managers. The only thing that no one ever knew then was how much it really cost to do anything – the locomotive fleet was common to passenger, freight, parcels and engineers' uses. Track and signalling seemed to be retained if there was a demand, no matter how small that demand might be. And, somewhat strangely, this was despite the need for greater cost awareness highlighted by the controversy over the closures policy of the Beeching era. The Parliamentary Select Committee examining huge railway losses in 1960 had reported that 'it appeared that neither the accounting system nor the costing techniques ... have yet been developed enough to show precisely where the loss is being caused'. So it was that on the basis of figures that were possibly spurious a lot of lines closed. Fifteen years later it was much the same, except, for some reason, the lines didn't close.

Nobody asked why we kept the straggling country branch line to Hemyock and I am sure that no one ensured that the full cost of its retention was included in the rates charged for the milk traffic that occasionally used it. This was because no one really knew how much anything did cost in isolation from the mass. In an article in *The Journal of Transport History* (March 1993), R.J. Irving makes the point that 'railway rates were not set on a product cost basis, and it was rare for the profitability of individual components of total railway business to be examined in anything like strict accountancy terms'. This was in the context of branch-line finances in the first decade of the twentieth century, but it seems to me that it applied equally to most parts of the railway seventy years later.

Similarly, we had lots of poorly used coal lines in the valleys. It some cases it was an all-day job for a crew and engine to traverse these lines, stopping to open and close rickety level crossing gates as they struggled along weed-strewn tracks, with probably only a few coal empties for a load. It seemed odd that after all the heartache of the heavy passenger closures during and after Beeching there were still so many lines left intact for occasional freight use. One might have thought that full costs would have been stripped out as soon as possible but this is something the railway was never very good at doing. Of course, some resources were removed. Loops and sidings slowly disappeared over the years as patterns of traffic changed but usually only when the mainline to which they joined fell due for renewal. This was then on the basis of saving engineering renewal expense by sacrificing operational convenience. Commercial justification for the retention of many of these facilities had ended years earlier but in the operations-led railway of the 1960s and '70s they remained as refuges, recess sidings and emergency stabling points, being pressed into service maybe a couple of times a year.

During this era, loose-coupled freights still shunted at every yard and the sight of a full freight yard was taken as an indication that we were doing well. Only later came the realisation that a full freight yard indicated only that the customers' traffic was standing still, that resources were idle and, consequently, that land, track, signalling, wagons and staff were all being used unproductively. Many railway people bemoaned the closure of freight marshalling yards such as Acton, Norwood and Feltham, overlooking the fact that freight should be moving and not hanging around in yards.

So much of the railway at that time existed for its own sake, or simply because it had always been there. The Regional Controls, such as the ones at Paddington and Waterloo in which I worked, were only there because there were Regions responsible to the Board for the running of the railway in their areas. But there were also Divisional Controls, which were more closely associated with the actual running of trains and which made arrangements during times of disruption. To some extent the Regional Controls merely relayed information to and from the Divisions, other Regions or the Board.

Hierarchical jealousies were rife: station and yard staff largely despised and made fun of Divisional Controls and they, in turn, regarded the Regional Controls with disdain. Appellations such as 'Fawlty Towers' and 'The Ivory Tower' abounded. There were closely guarded communication channels – only a Regional office could speak to another Regional office and the only Regional office that could speak to a Divisional office was that Division's own. So, for instance, if the Supervisor at Dover Town Yard had a special trainload of imported cars to go to Wakefield, which was quite a common occurrence, he would tell the Area 3 Controller at Beckenham Divisional Control. That Controller would arrange traction, crew and path, if available, and would tell the Regional Control at Waterloo. They would offer the train to the Eastern Region's HQ Control at York, who would offer it to Leeds

Divisional Control. Leeds would then offer the special to the Supervisor at Wakefield and the acceptance, or otherwise, of the special would make its way back to Dover by the same channels. Only then would wheels turn. The only function of the Regional Controls in this case would be to relay the message, reinforcing my point that they were only there because the administrative structure needed them for its own sake.

Some Divisions even had sub-Controls, adding another tier to every negotiation. The Western's sub-Control at Plymouth largely survived because of the awful state of the telephone system west of Exeter that made it difficult for staff at the West of England Divisional office at Bristol to communicate with locations in that area. The Plymouth Controllers tried their best to make sure that activities in their area were not understood by anyone else and that nothing happened that might provoke intervention by Bristol or Paddington. In this way they perpetuated their own retention. Similarly, the LMR's Stoke Division had a sub-control at Chester.

Rivalry between Regional Controls was common, too. I have mentioned the nightly locomotive feuds, in which the Eastern considered themselves to be the elite in one sense. Conversely, the Southern was universally ridiculed as the 'tramway' by the other Regions. In the eyes of the Western, London Midland, Eastern and possibly Scottish Regions the Southern had no proper locomotives and no real freight. On the other hand, Southern Region Controllers and Signalmen would laugh if they heard other Regions' staff talking about the 'rush hour'. Only Liverpool Street Control was considered by the Southern to know anything about a rush hour. Even outside the rush hour the Southern was much busier than the others in terms of total train movements: as Area 2 Controller at Beckenham in the late 1970s I had thirty-four passenger trains each hour starting, terminating or passing through my area. And that was the off-peak service, which was in addition to cement, coal and gypsum trains to and from Northfleet, Halling and Swanscombe, oil trains to and from the Isle of Grain, Cliffe aggregates trains, Hoo Junction wagonload services and other odd movements, such as Slade Green depot workings. The Area 3 Controller, whose post I covered regularly from 1976 to 1979, had the Dover–Dunkerque train ferry traffic to arrange as well as the distribution of coal empties to the Kent collieries. There were also parcel van train movements that peaked as Christmas approached, with specials being arranged and bay platforms at obscure stations being brought into service

More than 100 trains per hour were signalled over Borough Market Junction (near London Bridge) during the morning and evening peaks by one Signalman from this box. With this volume of traffic, the Southern defied other Regions to talk about the 'rush hour'. (Photo: Brian Garvin)

for just a few days each year for loading and unloading. Similarly, there were fleets of vans kept all year for the seasonal rush. So the Southern was, in actual fact, far from a purely commuter railway, just as the others were far from purely freight or InterCity.

Even within Regions there was rivalry. Whilst the other Regions poked fun at the Southern for its supposed lack of freight, the South Eastern and South Western Divisions of the Southern did the same with the Central Division, which really did have a negligible amount of freight, while the South Eastern jealously regarded the South Western's operation as child's play with all its flying junctions instead of the horrendous flat junctions every few miles that characterised the South Eastern. To this day, the commercial and operating aspirations of railway people are still governed to some extent by the legacy of Victorian railway construction, the well-engineered lines providing more opportunities for speed and for additional train paths, with the ones built by the poorer companies still suffering from congestion caused not only by volume of traffic but also by constraints of gradient, curvature, flat junctions, narrow track formations, small bridges, etc.

2

Go Anywhere, Do Anything

Our remit as Controllers in the 1970s was to attempt to run the full timetabled service and to provide resources for the clearance of surplus traffic. Nobody ever added the caveat 'at a reasonable cost'. So it was that train crews were offered huge amounts of overtime while engines and stock ran large distances light or empty to carry out special movements. Staff travelled miles in taxis, maybe just to work one trip from Grove Park to Bromley North. Whilst covering the South Eastern Guards Controller's job one afternoon I arranged to cover the last Charing Cross to Hastings service with an Orpington Guard on overtime, with a taxi to get him back from Hastings after midnight. Such extravagances took place every day. The Roster office gave the Guards Controller a daily list, known as the 'board', of duties they had been unable to cover. At the all too frequent times of chronic staff shortage the board could consist of more than forty trains and it was the duty of the Controller to attempt to cover these by juggling duties around and by offering overtime. Needless to say, there was a fair bit of sharp practice as well.

Some of us used to enjoy the logistical challenges this entailed. Moves could involve three-way swaps between Guards to get one of them to the right place at the right time. One day I arranged for Guards on up and down trains to change over with each other at Chilham, which is an unstaffed station in the Kent countryside, in order to avoid a delay to one of the trains at Ashford. Possibly that was the one and only time Chilham had seen a crew change. Much depended on staff passing on messages accurately and it may have been that the effort was at times out of all proportion to the benefit.

From 1976 to 1979 I was a Relief Controller on the South Eastern and we had a proud boast amongst ourselves that Relief Controllers would cover more Guards turns than the regular Guards Controllers, would run more specials than the regular Area Controllers and in general would get up to more jiggery-pokery than the regulars would to get things moving. One Saturday night I ran a special freight from Temple Mills to Dover Town. Because of engineering work it had to take a most indirect route, running round twice on the way. One of these runrounds involved the train being left in the platform at Swanley while the engine ran 5 miles to St Mary Cray Junction to cross over. This was the sort of move that the regulars rarely considered, simply saying that you couldn't expect to run a freight train on a Saturday night.

Despite our efforts to run the full service there were some of us who had misgivings about the benefit to the railway of running an intensive rush-hour service, with the inherent poor stock utilisation and empty running outside the peak. Particularly annoying and counter-productive to the railway as a whole was the Southern's notorious rush-hour freight 'embargo'. Sometimes there could be several freight trains queuing at Factory Junction in south London for up to three hours simply awaiting paths on to the South Eastern. Occasionally crews would come on the phone to say that if they were given a run they would do their best not to delay anything and there were some of us willing to give them the chance. One day Derek Peard and I decided to let a late-running Burngullow to Sittingbourne china clay train have a run down the Chatham main line during the evening rush hour, but to protect ourselves we told the Signalman at Shepherds Lane to make sure that he put the train down the Catford loop rather than letting it run via Beckenham Junction, where it would have to go past the windows of the Divisional office and might be seen by someone who supported the embargo policy. Having fixed it so that the train would be given a good, clear run, we awaited news that it had passed Shortlands Junction and was therefore well on its way. We were somewhat concerned a few minutes later to see the Operations Officer walk into the Control and hoped that no one would call in with news of the freight in such a way that he might overhear. Imagine then our further alarm when we heard the repeated sound of a locomotive horn outside the window and the freight went rushing by, its relatively short wheelbase wagons banging on the track as it did so. Shepherds Lane had seen a clearer run for it down the main line and the Driver was 'blowing up' to thank us for giving him a run.

'Something with a bad set of flats there, guv,' said Derek as quick as a flash before we both answered imaginary inward calls to divert attention. Luckily the train was hauled by a pair of Class 73s on electric power, so there was no telltale diesel noise.

On another occasion the same two of us told the signalman at Factory Junction to give a Northfleet coal train a run. Unfortunately, just as the 2,143-tonne train rolled through Lewisham an up Mid-Kent line train was disgorging its passengers, including amongst them the deputy head of the Passenger Trains Office. He complained the next day and we were 'spoken to' by Ron Crittell, the Chief Controller.

Some crews clearly enjoyed risky and complicated moves, too. There was a nucleus of 'go anywhere, do anything' crews who could be relied upon to understand (or suggest) and carry out unusual moves. Some of these flew close to the wind in terms of missing rostered breaks, working excessive hours and stretching the point when it came to route and traction knowledge. One night an Ashford Driver had been working inter-Regional train ferry specials to and from Dover in order to clear surplus freight traffic. The early turn Motive Power Supervisor at Ashford was alarmed to realise that this Driver was still on his way back from Willesden more than twelve hours after signing on the previous night. Arrangements were made for the Signalman to put the train into the platform at Ashford with a red light against it while the Supervisor instructed the Driver to come off. So the Supervisor and a relief Driver were standing on the platform as the train crept up to the signal. The Signalman meanwhile had thought the train had come to a stand, thus fulfilling the arrangement, so he pulled off the signal for the train to proceed to Dover. With a big grin, a 'Harvey Smith' gesticulation and a blast on the horn the Driver opened up again, leaving his Supervisor and relief standing helpless on the platform. By the time he'd been to Dover and back again to Ashford to sign off he must have done more than fourteen hours. Meanwhile, though, other Drivers would have been lying low and getting paid night rate for doing very little.

This kind of unofficial flexibility, bending of rules or ignoring of procedures was more common than many people would realise. The railway was far from the rigid and unimaginative organisation of common perception. I am still not sure, however, to what extent the management at that time (or now) knew about the ways in which the railway was kept running or to what extent they were prepared to turn a blind eye, only too happy to have more done than was theoretically possible. The Clapham disaster of December 1988 certainly put paid to this kind of attitude, though, highlighting as it did the excessive hours of signalling technicians.

Sometimes 'sharp practice' would be done on the personal authority of a local manager, at that person's risk. Following a derailment one day on the Sheerness branch, a string of wagons was moved along the running line entirely unbraked in order to clear the line. The manager who said to me that this was to be done made it clear that he would accept full responsibility if anything went wrong. Luckily for him the train did not run away. This same manager was later in charge of enforcing safety rules on behalf of the Director of Operational Standards at the Board.

From time to time there were mock incidents to test response times and communication channels. I was involved in these as a Controller and later as an Assistant Station Manager (ASM). One such was held at Lenham in Kent and was a mock nuclear accident. Nuclear flask traffic was a regular feature on the South Eastern Division, taking spent fuel from Dungeness Power Station and the naval dockyard at Chatham to Sellafield. The need to have clear reporting lines and rehearsed responses was vital, mainly to allay public disquiet. In reality it would take an unimaginable force to rupture a nuclear flask and, in fact, a new flask carrier had been derailed at Gillingham several times in 1977. The Lenham exercise was necessarily based on the so-called 'worst case scenario' in which a radioactive leak was supposed to have occurred. Of course at Lenham we only pretended there had been a crash – unlike the much publicised and televised British Nuclear Fuels stage-managed collision of July 1984, when they ran a Class 46 diesel at speed into a flask carrier in order to show how safe was the flask.

Another time we had a 'fire on a passenger train in a tunnel' mock incident. This was held in Greenhithe tunnel and tested the reporting lines between the railway and the emergency services as well as the procedures for stopping trains, discharging traction current, evacuating, providing line access for rescue, etc.

These mock incidents were good for highlighting preconceptions and misunderstandings on various sides, usually concerning the use of technical terms or jargon. One disadvantage of mock incidents, though, is that you can come away from them thinking that there is, or could be, a definitive way of dealing with the real thing. There never is, however, because each incident is different and the solution always requires the input of individual judgement, expertise and timing – not to mention temperament. It was on these occasions that the more imaginative 'go anywhere, do anything' people came into their own.

Most railway operating flexibility took place in freight yards and sidings away from the running line. In my personal experience the ultimate location for dodgy tricks had to be Angerstein Wharf, which is beside the Thames in the Borough of Greenwich. I had dealings with this place in the 1980s first of all as Assistant Station Manager at Woolwich Arsenal and later as Area Freight Manager, Dartford. In its heyday the numerous sidings there had been so busy that the Station Master (SM) for the Greenwich line was actually based at the wharf and not at one of the passenger stations, while in 1922 the South Eastern & Chatham Railway had wanted to build its own power station there to supply traction current for 94 route miles of its suburban railway. In addition to the maze of railway sidings there was also a network of tramlines serving the tram depot in the Woolwich Road, many of which were still visible from the wharf line's embankment. But by the 1980s the Blackwall Peninsula was largely derelict, the largest occupier, British Gas, having pulled out whilst retaining the land for strategic purposes in case coal-fired gas became viable once more. The tram depot had long since closed and rail freight activity was confined to sea-dredged aggregates and scrap metal. The sidings leading to the British Gas site remained in place in the hope of renewed traffic.

For a while there had been a resident Shunter who worked from a small building, heavily fortified against vandalism with bars, steel fencing and a solid steel outward-opening door. Because of this vandalism we couldn't even have point handles at the wharf – we had to fix them in each time we needed to shunt and take them back out again afterwards. The Shunter was underemployed a lot of the time and it turned out that he was spending most of his day in the pub. Eventually we had to take him out of the job and put him to work under supervision in Slade Green depot, but it was just at that time that traffic to and from the wharf picked up again with a new aggregates flow from Cliffe and trainloads of scrap from Dagenham. Some of this scrap was in better shape than the wagons used to convey it, these being redundant vacuum-braked 'minfits' from coal workings. Another thing about this traffic was that, although Dagenham is only just down the river from Angerstein Wharf (but on the other side), the scrap trains had to run via Stratford, Kensington and Lewisham in order to get to Angerstein's. Whilst we didn't complain about being given the traffic we did wonder if some sort of barge might not have been more efficient.

Occasionally I would have to assist train crews with shunting at the wharf. On one such day a Dagenham special was on its way even though the sidings were all still occupied with empties from the previous working. The only way we could sort it all out was by splitting the incoming train into four parts in different roads. We had just done this and were about to start the next move, which was to place one section in the customer's siding, when we realised that the last axle of one raft was foul of the interlocked far end of the points we needed to move, by a matter of only 2in or so. We couldn't get the engine on to the wagons without moving these points. What we should have done was to repeat in reverse order all the moves we had already made to get the engine on to the wagons concerned, move 2in and then start all over again. Understandably we didn't want to have to do this, so we found a crowbar, released the handbrakes on the first two offending wagons and tried to 'bar' the wagons along the line, which had a gentle downhill gradient towards the Thames. But they wouldn't shift, so we released the brakes further along the raft. Eventually we had the Driver and Guard standing alongside the brake levers of two wagons, me working the crowbar and the whole raft unbraked. It was at this point that the Driver lost his nerve, saying quite rightly that if they did start to roll they'd probably end up in the river, with us and entire scrapyard alongside. So we ended up doing all the shunts after all.

The Thames Metal Co. had a private locomotive in their yard that was used for shunting the scrap wagons. One Saturday when the yard was closed some children got in, started it up (it turned out that all you needed to do was to make contact between two wires), shoved it into gear and let it go. The loco trundled out of the scrapyard, taking the mangled yard gate with it on its buffer beam, proceeded along the exchange line and out on to the wharf line. It ended up derailing itself on the trap points where the wharf line joined on to the down North Kent line near Charlton. Having derailed clear of the main line it was nevertheless leaning towards it. Luckily the Signalman at London Bridge had noticed the track circuit flickering at Angerstein Junction just before the loco ran off the line and he cautioned the Driver of the next down passenger train, who stopped short of a glancing collision with the derailed private loco.

Following this incident, special precautions were put in place to prevent this engine from ever reaching the main line again, so I was taking quite a risk when I asked its driver one day to come out on to our wharf line to do some shunting. So fed up was I with repeatedly asking for an engine and crew from Hither Green to come and shunt that I just thought I'd get on with it. Fortunately for me the locomotive didn't become derailed and neither did it run away. Also luckily, no one saw. There were obvious industrial relations implications as well as those of safety.

In 1983 a new traffic flow started at Angerstein Wharf. Marcon RMC Ltd took over one of the sidings and started to bring in sea-dredged aggregates from Cliffe by rail. So passenger-biased was the Area management at the time that no interest was shown locally in the opening of this new freight terminal or in its resulting lucrative traffic. Having heard from Railfreight contacts when the first train was to run I went along to let them know that at least *someone* in the Area was interested. It was a good job I did go because the track improvements promised by the Civil Engineer had not been carried out and we had to work out how to shunt and position the train using the network of largely derelict sidings and loops.

To get the double-headed 2,200-tonne aggregates train into the Marcon private siding we had to split it in two and put the pair of Class 33 engines between the two parts so that they were propelling and hauling at the same time. This was the only way to avoid having one part of the train blocking the movement of the other. This had to happen several times a week and we became quite used to it, although various Drivers expressed surprise at what they were being asked to do.

On one such occasion we were conducting a propelling move along a siding that crossed the bridge over Horn Lane, the road to the scrapyard. To accomplish this move we needed to go quite close to the bridge and would sometimes go over it, depending on whether the train had twenty, twenty-one or twenty-two wagons. How fortunate it was that day that we only had twenty because when we looked later the bridge had gone. Under a previous management regime it had been decided that the siding was no longer needed but it had never been secured out of use. The Civil Engineers had been planning to remove the span whenever their resources allowed and had simply come in one weekend and done the job. We still used the siding after that – we had to – but no one came and installed a bufferstop for us and no one appeared interested in the fact that loaded 100-tonne wagons could have ended up on a public highway. It was difficult to get freight matters treated seriously at that time on the Southern.

If I needed to get to the wharf while I was based at Woolwich Arsenal I used to ask to be picked up at that station by the inwards train. I used to enjoy the deafening row made by the two Class 33s as they struggled to restart their own weight plus 2,200 tonnes on a reverse curve in a walled cutting. Sometimes it would take up to a minute of working flat out before sufficient amps could be generated and the wheels started turning. The din and vibration in Marks and Spencer's Woolwich branch, which was built on a raft over the walled cutting, must have been quite alarming as we rumbled underneath at around 10mph with 3,100hp working at full power.

Short-distance freight was viable with tonnages like this. 33046 and 33029 haul a 2,200-tonne aggregates train from Cliffe to Angerstein Wharf in August 1990. (Photo: Nick Pullen)

On occasion we had stone trains from Westbury arriving at Angerstein's and one day, when the drunken Shunter was still in residence, there had been a bufferstop collision as the train set back into the siding for unloading. The Shunter maintained that the train had not stopped as soon as he had thought it would after giving the stop handsignal. The same train left again the next evening to return empty to Westbury and having seen the train out (the Shunter had finished for the day and was, no doubt, in the pub), I rode out in the cab of the Class 56. As we were travelling between Erith and Slade Green the Driver noticed a metal bar placed across the up line. Seeing a signal a little way ahead he said he would stop at it so that the Secondman could get out and warn the Signalman to caution the next up train. However, the train simply didn't behave as it should and we rolled way past the signal, by at least a train length, before coming to a stop. The Driver went back himself to report the bar on the up line and also to say that he was unable to control the train properly and that we would have to go into Slade Green Carriage Servicing Depot, that being the first refuge point. We did this, much to the chagrin of the Supervisor there, who didn't like one bit having a dirty freight train in his sidings. It turned out that a special brake isolating cock had been turned, possibly maliciously, on several of the wagons, so that although the train appeared to be fully braked, in fact only a few wagon brakes were actually working. I couldn't help wondering whether it was possible that the train had run loaded all the way from Westbury like this, in which case the bufferstop collision on arrival was a lucky escape in comparison with what could have happened en route. The bar on the line turned out to be fortuitous in that the problem came to light before we might have had to stop at a red signal.

At considerable expense some years earlier, a system of lights had been installed to signal to the Driver of a train arriving at Angerstein's when it was safe to propel along the line to the wharf, which included crossing a public footpath. These lights were operated by the Shunter, who could ensure that the path was clear to cross. In an area notorious for its vandalism this installation was a rather naive idea, but there were still some people who thought we should be using these lights and therefore, presumably, have them repaired every day. In particular we still had Divisional Terminals Inspectors, most of whom were elderly and had been brought up to believe that if there was a procedure for doing something then that procedure should be rigidly adhered to, regardless of cost, practicality, time or convenience. The Inspector for the London end of the South Eastern Division, who retired shortly after we introduced the new aggregates trains, was a frequent (and, I have to say, rather unwelcome) visitor to Angerstein Wharf in his last few weeks. He was most scathing about the way we were shunting these trains and would have loved to have been able to stop the job, but his authority was already diminished as a new era of flexibility and local accountability was emerging. He hated seeing the 2,200-tonne train moving with its engines between the eleventh and twelfth wagons but when I asked him why he could only say, 'Well, it's hardly the normal practice.'

The Shunter's fortress lasted only a few days after we did away with his post, being predictably broken into and destroyed by fire. And what of the wharf? Tarmac Topmix, as successors to Marcon, expanded their use of Angerstein's, making it the landing and distribution point for sea-dredged aggregates rather than a delivery point and, in 1997, gave over control of the depot there and several others to the railfreight operator EWS* in an affirmation of their confidence in the new freight railway. And the peninsula itself? The site of the Millennium Dome, of course.

Whilst fire put the insignificant little hut at Angerstein Wharf out of its misery, it was the cause of a much more serious incident in September 1982 when a cable fire, possibly started deliberately, resulted in the loss of signalling control and phone lines from London Bridge box to the routes leading towards Dartford, Hayes and Chislehurst. This too presented an opportunity to test the flexibility of the system to its limits. The only way to move trains for several days was by the 'Time Interval' system, Regulation 25 (a) (iv) of the Regulations for Train Signalling, which can hardly have been devised with a failure of such huge proportions on one of the world's busiest commuter railways in mind. Suitably qualified people, such as Relief Signalmen and Assistant Station Managers, were posted at strategic places to calculate the stipulated time intervals between trains and to instruct Drivers to ignore signals and to proceed to the next point to await further instructions. Two such points were Kidbrooke and Blackheath on the 'Bunkum' (Bexleyheath

* 2018 update: EWS is now known as DB Cargo and no longer has exclusive use of the depot.

line). One Driver in the morning rush hour was told at Kidbrooke to proceed to Blackheath station and await instructions there. However, when he was in Kidbrooke Tunnel he decided that he'd better not cross Blackheath Junction without specific instructions, so he stopped with the rear of the train still in the tunnel. The required time interval of six minutes having passed (plus four as there was a tunnel in the section), the person on duty at Kidbrooke authorised the next Driver to proceed. Fortunately this Driver saw the red blinds of the previous train standing in the tunnel and stopped just behind it. This was a case that illustrates how important it is that everyone sticks to the rules, however 'degraded' the system is – the junction points had been secured in the right position for the first train and Blackheath station meant Blackheath station and not Blackheath Junction.

After any occasion that Time Interval Working was used, and it was pretty rare of course, the records of all movements authorised had to be sent to the Rules Section for examination, but in this case at least one Station Manager in the Dartford Area had simply not kept the proper records, having estimated the time intervals and just told Drivers to go carefully. For weeks the Rules Section kept asking what had happened to the forms, but then a lot of things got lost in the despatch system at that time.

I missed out on all this as I had been asked to help out at Maidstone West, the Station Manager and both Assistants being absent for various reasons. I arrived at Maidstone to hear of the London Bridge incident. We ran the Maidstone West line that week as a self-contained private railway as we still had our own crews at Maidstone at that time. One Driver set himself up to organise cover for all the trains and we retained the first two units each morning to provide a branch shuttle all day. Everyone was only too happy to leave us to get on with it as they had far bigger problems to think about. That was the closest I came to running my own railway.

3

Cash, Mangoes and Football

Freight shunting and dealing with mishaps provided a welcome break from the drudgery of working as an Assistant Station Manager on suburban railway stations in the early 1980s. That and all the personalities. Because we were all working long and unsocial hours (the railway ran on overtime) with the constant threat of assault and abuse, a camaraderie developed in which personal idiosyncrasies were exposed in a way that would not be possible in, say, a nine-to-five office environment. One of my Assistant Station Manager colleagues at Woolwich Arsenal had been an Army Physical Training Instructor and still liked to see some action from time to time. He caught someone breaking into cars in the station car park one day. Fetching an adjustable spanner from his own car, he proceeded to batter the miscreant's leg until he submitted and was led away. Another time a ticket dodger took a swipe at Mick, who then chased him out onto the street, lashing out with his right foot. Unfortunately for him, he missed his intended victim and injured his foot on the outside wall of the station. What with this injury and various skiing accidents, I was provided with many weeks of overtime covering for him. Years before I knew him he had been one of the first Freight Supervisors to be employed by BR at the then new Northfleet cement works. The story went that in order to get around the works he used an old army staff car. He would sit in the back as the Shunter drove him round, rapping on the dividing screen if he wanted to stop. He ended up by suddenly chucking the job in, marrying for the third time and running a guest house in Scotland.

Light relief was also provided on the Woolwich line by two of the staff at Erith station. Both in their early 60s, these two kept us amused (and fed) by sending up parcels of winkles and other shellfish when they knew we were in the office – which was mainly on Friday afternoons, being the day for checking all the staff timesheets. The phone would ring and the message 'parcel from Erith on the next up train' would prepare us. One of these gents, Ted, also gave us jars of red cabbage and other pickled goods, all made by him. The other, Bob, had a running battle of words with the Station Manager – face to face, in writing and on the phone. After a particularly vehement exchange one afternoon, an envelope arrived in the office from Erith. Inside was a noose. This then adorned the Station Manager's office wall for several months, being placed by him just above his own head.

Outside the station at Erith there was some derelict land, owned by the railway but formerly a tram depot. This was occupied one day by some travellers and we had to take advice from the Board's Solicitor on what should be done. The first step, apparently, and simply enough, was to ask them to leave. Jeff Waller (the SM) and I went down to Erith with this in mind, dressed in our long black uniform coats.

As we walked along the approach road, trepidation rising, Bob yelled out, 'Rather you than me,' but as we entered the area covered with caravans, dogs and scrap metal there came a loud guffaw from the station entrance. Bob was pointing at us and shouting, 'Look at them! A pair of bloody penguins!'

At least we went in with smiles on our faces to hide our worries. In fact, of course, for the travellers our visit was routine. Everywhere they went they were asked to move on.

Some of the staff had outside interests that were good 'earners' but which sometimes conflicted with what we required of them. One of the ticket barrier men at Woolwich Arsenal was a jazz saxophonist, playing freelance with some of the big names in London. Poor old Joe Akintibubo was hit in the mouth by a drunk one day while on duty and sustained a cut to his lip that devastated his playing ability for several weeks. This same Joe, rather sadly, thought he was going to retire in 1983 and had let this be known. When no retirement or pension papers arrived for him I made enquiries and found out that he was coming up to 64 years of age and not the 65 he had thought. So I had to tell Joe that he still had another year to do.

At Greenwich we had a Leading Railman who was a watercolour artist, exhibiting and selling his work quite successfully, while another was a regular film extra. Down at Belvedere there was a Leading Railman who also ran filling stations and owned properties for rent. He still asked for overtime though.

On my visits to Westcombe Park station I used to attempt to read the Urdu newspaper with the help of Abdul, one of the Leading Railmen employed there. About all I learnt was that the title of the paper translated as *The Daily War*, although I did find out from him why that was. Another ticket barrier man, from Jamaica, would give me presents of mangoes every so often, having heard me say that I couldn't find any for sale where I lived. At one station I could learn the difference between Creole and French, as spoken by Mauritians, while at another I was regaled by tales of the old days in the London docks by a former docker turned Booking Clerk. So there was no shortage of interesting people to meet when I was out on my rounds and I am sure my experience was representative of that of most Assistant Station Managers at the time.

The majority of an Assistant Station Manager's work on the Southern involved travelling from station to station and checking the booking office accounts, which I found boring in the extreme. I'd noticed that many Relief Station Managers had acquired the trick of signing the accounts not only without checking them but even without looking at the piece of paper they were signing. This must have taken years of practised lip-service to the accountancy procedures and some of their signatures had diminished to a scant initial. I found out also that it didn't really matter how you signed the accounts or what you wrote on them. One month I sent the accounts from Greenwich to the Division signed on every page 'G. Dogsbody'. Generally there were no repercussions, so long as things really did all add up. Every so often, though, the auditors would pick something up and all hell would be let loose, with the person who had signed the accounts being the first scapegoat. Sometimes they would identify or suspect fraud and police raids would be initiated. At one station, the Clerk somehow having been tipped off, the booking office was destroyed by fire the night before the auditors and police were planning to raid. The Clerk was never seen again.

We were expected to collect the takings each day from every booking office and take them to the main stations, where Chief Clerks prepared it all for banking or wage payments. There were no security arrangements at that time and no protection for us. Usually the money would be bundled into a brown envelope to be handed to us. The SM at Bexleyheath inadvertently left one such envelope on the seat of a train one day – a lucky find for someone. Another of my colleagues in the Dartford Area, Ron Doswell, had his eyesight permanently damaged by acid when he was attacked and robbed one morning. He never worked again but we were still expected to carry on collecting the cash as before. It was, of course, dangerous to get into a routine of visiting the stations in the same order and at the same time each day and I used to vary my route by using different means of getting about as well. Sometimes I would walk through Greenwich Park with the cash in a carrier bag or walk through Deptford market on my way to New Cross station with the money in my pockets. Sometimes many thousands of pounds.

Ever present in the London suburbs was the threat of armed robbery and every so often the police would claim to have had a tip-off. On one such occasion I was required to arrive at Abbey Wood station, having collected the cash from Erith and Belvedere, in the knowledge that there would be armed plain-clothes officers on the station. They had reason to believe that there would be a hold-up involving either me or the booking office itself. Somehow it all seemed to be part of the job, but writing about it now it seems outrageous that I and others should have been exposed to risks like that in our employment. Of course, there were real hold-ups from time to time but mainly at the smaller stations that had less sophisticated alarm systems. Some of these were difficult to investigate, especially when they occurred at times when the stations were single-manned by a Leading Railman as there was always the implication that no real hold-up had happened. The Police would send a 'SOCO' (Scene of Crime Officer) to take fingerprints, etc. but would also give the member of staff concerned a thorough grilling. While I was at Woolwich Arsenal we had three such occurrences at Westcombe Park in the space of a year or so, with nobody being apprehended. Some suspicion had to rest with the staff there, one of whom, it transpired, had falsified his references and had earlier 'done time' for stealing the cash paid as fines when he was a court usher in Ireland.

One time I had my eye on a persistent ticket dodger and had worked out his travel pattern. I requested police assistance in advance of his next trip but they did not turn up in time, so I followed the man into a single non-corridor compartment and there challenged him for his ticket, which of course he did not have. I told him that the police were on the way and that the train would not leave with him on board. He remained silent and after a minute or so a policeman turned up. I explained the circumstances and left the compartment. After a few seconds there was a flurry of shouts, waving and kicking from inside the compartment and a second officer went in to assist. The trio emerged with the suspect being frog-marched between the officers. Apparently he had pulled a gun (which turned out to be unloaded) on the first policeman, which I suppose he could just as easily have used on me.

The police on that occasion were the 'Met' police, whose responsibility did not strictly extend to stations as these were the domain of the British Transport Police. Some of the BTP's activities in our area were amateurish, to say the least. Part of their undercover operation at the Abbey Wood incident that I mentioned above involved a parked unmarked van with several policemen inside, ready to burst out if needed. One of the station staff (who were not informed of the stakeout in case the potential robbery was an 'inside' job) later told me that he knew something funny was going on because there was the ubiquitous dodgy Transit van outside the station with lots of people in the back laughing and rocking about. Every so often a trickle of urine made its way across the station forecourt, coming from a pipe in the van's floor.

On another occasion the BTP had decided to keep watch at one of the station car parks, following a particularly severe bout of thefts from cars. They kept this surveillance to themselves, so when a woman complained to the Station Manager that there was a strange man hiding in the bushes by the side of the car park he simply rang the Metropolitan Police, who duly came along to move the culprit on.

The reselling of used tickets was a favourite fiddle at the smaller stations and was easy to operate if the same member of staff was on duty all day. They simply failed to clip the ticket when it was issued in the morning, collected it back later in the day and sold it again in the evening, pocketing the second payment. We asked the BTP if they would set up an operation to catch someone at this and we decided to use Westcombe Park station for the purpose. So, at intervals throughout the morning, plain-clothes officers came along and bought tickets to London, noted the ticket numbers, came back later and handed them in. Other officers then came along in the evening to see if they would be sold any of the tickets whose numbers had been recorded. No evidence of reselling came to light, but the next day the Leading Railman told me how strange it was that so many plain-clothes policemen had been travelling to London at all times the previous day. Hello, hello, return to London, please, sonny.

Charlton Athletic were playing at The Valley in those days and, of course, are back there now. We always had BT police at Charlton station when there was a match, and whichever Assistant Station Manager was on late turn would also be present. There was one particular officer who seemed to think that there was no point in being there unless there was going to be some bother and would provoke people to swear at him or would jostle them, hoping that they would retaliate. One evening I had lost my uniform hat in the crowd, which was boisterous but not dangerous, and was moving with the supporters up the stairs to the exit. When I reached the top of the stairs one of these provoked scuffles broke out and I ended up being banged up against the wall by this officer. Recognising me, he gave me a grudging apology. Years later, working at Euston on nights, I came across another BTP officer who appeared to think that the whole purpose of policing was violence. Winos, pickpockets, prostitutes and pimps were easy game for him and all were regular visitors at Euston. If you saw him striding across the concourse in the act of pulling on his long black gloves you knew trouble was afoot for someone.

One evening at Charlton, when Chelsea were playing, the officer in charge of the Metropolitan Police on duty outside decided that things were getting out of hand at the station and sent an officer on horseback right into the station booking hall. As this was little more than a corridor in a 1960s' style 'clasp' pre-fabricated building there was hardly room to move, but no one misbehaved and all the supporters edged their way round warily. After all, who wants to be kicked by a horse? Dogs were usually used for this sort of control and, likewise, were rarely provoked.

Special train arrangements were supposed to apply when there was football at Charlton. One such arrangement was that up and down trains were not meant to be allowed into the platforms at the same time as each other. This was in order to stop people trying to jump from one train to another, especially as opposing supporters might well be travelling in opposing directions and might try to get at each other. A Millwall supporter had been killed at New Cross station in 1976 when he fell, jumped or was pushed from the offside of a train into the path of another during a running battle with West Ham fans, so there was good reason to be careful. Frequently, however, the London Bridge Signalmen would overlook this requirement at Charlton and there was no way of ensuring that both sides of both trains were safe for departure simultaneously. Also, all trains normally formed of four cars were supposed to be 'strengthened' to eight or ten, but again this sometimes didn't happen. So you could have four cars arriving at a platform with about 1,000 people waiting, another 1,000 trying to get into the station and other trains standing outside, unable to get into the station until you had somehow managed to persuade everyone to stop attempting to get into the short train. One evening there had been a shunting mishap at Slade Green depot that meant our two football specials were cancelled. The pressure of people on the platform, footbridge steps and in the booking hall was definitely dangerous, but in those days we had no radio communication with the police outside and so, if trapped at platform level by the crowd, there was no way of asking the police to hold people back. I often wondered why we didn't have more trouble than we did. We, the railway and the police, probably deserved to.

Reorganisation rose its ugly head once more during those Woolwich days. Senior management had begun to learn that they had to bulldoze things through if anything was to happen. A more confrontational management style was expected politically as the Conservative Government's industrial-

The cheap and grudgingly functional 'clasp' station buildings attracted vandalism and other anti-social behaviour. Charlton station also had to cope with football crowds, for which it was unsuited. (Photo: Author)

relations laws began to take their grip. So this is what happened with 'Local Traffic Management', known as LTM. With some amusement, it was noted by lots of us that while early correspondence referred to LTM as LTMO (with the O standing for Organisation), the pretence that it was an organisation was dropped on implementation. It was a very unsatisfactory set-up, which left Station Managers and their Assistants with many more stations than before. At Woolwich we took over five more stations as well as Slade Green depot. Our staff numbers more than trebled and it was no longer possible to know each member of staff at all well. In this way a lot of goodwill was lost. But despite the impracticability of managing day-to-day concerns with so many staff, the management of Slade Green depot gave us new variety in our work.

Slade Green was (and still is, after rebuilding) the home depot for the entire South Eastern suburban fleet of more than 1,000 vehicles and had developed piecemeal, without any coherent planning, over a long period dating back to steam shed days. One unfortunate result of this was the location of the carriage washing machine, which was squeezed outside one end of the running shed. Units had to run in one direction for the acid wash and then back in the other direction for the rinse, with the result that one end was rinsed off before the acid had worked properly while the other end had excessive acid action. So one end was not properly cleaned and the other ended up with acid streaking. Also, again because of the physical constraints of the site, there was no room for trains to queue for the wash clear of the main line, so if there was bunching of stock arriving at the depot only the first train would be washed, the rest having to bypass the washer in order to get 'inside clear' of the running line. Our Area Manager, John Norman, was keen to promote the idea of a new plant somewhere else in the Area to give a better standard of washing. He sent me to look at systems in use around London and this investigation reinforced in my mind just how cramped, busy and difficult the South Eastern really was in comparison with other lines.

At Hornsey depot I was shown the carriage washer for the Great Northern line fleet. This had a long approach siding that could hold several trains and which was also the reception road for the depot. This meant that every train coming into the depot went through the washer, without blocking back on to the running line. There was space too for the rinse to be situated sufficiently further along the line to make sure that trains were rinsed neither too soon after the first wash nor too late. In fact, every unit was washed so frequently that they didn't need to use acid cleaning at all, merely detergent. Thus they avoided a lot of safety rigmarole associated with acid soakaway and storage as well as having cleaner trains than ours.

Even the revamped depot at Slade Green cannot aspire to this sort of luxury, but at the time we thought we could install something like it if we used Plumstead Yard. The idea was that all empties would be routed via the North Kent line (as opposed to the Bexleyheath or Sidcup lines) and could then queue in Plumstead Yard, passing through the wash and rinse before rejoining the running line to go to on Slade Green for berthing and maintenance. It was the queuing that killed it – all our stock needed a Driver and a Guard in those days and the additional duty times made the scheme too expensive. Also, of course, in times of disruption, no one would be able to guarantee to route all trains via the North Kent line without causing further delay and, if stock was needed urgently, it might be run straight by Plumstead without going into the yard. So it meant that the benefits of the scheme could not be properly safeguarded. The complicated layout and staffing of the South Eastern had defeated its own objectives once again.

About eighteen months after LTM was brought in we faced LTM2, which really did alter things quite fundamentally and which made much better sense than the original LTM. With typical management aplomb it was left to NUR* members on our stations to read about it in their union paper and to tell us, their bosses, that our jobs were going to be reorganised again – but then the staff were generally the best source of information. Regional management now insisted that LTM was only ever a transitional arrangement to lead into LTM2. I thought at the time, if that's the case why was this never mentioned before, why was LTM 'sold' to us so persuasively and why, if there was to be another, was it not called LTM1? I think the answer was fairly simple: a growing assurance and even arrogance was abroad in senior management circles. With the dismantling of many of the industrial-relations laws they were learning that you could now do what you liked, when you liked and without the need for explanation. Explanation and expression of purpose were to come later with Network SouthEast – in the meantime the Regional management didn't deem either to be necessary.

* 2018 update: NUR is now known as RMT.

LTM2 abolished the Divisions, eleven years after I had been told that my first job on the railway was in jeopardy because the Divisional office was about to go. It brought in too the notion of 'functional' management and this was an important change in the way the railway was to be run. The Areas now had Passenger Managers and Operations Managers. The meaningless title of Traffic Manager was created for Station Managers but was soon dropped, thank goodness, largely at the request of passenger users' organisations. LTM2 enabled me to escape from the relative drudgery of suburban station management by becoming one of the Southern's first two Area Freight Managers, a post that I obtained simply through the outdated system of seniority and not through ability. As the 'senior' person in my grade in the Area I was called in to the office and invited to pick the job I wanted in the new set-up.

So it was that LTM2 paved the way for the separation of freight from passenger and parcels and also of passenger management from operations. It was the first tentative step towards proper business specialisation and resource accountability, and although we were still under the control of Area Managers it was a move towards the establishment of the 'retail culture' of later years. While I had found the booking office side of things tedious in the early 1980s and had enjoyed the relief provided by operations incidents, my successors on stations were soon to become one or the other – retail or ops. The days of the 'jack-of-all-trades' Station Manager were over.

4

Creating Our Own Jobs

One of the former Station Managers from the LTM era, Ron Lamb, shared an office with me at Dartford in his capacity of acting Area Movements Inspector for the newly expanded Dartford Area in 1984. Neither of us knew exactly what we were supposed to do in our new jobs and as no one else knew what they were doing in the new set-up there was nobody to tell us. We spent several days just touring around the Area together, finding out where places were and what happened there. Eventually we realised that it was up to us to create the shape of our own jobs, assessing for ourselves what needed doing. In the meantime we just had to put our trust in the goodwill of the staff.

I relied heavily on the Yard Supervisors at Hoo Junction and the Freight Supervisors at Northfleet, all of whom helped me find my way. I also had a TOPS office at Hoo and a Shunter at Plumstead yard. Other than that all the places I was responsible for were unstaffed. Originally I thought that this would mean that these were the easy places, but I soon learned otherwise. Being unstaffed meant that I had to do all the things that staff would have done if they had been there. So I travelled about, tidying places up, filling in potholes, pulling up weeds, erecting signs, checking that groundframes and handpoints were working and so on. On many occasions I had to see trains in and out of these sidings when Guards' detailed route knowledge was lacking.

One stormy night I was called out to Holborough cement sidings near Snodland to let a train in because the Guard was not 'passed out' (i.e. qualified) for this particular location. As I let him in he pointed to a house just behind the trees.

'I was born there,' he said. 'I used to watch them work this groundframe as a kid.'

But he wasn't officially passed out to work it, so I had to do it. I didn't tell him that I had never been there in my life before. As an on-call manager it was assumed that you were competent, whereas other staff had pieces of paper to prove whether or not they were competent to work each part of the railway, route by route, siding by siding.

Another of my unstaffed freight sidings was Allington near Maidstone. Amey Roadstone received daily trainloads of limestone there from Westbury. In the heyday of Kent motorway construction there had also been trainloads of shingle from Lydd and St Ives. If the weather was cold and it had been raining, the stone would be frozen into the wagons and I would have to help loosen it by smashing it with bars, along with the Amey Roadstone manager and staff. If it took too long to unload, the crew would be itching to get back home and might 'bale out'. We would stand to lose revenue because the wagons would be left in the siding, resulting in the next train having to be cancelled. As a specialist freight manager I obviously did not want to see this happen, so I had to help. This was the big difference between the new organisation and the old – freight and parcels were no longer marginal activities to be subordinated to the interests of the passenger railway; they had their own dedicated management now. At the same time, of course, it meant that they had to start paying their own costs and the pains this caused will be discussed later.

One winter's day a train was left at Allington due to late running and in the night it ran away towards the running line, derailing itself on the trap points and destroying the groundframe that controlled access to the siding. The Area Operations Manager, who was on call that night, reported from the site that the track was torn up and that there was no chance of using Allington Siding for a long time. Not surprisingly, the Railfreight people and Amey Roadstone were not happy about this. I went along to see for myself the extent of the damage and found that after all there was no real track damage – the wagons had simply run off the end and through the groundframe. We had the wagons rerailed and then devised a system to work the siding without the groundframe. The points were clipped and locked with a special padlock, the key to which was to be held in Maidstone West signalbox. A person authorised by the Rules Section at Waterloo HQ had to collect this key, go to Allington, let the train in when the Signalman gave permission to do so, reset the points, clip and padlock them and then do the same to let the train out again after unloading. Then the key had to be returned to the signalbox at Maidstone West. As the mechanism of the points was destroyed they had to be 'barred', i.e. levered across with a crowbar. And who was the lucky 'authorised person' who had to do this every morning at 6 o'clock for four weeks in the snow and rain? Some days I regretted ever having said there was no track damage. On many occasions I would go straight from Allington to Angerstein's to carry out the other unorthodox activities I described earlier. Having been one of three Assistant Station Managers whose 'patch' included Angerstein Wharf in the old regime I had now inherited it as my sole responsibility as Area Freight Manager.

One morning the Area Manager received an order from the London Borough of Greenwich to remove household refuse that had been dumped on our land along the wharf line. The Area Manager was liable to a personal fine if we failed to comply with the Council's order. Now at the same time as this occurred we had an aggregates spill on the wharf line as a result of vandals having tampered with a loaded train. Also, at Allington we had a lot of potholes that were ideal candidates for filling with this spilt stone. So I hired a pick-up truck, enlisted the help of the Area Cleaning Gang (a motley crew of individuals who were mainly on punishment), took the rubbish to the dump, loaded the gravel, took this to Allington and filled the holes. Three jobs in one and the chance to swan about all day in a hired road vehicle. To have got the jobs done through 'official' channels would have taken weeks of arranging. At Angerstein's it was very tempting, of course, to chuck the rubbish back over the fence into the gardens of the houses it had come from. Alternatively I had thought that we might clear it at night, as noisily as possible and with generators and bright arc lights borrowed from the Civil Engineers.

One of the strangest places in the Area was Swanscombe Cement Works, along the North Kent line between Dartford and Gravesend. At the time I took over as Freight Manager there was no traffic in or out of the exchange sidings at Swanscombe, but Ron and I wandered down there as part of our tour to make ourselves familiar with the Area.

From the running line it appeared that there were two parallel exchange sidings with a sharply curved spur leading off at the end to who knows where. We walked round this curve expecting to see the works and loading silos a few yards further on. But no, the line went on round an excruciatingly sharp curve until it had gone a full 180 degrees and then plunged down a slope. At the bottom of this slope it swung suddenly round a 90 degree curve and through a narrow tunnel under the A226. Then through a sea of chalk slurry and mud it finally divided into a fan of overgrown sidings, some of which led right down to the Thames.

This largely derelict, weed-strewn railway network was in fact only part of what there had once been. Another spur at one time ran back under the North Kent line and out into the chalk pits from where steam-hauled unfitted trains moved the chalk to the works in wooden-sided, spoked-wheeled wagons. In fact, this only stopped in the 1970s and was visible from the old A2.

Ron and I, having thought we were only going to be there for a few minutes, emerged an hour or so later with the conclusion that that would be the last we would hear of Swanscombe – a relic from the past now embarking on its final stages of decay. However, not only did it spring back into life but we also took modern air-braked bogie wagons right down, round all the curves, into the works. It turned out to be one of the most entertaining places in the Area.

The first thing that happened was that Blue Circle Industries (BCI) restarted the trainload cement flow from Swanscombe to Bristol, using ageing railway-owned Presflo wagons. These vacuum-braked wagons were set back into the exchange sidings at night as the train had to be split and shunted on the running line in order to get all the wagons into the sidings. There was no sufficient gap in the passenger service to allow this during the day. BCI then trundled the wagons down the slope a few at a time with one of their own small diesel engines. After they had been loaded and pushed back up the hill our engine and crew would call there and make them up into one train again before hauling them out on the way to Bristol Lawrence Hill depot. From our point of view this was a fairly painless, if rather time-consuming, exercise. The Guard on each trip was in charge of working the groundframe that gave access to the exchange sidings and, surprisingly, most Guards who were called upon to work this train seemed to be passed out to do so.

From this humble revival, though, things developed. Two ideas became apparent to me as Swanscombe blossomed again: first, that almost anything is possible on the freight railway if you put your mind to it and secondly, that however organisationally constrained and confused the railway may have been it wasn't a patch on Blue Circle Industries. I was in my office one day when the Traffic Manager at Strood rang to say that he had two people from BCI with him who wanted to look at the sidings at Strood in connection with the loading of chalk slurry for Aberdeen. I tipped off the Railfreight sales office and we set up some successful trial runs using existing Speedlink wagonload services that already called at Strood Coal Concentration depot. We were aware that the chalk slurry was coming by road from Swanscombe to Strood and naturally assumed that there was some internal BCI reason for wanting to do this rather than loading it at their own sidings and thereby obviating the need for transhipment. However, there wasn't any such reason – the complexity of BCI's management structure meant that the people in charge of organising this flow didn't know they even had a siding, let alone that it was in almost daily use. Many times I mention the continuing debate about whether the railway should be run by area, business sector or line of route and Britain's railways have shifted at different times between different combinations of these. BCI, though, appeared to have numerous conflicting management structures all operating simultaneously – there was a Works Manager at Swanscombe as a sort of site manager, then there was a cement products division located at Aldermaston that was in charge of cement making at many sites, then there was a by-products division located at Hull that was in charge of things such as chalk slurry production. Above all these was a headquarters organisation split between Stag Place, London and another address in Aldermaston that controlled the finances and transport arrangements.

The works manager had no idea the chalk slurry that left his site by road was then going back past Swanscombe by rail from Strood, while the by-products people had no idea that the cement division was loading to rail on site. We had to tell them. Eventually the works manager banged heads together and we arranged for the existing Plumstead Speedlink trip to call at Swanscombe for the chalk slurry traffic, hoping that it would lead to the cement people giving us more wagonload traffic, too. Sure enough, once they had realised that they could all work together, things started to take off.

Chalk slurry led to air-braked bulk cement and this led to bagged cement. We conducted trial runs with many sorts of bulk carriers and rail vans, some of which just scraped around the curves and through the narrow tunnel while others did not. Various wagon-owning firms sent their vehicles and salesmen there, hoping to secure the traffic for their own fleets. I had a couple of glorious afternoons riding precariously up and down the rickety track on the buffer stepboard of BCI's engine as we inched along through the weeds with what were really some very expensive modern wagons. Even at the slow speeds dictated by the state of the track I had to hang on for dear life as the locomotive lurched and bumped along the untamped line. Perhaps surprisingly, neither then nor subsequently did we have a derailment on BCI's track.

As traffic on the new trip picked up, so did our crews start to realise that the status of 'trial run' no longer applied and they started to complain about conditions at Swanscombe sidings. The sleepers on the exchange roads had apparently been salvaged from an electrified main line as they still had electrification insulating pot holders on them and these were a tripping hazard for the Guard as he did the shunting. The lighting was poor too and the stopboards that told BCI how far their engines could go and our crews how far BR engines could go were weatherworn to the extent of being illegible.

Luckily I found that the lighting, although on our land, was part of the works' internal system and the works manager got it repaired at no charge to us. The exchange tracks and the signs, though, were our responsibility. The local Permanent Way Maintenance Engineer told me he would have to programme for a weekend the work of clearing the weeds and removing the insulating pots, at overtime rates of course – and for three men. The cost, if not borne by the Area, would need to be charged to Railfreight and I would have to find an account number for the work and obtain the agreement of the account holder. I went to Swanscombe the following Saturday morning with my own wrench, undid and removed all the pot holders, cleared the weeds and was back at Dartford by two o'clock.

The next Monday I rang the Signing Group at Southern House, Croydon to get the stopboards made up. This would involve a site meeting, they said, in order to assess the size and fittings of the proposed boards as well as the wording. They would need a job number and authorisation to start incurring this cost. I rang a friend in Canterbury, the railway modeller Bob Fridd, and he made the signs in the traditional hand-painted way, being paid out of the Area's petty cash. Knowing that there was an odd-job man employed in the cement works, I sought him out and asked him how I would go about getting his bosses to agree to his fixing the signs.

'Don't worry, guv, I'll see to it,' was the response and within a day or so the signs were perfectly fixed with no fittings at all being visible from the front. No charge was made.

I was rapidly finding out that the freight railway of the 1980s was as much or as little as you cared to make of it. Many of the old constraints were crumbling and increasingly you could circumvent the procedures and get away with it. What's more, you usually saved time, money and heartache by doing so.

Because so many of us were piecing our jobs together in the new Areas of 1984 there developed a team spirit of mutual assistance. I had previous experience of crossing box operations so I helped out a colleague who was called out to Crabtree box where the night keeper had not turned up, while various former Station Managers gave me useful tips about the freight operations formerly under their control. As we discovered more things about our new jobs so we shared experiences and in some ways we were like a bunch of children let loose in an adventure park for the first time. As I said at the beginning of the chapter, there was little guidance from above as to what we were really supposed to be doing. One afternoon I went with the newly appointed Area Traction Inspector, Jim Leinster (who had been an Assistant Station Manager with me at Woolwich Arsenal in the previous regime) for him to show me his new 'toy' – a speed gun. We stood on the end of the platform at the old Eltham Well Hall station pointing this thing at trains traversing the infamous 20mph curve, at which the fatal 1972 derailment had occurred, making records of the digital speed readings flashing across the viewfinder. Several trains were doing nearer 30mph and warnings were duly issued to the errant Drivers.

5

King Coal and King Arthur

I was appointed to the post of Area Freight Manager, Dartford, in April 1984 when the notorious National Union of Mineworkers' coal strike was already under way. Only the Nottinghamshire pits were working, leading to the formation of the breakaway Union of Democratic Mineworkers. In the Dartford Area we had, of course, no collieries, although three remained elsewhere in Kent. Their miners were some of the most militant and were staunchly loyal to the NUM and its leader, Arthur Scargill. In fact, they had initiated the process that led to the national strike. There were two receivers of bulk coal in my Area – Blue Circle Industries at Northfleet and Rugby Cement at Halling. Other bulk coal passed through the Area on its way to the paper mills at Ridham. Household coal was received at Plumstead and Strood Coal Concentration Depots.

Northfleet coal came from Nottinghamshire while Rugby Cement was using Kent coal from Betteshanger. Both movements were affected by the strike. In addition we had aviation spirit and bitumen emerging from the rundown refinery on the Isle of Grain and oil was received at Reed's paper mill siding at New Hythe from the Thames refineries. These movements too were affected. It was a time of considerable brinkmanship and of the most severe testing of mixed loyalties. There was deep division between the traditional railway union loyalists and the growing body of those who saw 'solidarity' as destructive and old-fashioned at a time when road operators were queuing up to get their hands on our traffic.

Some train crews set out deliberately to break picket lines and to defy the strikers, some even coming forward with ideas for beating the blockades by carefully planned night manoeuvres, while others stuck rigidly to the letter of the orders coming from an organisation known as the Railway Federation of Unions – which was a specially formed grouping of railway unions and, locally, of Kent miners. A large part of the effort of the Federation was wasted, however, because they failed to stop the movement of coal by road. Indeed, they did not even attempt to picket road deliveries and in this way betrayed the so-called solidarity between railway and mining workers. All that happened was that railway staff lost out on overtime, night allowances and job security while lorry operators made a quick killing. As a last-ditch, all-out protest against the Thatcher Government's policy of industrial decimation and social division the coal strike was a tremendous, if suicidal, display of sacrifice and fellowship on the part of many thousands of working people but the lack of attention to the detail of its implementation meant that the overall effect was largely reduced to nothing more than a gesture and so the pain was for the most part wasted.

Blue Circle (as Associated Portland Cement Manufacturers) had started to build Europe's largest cement works on the south bank of the Thames in the late 1960s and it was opened, in part, in July 1970. It replaced many small plants that had at one time been scattered along the North Kent line and it incorporated the first railway merry-go-round loading/unloading system to be installed by the private sector in Britain. Blue Circle also invested in a fleet of new 102 tonne wagons for the transport of bulk cement powder.

The new works was built at a time when energy was relatively cheap, so they went for a 'wet' process, pumping clay slurry under the Thames by pipeline from Ockendon to Swanscombe, mixing it there with local chalk and then piping the mixture to Northfleet. They then used a massive coal-fired system for the process of making and drying the cement powder. The huge energy cost inherent in this meant that the Northfleet plant never worked to capacity and in the 1980s the higher cost of fuel had reduced it to a fraction of its original capability. When it was opened in 1970 it was hoped that traffic would build up to sixty outwards cement trains per week and twenty-eight inwards coal trains, with about half the cement tonnage going long-distance, including as far as Scotland. The revenue to the railway, were this to have been realised, would have been immense. But by the mid 1980s loading to rail was restricted to the night shift, as was the receipt of coal. Destinations for cement were Theale, Dunstable and Totton – all relatively short hauls (Berkshire, Bedfordshire and Hampshire respectively). Just occasionally we ran specials to Uddingston in Scotland when there were production problems there and we charged premium rates for doing so, but it was a far cry from the nightly long hauls envisaged in the early days.

On the railway side of the operation we had an early-turn Supervisor and Shunter each weekday for the sole purpose of receiving the gypsum train from Mountfield in Sussex. All other traffic was received by the night turn Supervisor and Shunter and traffic was worked on the slow-speed merry-go-round system with a full signalling system controlled from a panel by the Supervisor. Expense had been no object, apparently, when the place was built. And how much traffic is received and despatched now at Northfleet? None, Blue Circle having pulled out of renewing its rail contracts through uncertainty over the future ownership of Railfreight as privatisation loomed.

During the miners' strike Blue Circle switched to road for the receipt of their coal as railway staff were not moving 'blackleg' Nottinghamshire coal. Fleets of lorries came down the A2 to unload at Northfleet. They arrived there and unloaded without ever seeing a miners' picket. One husband-and-wife haulage business reputedly did two trips every twenty-four hours, one

Europe's largest cement plant, at Northfleet in Kent, needed huge amounts of coal but never lived up to its promise of up to sixty cement trains per week. 47355 is seen returning empty merry-go-round coal wagons to the Midlands in February 1975. (Photo: Brian Garvin)

each, in the same truck and doubtless did very well out of it financially, even if they didn't see much of one another. The Blue Circle management told me at the time that they were very pleased with how things were working out, but when the strike ended they confessed that it had been a logistical nightmare getting all the lorries in and out amongst their own traffic, never knowing when they would arrive or in what numbers and having to deal with so many individual drivers and different vehicles. They also had to pay more per tonne for road haulage as the hauliers were exploiting the monopoly created by the railway workers' refusal to move the traffic. Despite the fact that 'blackleg' coal was being used there was no effort made to stop outwards movements of cement, partly because of the so-called 'secondary action' laws passed by the Government that forbade stoppages or picketing that might affect any part of a process subsequent to the one actually in dispute. Nevertheless, one might have expected at least a murmur of dissent.

Rugby Cement had a smaller plant on the west bank of the River Medway at Halling and they had other problems connected with the strike. They had been using high-carbon Kent coal, none of which was available during the strike. There being no Kent coal available, Rugby Cement decided to switch to Nottinghamshire coal and a terrible time they had of it, too. All coal-fired plants, in whatever industry, are designed for particular fuel characteristics and Notts coal is by no means the same as Kent coal. Most bulk purchasers take samples from each delivery for analysis in order to ensure that the coal meets their specified requirements in terms of carbon, sulphur, ash, etc. On occasion at Northfleet, for example, we were paid to take entire trainloads back at the Coal Board's expense because the product was not up to standard. By the time the strike ended there was a mountain of Nottinghamshire coal at Halling that the company had been struggling to use but which was not suited to their needs. They then tried to sell it on to someone else and at one time approached us about moving it back to the Midlands, which would have been a nice irony – blackleg road-delivered coal being returned by rail. However, the cost of reloading it coupled with the fact that there was a smouldering fire somewhere deep in the stockpile made this impracticable. Most of it ended up slowly disappearing into ash as it burned from the inside out. The occurrence of such fires is not unusual in these circumstances, being caused by a combination of released gases and trapped air. Once they have started it is difficult to stop them too, unless the whole pile is opened up and the source located. Production at Northfleet was occasionally brought to a complete standstill by the need to deal with stockpile fires in the enormous coal bunkers.

Perhaps somewhat bizarrely, all the while the coal strike was dragging on, Reed International at Aylesford Paper Mills were preparing to switch back from oil to coal for their paper production. The siding to be used, which was known by the railway as Brookgate, was relaid and coal discharge equipment installed. Creep signals were put in to regulate the speed of trains during unloading. I attended several friendly meetings with their management and with the Trainload Coal Development Manager from Nottingham (a character known as 'Captain Beaky') and a good many lunches were consumed at Reed's unquibbling expense. Not only was this at a time when there was a national coal strike, supported by railwaymen, but on top of that their own inwards oil trains were being picketed, thus disrupting their production. Their tolerance of the railway industry was truly amazing. Maybe it had something to do with their Production Manager being a closet railway enthusiast.

The reason stated for picketing the oil trains was that Kent miners' leaders seemed to think that Reed's were generating surplus electricity at their plant and then selling this to the National Grid. Apparently this was technically feasible and so they may have been doing so. But what a tenuous connection to have dreamt up in comparison with the obvious movements of coal being delivered by road not so very far away, which passed, as I have said, unpicketed. Anyway, orders went out from the self-appointed leaders of the Federation that the oil trains were to stop, but several got through as not all crews and Signalmen could see the sense in stopping oil trains as well as coal. However, one train of ten 100-tonne tanks ended up being impounded at Reed's, blockaded there largely by the actions of local Signalmen, some of whose loyalties we had tested to the limit. On its way into Reed's this same train had got from Ripple Lane (Barking) as far as Maidstone West without interruption but at a time when the next box, Aylesford, was manned by one of our Area's most militant Signalmen, known as 'Lord Lucan'. Lord Lucan inadvertently gave 'Line Clear' to Maidstone West for the train and it duly entered the section to Aylesford. His suspicions being aroused, he rang the box at Maidstone West to find out exactly what Class 6 freight he had just accepted and was not amused to find what had been done to him.

The train came to a stand at Aylesford's outer home signal while Lord Lucan made several angry phone calls to the Area management to the effect that the train would stay there on the running line until the end of the miners' strike. Eventually he realised that his action would not only be most unprofessional for a Signalman (all Signalmen have high principles regarding unnecessary detention of trains on the running line) but also that the action he was proposing was, in legal terms, 'secondary' and so we could dismiss him if he failed to carry out his job properly. Reluctantly he 'pulled off' the signals to let the train pass, no doubt seething as the Crompton thrashed its way by the box, its 'blackleg' crew a few feet in front of him.

Unfortunately there had been so much disruption and picketing at Reed's that they stopped taking further deliveries by rail and no Signalman would let the empty tanks out. We ended up having to pay Shellmex-BP, the owners of the tanks, compensation for their non-return. As soon as road deliveries started, however, the pickets miraculously disappeared just as they had at Northfleet and Halling, indicating once more that the miners had no interest in safeguarding the railway jobs of the men who were so foolhardily and one-sidedly supporting the struggle for mining jobs.

As the strike wore on new targets were found in an effort to intensify the pressure on the Government and the Coal Board, and one such was BP's Grain refinery. Pickets tried to stop the movement of aviation spirit and bitumen, the only two commodities still produced there. Quite how these products were supposed to be being used as coal substitutes was never explained – there being, of course, no explanation. This picketing was a sign of increasing desperation on the part of the miners, who now wanted to expand the stoppage to all areas of energy supply, in direct contravention of the new laws on secondary action.

As the desperation grew, so did the tactics become more daring and foolish. On one occasion when pickets and Police were at Grain Crossing a picket lay down across the line after having failed to stop an inwards empty oil tank train, the crew of which had told the pickets that they had every intention of coming back out with a loaded train. A policeman approached the Driver as the outwards train was being prepared to tell him about the man on the line at the crossing, thinking that the Driver would probably agree to avoid trouble and would go back light engine only. He was wrong, though. The Gillingham-based Driver told him that he had more than 1,000 tonnes behind him and that once he had got 'the road' to start he would be doing just that and furthermore that he wouldn't be able to stop the train suddenly even if he wanted to. The policeman could tell that to the man on the line. The picket's nerve broke and the train went on its way to Stansted, but the police were sufficiently concerned about this development to ring me at Dartford with a request to suspend further moves for the day in order to let things calm down. I refused.

Not all crews would work these trains, though. In the case of aviation spirit this sometimes resulted in reloading to road, which of course was not picketed. This was costly enough but in the case of bitumen trains the costs of reloading were much greater as it was loaded hot. The destination of the train was Cardiff Tidal Yard and, in an early example of Just In Time, the train was timed to arrive there while the bitumen was still warm enough to flow out of the wagons unaided. So it was vital that the train left as soon as possible after loading and that it wasn't delayed during the night journey to Wales. However, during the time of picketing, several trains failed to get away and BP had to pay Grain Power Station for the supply and piping of steam to heat up the wagons in order to make the bitumen flow, either for reloading to road, at our expense, or for another attempt to get there by rail.

The oil derivative trains from Grain ran largely, or in some cases entirely, through the Power signalbox areas, as opposed to the Absolute Block single-manned boxes on lines such as the Maidstone West branch. It was notable that the powerbox Signalmen and Regulators were not militant. There was no trouble in getting trains through the Dartford, London Bridge and Victoria signalling areas once they were on the move. Dartford had been the first of thirteen projected boxes that were intended to cover the entire Southern Region by 1985. Had this scheme been implemented as planned maybe the running of 'blackleg' trains would have been much easier but a wealth of signalling interest would have been lost, too. Even now there are several former Southern routes still signalled by Absolute Block with old-fashioned signalboxes.

In my capacity as Area Freight Manager I issued a periodical newsletter with information on freight staff appointments, local freight intelligence, etc. It had struck me in particular that train crews had been left for too long in ignorance of the commercial ramifications of rail freight activities. Because of the way in which railway grades had developed, with clear divisions of labour, and because most Drivers were traditionally represented by a separate trade union that encouraged an isolated elitism amongst its members, a culture had developed in which the cab of the train was a different world and not really anything to do with what went on behind.

Many Drivers, it transpired, were very interested in being told what was going on regarding new traffic flows or about which flows were at risk and for what reasons. Similarly, shunting staff who had previously been told just to get on with the job became more motivated when they knew that the wagons weren't just there for their own sake but were part of a wider industrial process, affecting the lives and livelihoods of countless other people. *Area Freight News* also helped to raise the profile of freight amongst my fellow managers in an Area heavily dominated by rush-hour passenger traffic along with busy booking offices. To put it into context, originating freight revenue in the Dartford administrative Area in the mid 1980s was around £3 million per annum, while passenger revenue amounted to more than ten times that amount. The value to the railway of freight traffic received in the area, incidentally, was around £5 million at the time.

As a result of this fostering of freight interest, I received a long letter from a Driver based at Hither Green diesel depot. This Driver, by the way, was the author of several railway history books and was at the time an Independent councillor on Tonbridge and Malling Council. His letter to me was full of tips for new freight opportunities and I duly forwarded it to the freight sales people for investigation. But his letter included something else – he wanted to speak to me about the several stranded coal trains in various parts of Kent as he had a plan to get some of them to their destinations. The strike, of course, was still on. He made clear, however, that he did not want to be seen meeting me as his attitude to the strike was well known and he was closely watched by union activists.

So I went down to Dover one day, telling only him, and he picked me up from the end of Dover Priory platform whilst working the 1530 Dover Town Yard to Toton Speedlink service as far as Hoo Junction. As the Class 33 forged its way through the heavily graded Kentish countryside he gave me details of a nucleus of Drivers and Guards who had got themselves together discreetly and were prepared to travel to places such as Faversham, where there were two impounded coal trains for Ridham paper mills, and to work these trains to their destinations at times when sympathetic Signalmen were known to be on duty. To avoid attracting attention these movements would need to be carried out at the dead of night, he said. He was asking me for management help in getting information and in arranging rosters and resources to facilitate this, but without doing so too obviously. It was an intriguing idea and with my views on what I saw as the betrayal by the miners of the railwaymen's interests, I was willing to give it a go.

The problem from my point of view was that there were no coal trains actually stranded in my Area. Neither were any of the crews or signalmen concerned under the authority of the Dartford Area. If the whole thing could have been contained within my authority, or with just the help of one or two close colleagues at Dartford, I would have done it as much for the adventure as anything else, but the management in the adjoining Areas, whose co-operation was vital, would not take the risk. These Areas did not have specialist Freight Managers like me and so I was dealing with people for whom freight was a lower priority. They were afraid that the passenger railway might be brought to a stand by strike action if a coal train moved with their authority. So once more an organisational constraint stopped something from being done – possibly, I have to say, for the best. The idea was inflammatory in the extreme.

At last, in March 1985, the strike ended. The National Union of Mineworkers was terminally damaged but the folk-hero status of Arthur Scargill remained mostly untarnished amongst his supporters. Coal and oil trains that had been standing still for a year creaked back into action. I watched from an upstairs window at the office in Dartford as a Class 56 hauled the first coal train through the station on its way to Northfleet, having stood at Cricklewood Recess Sidings since the first day of the strike. It seemed pretty momentous to me but no one else gave it a second look. Things were back to normal, that was all.

I imagined there would be all sorts of problems with coal unloading gear, creep signals, points and everything else connected with these trains and the sidings they used but within a couple of days it was as if there had never been a stoppage. All staff, including those whose actions had directly resulted in traffic being blockaded, co-operated in the running of specials to catch up with the backlog and there were remarkably few recriminations from any quarter amongst local freight staff and crews, bearing in mind the wide diversity of opinion that had manifested itself during the strike. It had been a much longer stoppage than anyone had anticipated or wanted and most people, regardless of their loyalties, were simply relieved that it was all over.

The notoriously 'solid' Kent miners were ruthlessly wiped out after the folding of the strike and Britain's highest-quality coking coal supply was sealed off, many would say as a lesson by a vindictive Government bent upon breaking trade-union power, regardless of the cost. The economic and social consequences of the Kent coalfield's obliteration were mitigated in the short term by the large number of underground workers required for the construction of the nearby Channel Tunnel and so the wiping out of an industry went largely unnoticed.

For years after, though, there was a heavy financial burden from the coal strike for Railfreight. As well as lost revenue there were compensation payments to be made to customers. While fuel, maintenance and staffing cost savings had been made during the strike, Railfreight still had to borrow more than £200 million at commercial rates in order to survive. The crippling interest and capital repayments took more than five years to recover from and undoubtedly put paid to many freight developments that might otherwise have taken place. The eventual cost to Railfreight totalled £300 million and none of this was recoverable from anywhere other than its own revenue. Cross-subsidy from other railway businesses was not permissible and Government financial support for freight by rail had been withdrawn in 1979, under the Labour Government. William (later Lord) Rodgers, Minister of Transport, had said at the time, 'I cannot see the merit in protecting rail from legitimate competition' and so all subsidy ended. The succeeding Conservative administration, with the added determination to punish railway workers for their support of the miners, had stuck to this resolve, leaving Railfreight to find its own salvation in the matter of the miners' strike.

6

Striking Off

The quick resumption of normal working relations after the demise of the miners' strike was in stark contrast to the lasting malice that had arisen from the ASLEF 'variable-day rostering' strike of three years earlier. During this strike, which took place in July 1982, some ASLEF Drivers had continued to work, in addition to Drivers who were members of the NUR. The latter were few and far between but tended to be in pockets, such as at Ramsgate.

So it was that the occasional train would creep its way up from Dartford on the Woolwich line where I was working at the time. During the morning rush one day a ten-coach train came up when I was on duty on the platform at Woolwich Arsenal. It was packed to bursting and it was obvious that nobody else could realistically expect to be able to board it and therefore that there was no sense in it calling at any other stations to pick up. The Driver, rather than the Guard, got out of his cab and came back to see me to make this point and I noticed with some surprise that he was proudly wearing his ASLEF badge on his lapel. Divisional Control, who simply wanted to be able to record that they had supplied the Greenwich line with a service, refused to allow the train to run fast to London Bridge but of course this is what it did. It just would have been neither safe nor practical to have called at the intermediate stations.

Drivers such as this were ostracised at that time and for a long time afterwards. One Driver, based at Charing Cross and living on our line at Belvedere, had always travelled up in the cab on his way to work and had been a popular character amongst his contemporaries. Never again, though. For years Nick's colleagues would not speak to him after he worked during the strike and he drifted into station staff rooms to avoid the stony silences that greeted him in Drivers' messrooms. Ten years later I appreciated the flexibility and greater understanding of other people's jobs that this experience had given him when he came out of his cab at Charing Cross, back into the Conductor's compartment and made a passenger announcement apologising for the fact that we were being delayed awaiting the Conductor. Other than on Driver Only trains I had never heard, or heard of, a Driver doing such a thing. In the context of freight operations I mentioned earlier that Drivers had tended to live in a calculatedly exclusive world of their own, removed from other staff, passengers and customers. Nick, despite being 'sent to Coventry', had evidently found a whole new life on the railway by losing his exclusivity.

During the 1982 strike we occupied ourselves as station management by ensuring that all stations were cleaned and, in some cases, repainted. Weeds and bushes were cut back, flowerbeds tidied, holes in car parks filled, window frames and waiting room walls painted, platform edges whitelined and poster boards repaired – all by station staff. Of course, we had to cancel all overtime and rest-day working that might otherwise have been worked in order to reduce costs, so it was a tough time for many. The railway at the time relied heavily on such working in normal circumstances simply to keep going.

I would drive from my home in Tonbridge to Woolwich each day during the strike, calling at Shortlands to pick up Jeff, the Station Manager. We then used my car to get about the line, usually stopping off at Erith for a lavish cooked breakfast at the café just up the road from the station. Car mileage allowances were kindly suspended by the Divisional Manager so I was not paid for using my personal vehicle on railway business, for which I was also not insured. Not only did we visit the stations to see that the staff had things to do but we also collected the limited takings and distributed the reduced wages. Parking at some of the stations was not easy and we had to walk along some pretty shady streets with the cash in some cases. Deptford was the worst from this point of view, with its dodgy car repairers in yards guarded by mangy Alsatians and its seedy businesses in the railway arches. This said, though, Deptford was one of my favourite stations, with its friendly staff welcome, its vast, mouldering, unused upstairs rooms, its ramp that was part of the original London and Greenwich Railway and its bustling street market, complete with hot bread shop and exotic fruit and vegetable stalls.

After a while, so much cleaning and painting had been done that Jeff and I let it be known that with effect from the next Monday we would go round the stations and paint in gold the decorative heads of the canopy columns. This would be the finishing touch to the staff's efforts. The strike ended, however, before we could do this so they remained black until the more imaginative colour schemes came in a couple of years later.

ASLEF was broken by the strike, much as the NUM was by the later miners' strike. The strike had been over the issue of so-called flexible (or, officially, variable-day) rostering. ASLEF had achieved the goal of the fixed eight-hour day in 1919 and seemed to think that it was sacrosanct. The management wanted to be able to vary the length of shifts between seven and nine hours in order to meet traffic and commercial requirements, with hours balancing out over a specified period. After two weeks of striking over this matter, ASLEF was told by the TUC to call it off. The union movement as a whole thought ASLEF was being unreasonable in its action, helped by the fact that the larger NUR had signed up for variable-day rostering in December 1981. Soon after its defeat on this issue ASLEF lost its place on the TUC General Council and never recovered the stranglehold it had once held over the railway management or its influence on the whole trade union movement. For such a small union, ASLEF and its General Secretary Ray Buckton had held a disproportionately high profile in the heady industrial relations climate of the 1960s and '70s. The variable-day strike was the ignominious swansong of ASLEF and of Ray Buckton, who retired soon after.

This strike, coming as it did on top of ASLEF and NUR one- and two-day stoppages over pay earlier in the same year, cost the BRB an estimated £240 million. Always one to look on the bright side, the Chairman, Sir Peter Parker, described this huge loss as money well spent on achieving the principle of variable-day rostering. He regarded it as an investment for the future.

There was deep mistrust on the issue of flexible working, which was widely thought to be a management ploy to reduce earnings and to make employees work unreasonable numbers of hours for no reward. As with so many national management initiatives, it had been badly 'sold' down the line. Had seeds of the idea been sown earlier in co-operation with local management, confrontation might have been avoided. The word could have been spread and fears allayed. Instead, of course, local management were just as much in the dark about it as the staff. The policy at the time was to present the unions nationally with a proposal, thus giving them the opportunity either to support it or to oppose it, with whichever way they chose to go having effect over the entire country. The national decision of the union then permeated downwards, whereas with better groundwork a more constructive approach might well have come upwards.

When the new rostering system came in we were able to re-arrange staffing hours to suit the times when staff were actually needed and in this way all the station jobs became more worthwhile. Short-rostered weeks were balanced with long ones so that overall hours and pay were not lost. In this way longer breaks from work could be given within the normal roster and the system was generally seen as a good idea, once the original fears had been dispelled. Later on I shall mention the way in which variable rostering, won at such expense and with such publicity, was still thought too controversial to be introduced for Sleeping Car Attendants, all of seven years later. Different parts of the railway moved at different paces, as I discovered on several occasions as I moved about the industry.

At around the same time as the variable-day rostering issue was at the forefront of industrial relations changes on the railway, the working week was reduced from forty to thirty-nine hours and even this was seen by many to be a way of cutting earnings. I remember having to explain to a Charing Cross Guard that if his pay remained the same but he only worked thirty-nine hours instead of forty his hourly rate would be higher, making his overtime rate greater and meaning that any overtime would start one hour earlier than before. He would have none of this, insisting that what it really meant was that management were going to cut one fortieth of his pay.

Like many Guards at that time, this one was distrustful of management, possibly because there were the first rumblings of Driver Only Operation (DOO), which would do away with Guards. This proposal had been launched under the title One Man Operation (OMO) but the 'political incorrectness' of this was soon realised in an organisation supposedly committed to equal opportunities for both sexes. Amidst considerable publicity the first female Guard, Pat Mitchell, had been appointed at our own depot at Plumstead just a couple of years previously.

Drivers, Signalmen and Guards all knew that Drivers and Signalmen would gain financially through DOO as special allowances would be payable to them. In this way the NUR, which mainly represented Guards and Signalmen – but also some Drivers – was put in the tricky position of having to negotiate for payments to some of its members in return for abolishing the jobs of some others. There was some unrest in the autumn of 1985 amongst both Guards and Drivers as the first DOO freight trains began to run. Freightliner trains from Willesden were used to test staff attitudes and to assess the operational impact of DOO. Guards took different ways of protesting as DOO spread and as proposals for passenger DOO were developed. Some tried to demonstrate how you could never do away with them, by helping passengers, making announcements, seeing trains away from stations unaided, etc., while others used the tactic of drawing attention to themselves by waiting for minutes on end at stations when they thought there should be staff to see them away. On the South Eastern at the time there were no corridor trains on suburban services and therefore no ticket duties to perform and only limited public relations possibilities. Starkly aware of this, Guards sought other means of trying either to look indispensable or to create nuisances of themselves.

In fact it took another ten years before rolling stock suitable for DOO was delivered to the South Eastern and so for another decade Guards were employed to go 'ding-ding' at each station and then put their feet up until the next station. This was despite the fact that the experimental sliding-door PEP train was not only tried in passenger service on the South Eastern as long ago as 1972, but large sums of money were spent on raising platform levels for it.

DOO was established as the norm for freight trains fairly soon after the principle had been agreed but many people thought that short cuts had been taken in order to bring it in. It had been generally understood that one of the requirements for DOO was for there to be radio contact between Driver and Signalman, regardless of the type of train. In late 1985, however, freight trains were running single-manned without such equipment having been installed. The early doubts evaporated and by the time it reached the South Eastern in early 1986 everyone concerned seemed happy about it, from the Shunters who received special allowances for train preparation to the Drivers who were paid extra for any shift that contained an element of DOO, and the Signalmen who likewise received an allowance if a DOO train passed through their area. The Guards protested in vain and half-heartedly. There really wasn't anything for them to do any more and they knew it. TOPS had taken away a lot of the train preparation work, as had the standardisation of wagon types; continuous braking had removed the need for brakevans at the rear of each train and also for the need for much of the Guard's vigilance in running to ensure that the train did not run away; track circuiting had taken away some of the train protection duties in cases of breakdown, mishap or delay; and the requirement for Guards to keep a lookout ahead by means of periscopes or side windows had long gone. Only when certain categories of dangerous goods were being carried was there still a need for a Guard and even today you can see the rather incongruous sight of a traditional brakevan at the end of trains conveying nuclear flasks from power stations, dangerous gases, etc. Guards and vans are retained on these trains so that, in case of mishap, help can be summoned and protection put in place from either end of the train without the crew having to walk by the affected wagons.*

While the abolition of Guards and also the single manning of cabs came in relatively painlessly, with only small pockets of resistance, this was in marked contrast to the industrial relations climate of the early 1970s. Looking back now at when I joined the railway it seems that all the management could do was to try to hold their heads above water. There was either no time for far-reaching schemes such as DOO, or there was no inclination, or, perhaps, they just didn't dare. It was the era of massive pay inflation – one year we had a 25 per cent increase – and this was where all the pressure was. The miners' strike of 1974, coupled with the oil crisis, compounded the problem in that the energy shortage led to the Government's issuing of petrol coupons. This then gave the railway trade unions a further lever in their demands and at the height of the crisis I remember having to walk from Bromley South to Beckenham Junction each day because ASLEF had declared a 'work to rule' in which Drivers were refusing to work trains that were not fitted with speedometers, which meant that most of the South Eastern's suburban fleet was at a stand just when BR could have been cashing in on the fuel crisis, both in terms of additional business in the short term and in the public relations terms of establishing itself as the energy-efficient carrier of the future. What on earth, though, were we doing as late as the 1970s having a suburban fleet with no speedos? There were times when the management gave the unions items of contention on a plate.

* 2018 update: There is no longer a requirement for Guards on these trains.

In the heady days of industrial confrontation it always seemed that it was the 'innocents' who had to take the stick. It was the Booking Clerks and platform staff who had to deal with the irate passengers, whereas the industrial action was usually taken by Guards, Drivers or Signalmen. Horrendous queues would grow for season-ticket refunds, for example, with tempers getting ever shorter as Clerks worked excessive hours to try to clear the backlog. Time and again those of us on stations were left unsupported by Regional, Divisional and Area management as we did the business of clearing up the mess. Right up until the variable-day strike of 1982 there was the feeling that we were trapped between the demands of over-powerful unions on the one hand and a drifting, purposeless Southern management on the other. It was that strike that turned the tide, though, as ASLEF's credibility was damaged by it. Perhaps that was the real investment for the future that Sir Peter had referred to rather than simply the achievement of the variable-day principle itself.

7

Runaways and Other Misdemeanours

In the last chapter I mentioned the way in which the advent of continuous braking of freight trains had contributed to the abolition of freight Guards. It also led to the demise of the traditional 'goods' train. Loose-coupled trains provided a whole wealth of railway lore: brakevans with smoking stoves and open verandas, catch points on the track, clanking trains with wagons cannoning into each other and then snatching, breakaways and runaways. Amazingly (or perhaps not, depending upon your point of view), trains without continuous braking continued to run well into the 1980s.

Towards the end of the loose-coupled era, which came sooner on the Southern Region than elsewhere, a colleague of mine had been Signalman at Canterbury East and was on duty one weekday night. The last down passenger train had arrived and was crossing over in order to return empty to Faversham. Meanwhile, the loose-coupled 0030 Shepherdswell to Cricklewood coal train had been accepted from Adisham signalbox, running a few minutes before time. Canterbury is in the valley of the River Stour so there is a long gentle gradient down towards the station. As the 0042 empty coaching stock train was negotiating the crossover from down to up lines, the Signalman heard the distinctive, plaintive one-tone chime whistle of an electric Class 71 locomotive and, just as the passenger stock pulled away from the platform, the 0030 Shepherdswell came careering around the corner out of control. It raced through the station with sparks flying from the locomotive's brakes and only came back under its Driver's control when the gradient changed after crossing the river. Collision was averted as the passenger stock was by then sufficiently far ahead, but the incident went to prove just how vital to the control of the train the Guard's contribution should have been. He had fallen asleep on the slow, relatively smooth climb at the start of the journey and had not woken up in time to start screwing down the brake in his van as the train tipped over the change of gradient. So the Driver lost control and the locomotive was pushed down the slope by the weight of its own unfitted train.

When the decision was made to ban loose-coupled movements on the Southern Region the need for catch points on gradients evaporated. These had been installed on uphill gradients in order to derail unbraked wagons running away in the wrong direction after splitting from their train, or indeed, complete runaway trains. However, most catch points remained in place at least until the section of line they stood on was due for renewal and most were not even clipped out of use. One such set was on the down line near Mottingham on the Dartford Loop line and, in combination with a train crew's lack of detailed route knowledge, led to a very expensive and messy derailment in the early hours of 11 October 1977, while I was a Controller on the South Eastern Division.

Northfleet coal trains at that time ran from Welbeck Colliery (near Mansfield), being hauled by a Class 45 and assisted from Cricklewood onwards by a Class 47 to cope with the tight curves and gradients on the Southern. This was, incidentally, an expensive way of doing things as the traction could not run in multiple but had to run in tandem with crews on both engines. On the night in question one of these 2,143-tonne trains was in difficulty with wheelslip on the uphill gradient near Mottingham, despite its combined 5,250hp, and had slipped to a complete stand. In attempting to restart, the Cricklewood Driver had allowed the train to roll back a few yards and by the time it got going again the rear wagon had been derailed by running back through the catch points and was being dragged along, foul of the up line and tearing up the track of the down line.

Meanwhile, the 0324 Northfleet to Dunstable cement train, double headed with Class 33s in multiple and crewed by Hither Green men, was heading up the line. The leading loco struck the derailed coal wagon and the cement train, more than 2,000 tonnes of it, tipped over and down the side of the embankment. It ended up strewn along a series of suburban back gardens. Local residents rushed out in the night to find the crew shocked but not seriously injured, lying in the leading engine, which was on its side.

Some of the cement wagons had split and cement powder was spilling on to the gardens.

It was vital to clear the wreckage before any rain turned the cement into weak concrete and to do this the back gardens had to be commandeered by the railway, access between houses had to be made and lighting installed. A combination of railway heavy lifting cranes and road equipment was used to rerail the locomotives and wagons. Cutting gear and road tankers dealt with wagons that were condemned and with their contents. When it was all finished the gardens, fences, driveways, greenhouses, flowerbeds, etc. all had to be made good again. The total cost of recovery approached £1 million and took several weeks to accomplish. The railway, one of the country's busiest commuter routes, was closed for most of this time as both lines were torn up. A very expensive mistake by the Driver and a costly set of redundant catch points.

Returning though to the Signalman at Canterbury East: this same Signalman was in his early 20s at that time and so were many others who worked the small Absolute Block boxes, which were the starting grade boxes as they were on lines with relatively few trains passing. To some extent this was a topsy-turvy arrangement because it meant that young, inexperienced Signalmen were left to work unsupervised while older, possibly more responsible Signalmen worked together under the supervision of Regulators in the busier power boxes, a situation that persists today.

Stories abounded of antics that took place in remote signalboxes at night. After all, a signalbox was warmer and more roomy than the back seat of a Ford Cortina and if the Signalman had set up an early warning system in case anyone approached there was time to make things appear straight again. Some boxes had creaky steps leading up to them, deliberately kept that way by the Signalmen, while others even had specially rigged warning devices under the boards of walkways.

Another colleague of mine had at one time been a Signalman at North Kent West Junction box, which was on the approaches to Bricklayers Arms. He had an arrangement with a woman whose house backed on to the railway – if there was a packet of OMO washing powder in her kitchen window it was OK for him to slip over between trains, which were few and far between. Why OMO? Old Man Out (definitely not to be confused with One Man Operation, mentioned in the last chapter!) At one time this same colleague had worked at Chelsfield box on the South Eastern main line. His mate was

Redundant catch points near Mottingham, south-east London, contributed in October 1977 to the derailment of a 2,000-tonne coal train, which was then run into by a cement train. Two steam-powered recovery cranes are seen lifting cement wagons, some of which were strewn along a series of suburban back gardens. (Photo: Brian Garvin)

in the interlocking room under the frame with a girl and my colleague was dripping cold water on to them through the gaps in the floorboards. This was a box that apparently had an early warning system in case the SM or Area Inspector visited. Incidentally, he used to tell us just how unsatisfactory the signalling system was in those days, with dimly lit semaphores and steam-hauled trains with their poor forward sighting and their crews striving to keep up steam on the long drag up to the summit at Knockholt. Apparently it was not uncommon for a rush-hour express to pass all his signals at danger, the crew not even being aware of where they were. It was precisely this problem that was the major factor in the Lewisham disaster of December 1957 in which ninety people died.

It was not only Signalmen who got up to tricks. A Relief Crossing Keeper told me how he had brought a girl into Crabtree crossing box one Sunday afternoon and a steamy situation was developing when he heard the Station Manager's motorbike arriving. He quickly bundled the girl into the toilet, locked the door and tidied himself. Just as the SM came up the steps he noticed the girl's bra on the floor, which he quickly stuffed into the back pocket of his trousers without being able to be sure that it was not protruding. Keeping his back turned from the SM, he took him through all the box equipment, let him inspect the Incident Book and somehow managed to let a couple of trains pass. Then, as part of checking the cleanliness of the box, the SM asked him the question he was dreading. He asked for the key to the toilet. A sudden burst of inspiration enabled the Keeper to say that the regular Keepers must have hidden the key (and because of persistent rivalry between resident and relief staff this was quite likely and therefore a good story), knowing all the time, however, that he had rather foolishly hung the key back on its normal hook. Luckily for him the SM did not spot the key and told the Keeper that he had his authority to break the door open. Again luckily for the Crossing Keeper, he did not insist on this being done in his presence. Sidling along the wall, the Crossing Keeper said his goodbyes to the SM and breathed a sigh of relief when his bike roared off into the distance.

Having been sworn to secrecy, I was shown photographs taken in another Crossing Box of one of the well-known local girls draped across the lever frame. The staff room at one of the local stations was being used as a darkroom for the developing of such photographs on nights. For some reason railway station staff in those days seemed to attract 'groupies' who would hang about the stations, fetch things for them, flirt with them and in some cases end up in a locked staff room with them. Bear in mind that we still had night turns of duty on most stations then. Indeed, we had staff on most stations then. But why did we allow this sort of thing to go on? Obviously we didn't condone it officially, but with staff being required to work up to eighty-four hours per week and with us struggling each week to cover certain vital, but unpopular jobs, there had to be a bit of give and take. Some staff were so rarely at home that they brought their private and social lives to work with them.

Following a spate of such incidents at one of the most notorious North Kent line stations, the wife of one of the staff came into the Booking Hall one rush- hour morning with a collection of loaded carrier bags. She stood in the middle of the doorway to the platform and tipped out the contents, which were all her husband's belongings, on to the platform, shrieking abuse and threats as she did so. We transferred John to another station, largely for his own safety. He once told me that he had seventy-six stitches, mainly on his head, following a series of violent attacks by his wife. I remember wondering how many she had.

God alone knows what the passengers made of all these antics, but then the whole area was populated with people who openly brought all their domestic wrangles to work with them or fought them out on the streets, in the pubs or in the shops. It was *EastEnders* come true! Many of our staff and hundreds of our passengers lived in places such as the high rise and notorious Kidbrooke estate or the sprawling and equally infamous Thamesmead estate, which had rehoused thousands of people from the most deprived areas of inner London. Unemployment, drug-dealing, mugging, glue-sniffing, promiscuity and parental neglect were just some of the most blatantly obvious signs of how life was lived from minute to minute with little thought for the future. In a strange way this was tremendously invigorating, if sordid, in comparison with the stifled behaviour of other parts of south England. In that sort of environment we certainly weren't just playing trains – the railway was a very human industry with all the complications that arose from that.

Other than sexual indiscretions, the two main activities amongst errant railway staff in south-east London were drinking and stealing, or, to use the south London vernacular, "fievin". Numerous staff were dismissed or transferred for drinking and the problem of drink and of changing attitudes towards it will be one that I come back to. In the meantime, though, an amusing chapter of disasters that culminated in a drunken outburst from one of our staff in rather inappropriate circumstances. In an object lesson in incongruity, the Royal Train was coming to Charlton to take Prince Charles to Scotland following an evening engagement at Woolwich Barracks. The story started for us in the early afternoon when the SM belatedly realised that he hadn't got the required bowler hat to wear on formal occasions. I was sent out to get one for him, which wasn't easy as Woolwich is not peopled to any large extent by the wearers of bowler hats. Anyway, I found one eventually, in Lewisham I think, and the SM went home to get changed, the train being due at around ten in the evening.

Next hiccup was a points failure at Factory Junction, coupled with the fact that a wrong signalling description for the empty Royal Train from Wolverton had been given to the new Victoria box. Seeing a Class 5, i.e. empty coaching stock, train waiting at the junction, the Signalman in the newly commissioned panelbox decided to leave it there and not have the points wound over manually for it until there was a good long gap in the service to and from Victoria. The Driver, speaking to him from the signalpost telephone, did not think it was necessary to say exactly what the train was as everyone concerned should have received the special notice detailing the run. So he sat tight, having been told to wait for the points to be wound over. Eventually the train manager came up to ask what the delay was for, all was revealed, the Signalman re-described it correctly as a Class 1 and the train got on its way – late, of course.

Along the North Kent line approaching Woolwich there is a series of short tunnels and the Royal Train was limited to 10mph through two of these because of the limited clearance for Mk III rolling stock. The two tunnels were specified by name in the Special Notice, but it turned out that the Driver did not know the names of the tunnels so he went through them all at 10mph. By the time the train had run round at Plumstead Yard and returned on the up line, back through the same tunnels at 10mph, it was more than twenty minutes late and Prince Charles was waiting in his car at the end of the red carpet. Just as he got out of his car a drunken bellow of 'Good on yer, Charlie boy!' reverberated through the tense air as Danny, one of our Leading Railmen, along with his mates, decided to visit the station in between pints at the pub on the corner. He shouldn't even have known about the Royal Train as he was not on duty. One other thing – the Driver overran the specially erected stopboard by a yard or so, so the red carpet across the platform did not actually lead to a door. What a night.

Drinking and dishonesty were inextricably linked for many staff on stations at that time as there were large pickings to be made from excess fares, which then funded the other activities. Wives (virtually all our staff were male at the time) might expect to see payslips so illicit earnings were a boost for staff and could be spent on things of which their spouses might not approve. Although we tried to enforce proper ticket barrier control when passengers came on to stations, the staff would turn away again as soon as we had left, letting people through without tickets. This was a universal practice and resulted in large numbers of people arriving at other stations offering 50 pence or so to the staff there. Of course, the same staff who failed to check the tickets of joining passengers made sure they were on the barrier when passengers got off. In the rush hour a lot of money could be pocketed in this way along with a few pounds that would be accounted for properly in order to keep management off the staff's backs.

When Inspectors or Managers carried out ticket inspections, as we did from time to time, the excess fare takings soared through proper charging and accounting. When challenged about this, the staff would say that passengers were intimidated by all the gold braid and would therefore pay the right amount. To some extent this was true.

At Abbey Wood station I kept a league table of the amounts paid in by each member of staff. One person consistently topped the league but it was rumoured that he was also making more for himself than anyone else. He was just being more vigilant. Looking back on it all now, we should have kept on hammering home the need to ensure that passengers had tickets before they joined so that the excess fiddle was contained. Ideally, there should never have been a need to take money at the end of a journey. Nowadays, with open stations, corridor trains and Penalty Fares legislation, the problem has been largely solved – but others have been created, more about which later.

It was generally understood, though never openly stated to management, that there was a hierarchy of ticket-barrier positions on the Woolwich section of the North Kent line. The full-time ticket collectors on the busy barrier at Woolwich Arsenal itself had the prime positions and staff at other stations aspired to these jobs. I mentioned earlier the case of Joe Akintibubo, the saxophonist, who worked on this barrier and who thought he was about to retire. When it turned out that there was to be no vacancy after all several people's aspirations were ruined, not least those of my league champion at Abbey Wood. I think it is probably reasonable to say that in the early 1980s the three Woolwich Arsenal ticket barrier staff were making well over £50 a week each from fiddles. In all other jobs we had a very high turnover of staff, some people lasting only a few days, but these three hung on to their jobs with great determination, refusing higher-grade duty and other opportunities that might have arisen, retirement notwithstanding.

Many passengers, when handing over small amounts, wouldn't even bother to say where they had joined the train – or were pretending to have joined, of course. Others would say the name of the adjoining station but either way it was understood that the money was going into the collector's pocket. Occasionally we would stage ticket 'blocks': the other Assistant Station Manager, myself and some Inspectors would block the small stations, ensuring that no one got on a train without a ticket. Other Inspectors would then man the barriers at the major stations and challenge everyone who offered a short fare or purported to have come from one of the blocked stations. We frequently launched large-scale blocks with Police assistance and in most cases numerous prosecutions resulted. The sensible passengers, though, seeing a sea of gold braid and Police helmets, would offer the full fare from London and then go back to a 50 pence piece the next day. Of course, if there had been proper control of boarding passengers at the ticket barriers at Charing Cross, Waterloo East and London Bridge, the scope would not have existed for short payment on such a scale. Cannon Street was always more tightly controlled, showing that it could have been done at the others if only their managers had put their minds to it.

Basically, the revenue protection system was deeply flawed and although the passengers and staff were often in an unspoken complicity of dishonesty, the railway got no more or less than it deserved. At busy times, with people legitimately rushing for trains, not even the sharpest person could check in detail every ticket so some people were bound to get through. Long booking office queues always peeled off as the train drew in and passengers rushed through without tickets. At the other end of their journey they simply wanted to get on with their business and not have to wait for receipts for any money tendered. In the rush hour it was simply impossible anyway to stop and write out a receipt for one person without letting another dozen through unchecked. Staff were supposed to record all the amounts taken on slips variously known as 'long johns' or 'slim jims', but even this could not be done at the actual time of each transaction without missing another few tickets or fares. After each rush had passed, staff would enter a few figures on the slips, usually purporting to be full single fares from London. If £15 had been taken from about twenty people, an entry showing four singles from London at £1.60 each might look reasonable.

Some Booking Office Clerks were notoriously slow at their work, contributing to this situation. However, lots of the slow ones were also the most accurate and trustworthy and there were only a few Clerks who were both quick and accurate. The cumbersome ticket ordering and storage systems in use at the time also led to delays. Relief Clerks in particular would not always know where tickets were kept in each office and would end up writing out 'blanks' instead of using existing printed stock. All this was very time-consuming and one such incident in the morning rush hour could easily add another twenty impatient passengers to a queue, who would then run through the barrier as the train arrived. The abolition of Edmondson card tickets and the advent of APTIS (All-Purpose Ticket Issuing System) machines for ticket issuing did away with pre-printed stocks and thus sped up the process. Incidentally, another benefit was that ticket offices no longer needed so much storage space with a consequent saving on land and building costs for new station buildings. The drawings for the replacement station building at Abbey Wood were amended with this in mind as it was one of the first rebuilds to be carried out after APTIS was brought in.

With the early 1980s on the suburban South Eastern being typified by long queues, slow service, lethargic platform staff, ancient rolling stock, badly washed trains, cancellations due to chronic shortage of train crews and delays nearly every day it was not surprising that passengers sometimes became abusive or even violent. Assaults were common and abuse was almost taken for granted. It resulted in staff adopting a carefree attitude to the job and towards passengers. If your job didn't allow you to rise to each insult or slur then you coped with it by shrugging everything off. Hence the notorious indifference shown by so many railway staff – the calculated way in which staff carried on walking by when being addressed by a passenger and would never meet the passenger's eye. If you didn't get involved, nothing could develop. It was a depressing time for passengers and staff – the South Eastern was going nowhere at the time and its management, under Bob Newlyn, seemed to lack direction. Malcolm Southgate, while Regional Operations Manager for the Southern in 1979, had said to a group of us that we were saddled with the legacy of a 'utilitarian age', while Gordon Pettitt, General Manager, depressingly told us a couple of years later that there was no financial case for renewing the South Eastern's suburban fleet. We felt we were in a rut, being bypassed by developments elsewhere. It took the initiative of Chris Green's Network SouthEast to break the mould.

Despite these problems there were some surprising unofficial rules to which staff adhered. For instance, it was understood on the Woolwich line that staff would not smoke in the view of passengers. Yet today, even after a general decline in smoking, there are stations where you can see staff smoking on the platform or in booking offices. Another discipline we had was in the recording of train times, the timing of announcements and the operation of destination indicators. This discipline is manifestly lacking at many stations still.

To some extent the emergence of the 'retail culture', which had at least the merit of giving purpose to the operation, was at the same time responsible for the dismantling of these station operating systems. Divorcing train running management from station management perhaps resulted directly in trains staying over time at stations. How many of the specifically recruited retail staff would have known that an electric multiple unit train is booked to stand at the platform for twenty seconds and a DMU for thirty unless specifically shown otherwise in the Working Timetable, for instance? Another consequence was the higher incidence of doors not being properly closed on slam-door stock. One of the most enjoyable, if dangerous, aspects of platform vigilance was the indication to the Guard of a train that you would close a door that was 'on the catch' after the train had started. As the train accelerated, you would position yourself alongside and give the door a sharp rap with your fist or foot as it went by, thus slamming it shut and making the person sitting next to it jump out of their skin. The faster the train was moving, the more of a bang it made and the more satisfying it was. Another trick, incidentally, was in the accepting of packages from Guards. If the Guard was riding 'behind 8' of a ten-car while you were near the front of the train and he indicated that he had a package for you, you would hold up both hands as if about to clap. The Guard would then know that you intended to snatch the package as he went by. Again positioning yourself alongside the train, you would stand with your hands nearly together at just the right height and distance to swing round and grab the package from the Guard's hand as he sped by.

The spread of open ticket barriers, implemented in some cases so half-heartedly that staff were sometimes still seen on barriers and sometimes not, had the direct consequence of the deterioration in the timing of announcements and of indicator changing, as well as ending platform vigilance. The dismantling of systems without adequate replacement is one thing the railway proved itself to be adept at as the pace of change increased and it was a sign of the newly found freedom of management from the shackles of having to negotiate everything at length with Staff Representatives before any new ideas could be brought in.

8

Files and Affectations

The most dreary job I had on BR was surely in 1974 when I was a Clerical Officer in the Chief Passenger Manager's department at London Midland Region HQ, then at Euston House. The building was in its original state at that time, full of dark wood panels and small rooms. I worked in the dingy room 414A on the fourth floor, overlooking the gloomy central well of the building and therefore largely denied natural light.

The railway of the 1970s had huge office buildings like this all over the country, largely occupied by vast teams of Clerical Officers and junior managers who perpetuated a culture of obstruction, long-windedness and affected office mannerisms. Virtually all this was swept away subsequently with the arrival of greater levels of accountability, increased use of information technology and clearer ideas of the aims of the industry. Whereas in those days letters were dictated into dictaphones to be typed in huge typing pools overseen by sadistic slave mistresses, they were later mostly produced in a fraction of the time by their own senders directly on PCs. The massive scale of the reduction in the number of administrative departments and in the tiers of management meant that fewer letters needed to be written too, that there was a lot less toing and froing of correspondence and therefore that files were smaller and their contents more concise. Eventually, of course, a lot of it was sent and stored electronically, but this was a far cry from Euston House of the 1970s. There we had File Registries that worked rather like lending libraries. A lot of time was taken up in booking files in and out of these Registries, which were staffed by obstructive pedants who vainly fancied themselves to be archivists.

Office economics, office buildings and office personalities of the time had a marked resemblance to the unsustainable, corrupt, isolationist unreality of

Mervyn Peake's *Gormenghast*, particularly in the way that each person seemed to be needed solely because there were other people who expected them to be there.

The passenger department organisation on the old London Midland Region was ludicrously complicated: the Chief Passenger Manager had an Assistant and also two Service Group Managers for the InterCity lines. One was for the West Coast Main Line and one for the Midland Main Line/Cross Country services. It must be remembered that neither of these two service groups was exclusive to the LMR and so other Regions also had managers who had some input to these services. Then there were other generalist or specialist managers whose purpose I never understood, even though I worked directly for some of them. Owen Edwards, Ray Pinnock and Mike Tham had nondescript titles such as 'Passenger Officer', 'Passenger Planning Officer' and 'Passenger Services Officer', but basically they all trod on each others' toes and attended vast meetings at which things were endlessly debated without conclusion. More letters would be sent to more people as the result of each meeting and so the files would grow fatter and fatter, as would the egos of their custodians. Of course, there were teams of support staff to back up these managers and what really happened was that everyone provided work for everyone else in a vicious circle of mutual justification that bore little relevance to the railway outside, let alone its users.

In addition to this unwieldy Regional set-up there were Divisional Passenger Managers, one for each of the seven Divisions on the LMR. Then there were people working at the Board for the Executive Director, Passenger. The Divisional Passenger Managers reported to both their own Divisional Managers and to the Chief Passenger Manager thus creating another fudge in accountability. They too, needless to say, had teams of clerical support. Divisions had been established following the requirement for decentralisation made by the Transport Act, 1953, which in turn had reversed the centralisation imposed under nationalisation. Each change seemed simply to have resulted in new layers of bureaucracy being added, without the previous ones having being disbanded or reduced.

What makes all this rigmarole even more ridiculous to look back upon is the fact that at that time the 'point of sale' staff, i.e. Booking Clerks, were not even part of the passenger organisation. The passenger departments, huge as they were, had no direct involvement in the running of the railway, not even to the extent of managing the booking offices. This was left to the Operations department, through the Area Managers, an anomaly only rectified by the so-called 'Organising for Quality' reorganisation of the early 1990s, which at least had the merit of creating a professional retail body to sell the railway's services, allied to the specification of those services. The old-time Passenger Managers, hidden from reality in the huge grim offices of the former railway companies, would have had a rude awakening if they had been required to perform the 'hands-on' type of work undertaken by their Retail and, now, private sector successors.

With this unwieldy structure it is no wonder, for example, that the 1970s' proposal to reopen the Snow Hill Tunnel between Farringdon and Blackfriars drowned in a sea of conflicting paperwork between the London Midland Region, Southern Region and the Board. This element of the railway's contribution to the 1974 London Rail Study, unnecessarily complicated by the Regional divide, was relegated to the category of secondary importance by the planning authorities. It was estimated that it would cost £10 million to reopen the route. A decade later the relatively streamlined Network SouthEast organisation was able to see it through under the properly co-ordinated brand name of Thameslink, and at a lower cost. While the 1974 scheme floundered in the operational nightmare of two distinct railways operating over each other's lines (LMR to Croydon, etc. and SR to West Hampstead – not to mention the Divisions within those Regions), Thameslink was run as part of Chris Green's 'one railway for Londoners' policy. One railway? Now, of course, there are fifteen separate passenger companies operating into London, but then that's progress!

Other schemes we were working on at LMR HQ in 1974 included the BRB proposal that where there were two or more stations in a town or city, one should be designated 'Main', so that, for example, Manchester Piccadilly would have become Manchester Main and Warrington Bank Quay would have been Warrington Main. Thank goodness that never happened. Remember that this was the era in which one of the few of the BRB's visible interventions in the running of the railway was the imposition of the Corporate Identity, which attempted to establish a uniform level of dreariness on everyone.

Then we were looking at the implications of transferring major engineering works from Sunday to Wednesday in order to save paying time-and-three-quarters to engineering staff. This would have devastated the InterCity business market as well as infuriating commuters and freight customers. Of greater benefit was the proposal to develop battery-powered locomotives for the Holyhead line, Blackpool North line, etc. The idea was that the batteries would be charged while the loco was 'under the wires' from Euston and it could then go through to its destination and back on battery power, thus doing away with the need to maintain a separate fleet of diesels and saving the time and operational hassle of changing engines at Crewe, Preston, etc. It would also, of course, save the cost of electrifying the branches. Battery technology was certainly up to powering a lightweight train for around 50 miles at moderate speeds and had, in fact, been used on the Ballater branch in Scotland as long ago as 1958. In the 1970s, as it became apparent that further development might be possible, BR, the Electricity Council and Chloride had formed a consortium to develop the idea. Nothing came of it directly, but as with so many abortive railway developments, most notably the Advanced Passenger Train, there were technological spin-offs that benefited not just the railway industry.

Other ideas being promoted were the concept of Parkway stations to attract roadborne railheading – Alfreton & Mansfield Parkway and Bristol Parkway were early examples – and the extension of Birmingham New Street as the hub of an expanding North-East/South-West InterCity passenger service. Indeed, the NE/SW routes were showing the fastest growth of all InterCity services at the time. The great tradition of changing trains at Crewe for just about anywhere was slowly being replaced by a co-ordinated network of through cross-country InterCity trains calling at Birmingham New Street, a concept retained by the present operators, Virgin XC.* We were also putting together plans for new stations at Birmingham International and Milton Keynes, the latter causing much debate as neither Wolverton nor Bletchley was ideally positioned for the new town, resulting eventually in there being three stations within a few miles of each other along the same line. Even then we realised that, from the railway point of view, Bletchley would have been the place to have developed as it offered the chance to revive the east–west service from Oxford to Cambridge that is now being spoken of again.

* 2018 update: Cross Country Trains are now operated by Arriva, not Virgin.

The main event during my time as a Clerical Officer on the LMR was the launching of the 'Electric Scots' in May 1974. The new Class 87 locomotives had been built specially for through electric haulage between Euston and Glasgow Central now that electrification was complete. I went to see the first five-hour Royal Scot arrive at Euston, having averaged 80.3mph all the way from Glasgow Central, including stops. For a brief period the West Coast Main Line had the fastest timings between London and Glasgow/ Edinburgh, soon though to be overtaken again by the East Coast Main Line. The up Flying Scotsman in the last days of InterCity averaged 94.5mph while the Royal Scot of the same period was hanging precariously to its 1974 timings on a WCML again notorious for rough-riding and speed restrictions. The ever-cyclical nature of railway investment is heading back towards the WCML now, of course, with Network Rail rebuilding the line.

In those days so far removed from the notion of separate 'businesses', except as brand names, much play was made of the fact that the new Class 87 locos would work during the day on express passenger work and then overnight on fast freights. In practice they couldn't maintain the tight timings required by some heavy overnight Freightliner services over Shap and Beattock summits and so ended up being diagrammed in pairs, which put paid to some of the cost benefit.

The Chief Passenger Manager on the LMR when I was there was Myles Herbert, one of the last of the military-type, true gentlemen railway managers. I hadn't realised that there really were such people, other than in war films, until I met him. He presided over his vast, crumbling and inefficient empire with the grace and good manners of a bygone, colonial-style age. I was the most lowly graded person in his department, but he nevertheless found time to thank me personally when I had helped out at Euston Telephone Enquiry Bureau during a day of disruption caused by the derailment of a Freightliner at Tring. Similarly he sought me out and apologised for being curt to me over the matter of a lost file, which he had eventually found on his own desk. When I left, on promotion to the post of Assistant Controller on shifts with the Southern Region, he called me into his office to wish me well and to warn me of the dangers of staying in shift work for too long. He drew on his experience of staff who worked for him when he had been Divisional Manager at Inverness for this warning. Could there really have been a Divisional Manager at Inverness, I wondered? What for? And could

Completion of West Coast Main Line electrification to Glasgow saw the launch of the 'Electric Scots' and the introduction of the Class 87. An express passes Linslade in November 1980. (Photo: Caley Photographic)

In the days when we all worked for the same railway, the 87s were common to both passenger and freight and so achieved day and night utilisation. A Freightliner train passes Linslade in November 1980. (Photo: Caley Photographic)

it really have been Myles Herbert? One could imagine a white-moustached English gentleman of military bearing huntin' and shootin' in his tweeds on the moors while the staff were shuntin' and hootin' in the stations and yards. It was impossible, though, not to respect the man's ingrained integrity and good manners.

There were still then several managers in the dim corridors of Regional Headquarters offices and at the Board who had military titles, some probably spurious. At the same time there were names redolent of the British Establishment and of railway heritage – Bonham Carter and Huskisson, for example, the LMR General Manager and London Divisional Manager respectively.

The Board's offices at 222 Marylebone Road, which I had to visit from time to time, had separate toilets and restaurants for different grades, its wealth of both being a legacy from its days as the Great Central Railway's hotel. So too did some Regional offices. The higher grades were known as 'Officers' and they ate in the 'Officers' Mess'. This elitism lasted right through to the 1980s. The Officers' Mess at Waterloo, for instance, was through a grand door in the hallway next to the Victory Arch, while the rest of us had a grotty canteen overlooking the platform that was used for Exeter departures and so was full of diesel fumes. In the early 1980s the two were abolished and replaced by a 'staff restaurant' for all grades but the Officers were then discreetly given vouchers for meals at the Charing Cross Hotel.

General Managers had private saloons for attaching to loco-hauled trains or for running as specials. These were used for inspections or for entertaining. The GM on the Western regularly entertained National Coal Board members in his saloon on the way to see the rugby at Cardiff Arms Park, the saloon in those cases being attached to the rear of a service train in the days of Class 47 haulage. Over the years the use of these saloons has declined, partly with the trend towards fixed formation trains such as the HST and partly with the abolition of privilege. Later use of saloons was more for publicity and fund-raising efforts. In March 1991 I was one of a party riding around south London in the Southern GM's saloon, entertaining officials and councillors from a couple of London boroughs. We had been fortunate in getting financial assistance from them to help with environmental improvements and we were able to show them a great many more places where money might be spent. Morning coffee was served on board, followed later by lunch and it was all very civilised, although it has to be said that you feel a trifle ridiculous being seen in a vehicle with all-round windows eating lunch as you go through places such as Catford and the Elephant, with all the Del Boys on the platforms staring at you as if you come from another planet.

Chauffeurs were also employed for many senior managers, another facility that declined as time went by. Other symbols of prestige were the leather, silver and gold passes for travel on the railway and on ships and hovercraft, all of which really were made of those materials until a few years ago. By the time I came to qualify for what used to be a 'leather' it had become a piece of plastic like a credit card. Later still it was reduced to a thin card like a season ticket. At least it had the benefit of looking roughly like an ordinary ticket, so that in a crowded carriage other passengers wouldn't have to know you worked for the railway when a ticket check was made. I often wondered whether the very senior managers ever felt a bit silly showing a gold medallion to a ticket Inspector. But then I suppose if you manage to reach those dizzy heights you must have to have the confidence to carry it off.

Staff travel concessions were at one time very valuable as the railway operated hotels, ships and hovercraft as well as trains. Staff could even obtain a discount on a cup of tea at station buffets – but only tea, not coffee, which presumably was not thought to be drunk by 'workers'. Until 1982 these perks, which all employees received to a greater or lesser degree, were tax-free, the Inland Revenue not yet having woken up to the considerable value involved. By the early 1990s, though, middle managers on the railway were typically paying an additional £300 per annum in income tax for travel facilities, which had by then been considerably reduced by the privatisation of ships, hovercraft and hotels. And, of course, of station buffets – so no more cheap cuppas.

The system for issuing concessionary tickets to staff who were not passholders was a prime example of the way in which railway staff until the 1980s seemed to justify each others' jobs. Each personnel office had a Travel Facilities Section. Staff had to apply to this office each time they wanted to use one of their annual entitlement of free tickets. Clerks wrote out these tickets, recording all the details and ticking off each individual's total to ensure that they had no more than was due to them. Most people applied for such tickets because they had specific journeys in mind, but large numbers of us applied for tickets that simply gave the maximum travel possibilities. Thus, most of my applications were for returns from Calais to Falkirk High, so I could travel the entire length of both West Coast and East Coast routes as well as having a trip to the Continent, or Lowestoft to Fishguard Harbour. When you consider that journeys could be broken any number of times en route you will see that the possibilities were enormous. There was little to stop you from giving away your tickets to others until photo identity cards were introduced in the late 1970s. Indeed, I must confess, I was given someone else's ticket to use on a trip to Brighton before I'd even joined BR. When the photocards came in a colleague and I had our photographs taken by a machine at Canterbury Bus Station after a heavy lunchtime session on a midweek rest day in 1978. My glazed expression and full head of hair remained to torment me for the remainder of my railway service.

The Travel Facilities Sections were done away with on the introduction of cards on to which users entered their own details as and when they wanted to travel. This was part of a drive to shake off the culture that had persisted for so long that meant that the more staff there were on the books, the more staff were needed to support them. Once this upward spiral is reversed, as on the railway, huge savings in staff costs and office space can be made as well as massive gains through the streamlining of reporting lines. The abolition of the cumbersome Regional departments, such as the monster that was the LMR Chief Passenger Manager's, was part of this process. Railway culture changed over the years to an almost obsessive belief that the fewer resources of any kind you had, then the fewer still you would shortly require. This was certainly valid in the days of enormous waste and duplication in which each resource, human or otherwise, needed another to keep it going, but when most of the fat had gone it did lead to some nonsensical reductions in which valuable expertise was lost in the drive to cut staff numbers at any cost. But more about that later.

So with the demise of the Travel Facilities Sections went another chunk of administrative cost. Gone was the need to give notice of the intention to travel free. Gone too, though, were lots of the travel opportunities – a few more branch lines, such as Alston and Bridport, the ships and the hovercraft: the ships for a fraction of their value and the hovercraft for the ubiquitous 'nominal sum'.

9

Sailing into Stormy Waters

For many years BR had run its ships through the Shipping and International Services Division (SISD). Together with the SNCF and SNCB the marketing name Sealink had been coined in 1970, being, of course, a BR initiative. The main business was cross-Channel, with Sealink running in competition with other operators, notably Townsend Thoresen. For some time there was a price cartel on the short-sea routes from Dover and Folkestone but this was broken not by the company that sailed its ships under names that all included the words 'Free Enterprise' but by the state-owned Sealink. This triggered two things. The first, quite obviously, was a price war. The second was Townsend's decision to turn the crossings into a race. They sped up their journeys so that they could overtake Sealink's ships *en route*, but this was at the cost to them of enormously inflated fuel consumption. Sealink's Chief Engineer, at a training seminar I attended in 1980, estimated that Townsend might have increased their fuel costs by as much as 50 per cent in order to achieve the kudos of overtaking the Sealink vessel. Both the time and price wars contributed to the Zeebrugge tragedy of March 1987 in which Townsend's *Herald of Free Enterprise* capsized when leaving the port before having closed its bow doors.

Sealink, being part of the international railway organisation, had a monopoly on the so-called 'classic' market, i.e. people who caught the boat train from London to the port, took the boat across and then went by train to Paris, etc. This had been the mainstay of the railways' international business from the days of the Channel packets but was now being overtaken by car ferry traffic in which they ensured they also had a stake. The Southern Region ran connecting boat trains and in the 1970s we sometimes had up to three trains meeting each sailing. Trains would run non-stop to Victoria in

BR ran ships and hovercraft. Fourteen-car boat trains met each 'classic' sailing at Dover and Folkestone, running non-stop to London Victoria. Sealink's *Invicta* waits at Dover Western Docks in 1971. (Photo: Brian Garvin)

convoy. At the time all boat trains ran with fourteen cars – Motor Luggage Van, Trailer Luggage Van and twelve coaches, including a buffet.

On 1 January 1979 SISD was turned into Sealink (UK) Ltd, still wholly owned by the three railways. Even in those pre-Thatcher days many railway people could see the ultimate motive for doing this, but a sell-off was strenuously denied by the Board. Indeed, this was confirmed in March 1980 by the Minister of Transport, Norman (later Sir Norman) Fowler, who said that BR's shipping and hotel interests would not be 'hived off and got rid of'. Sure enough, though, the hotels went in 1983 and Sealink was sold to Sea Containers in July 1984 for £66 million. So the railway, which had developed the short-sea routes as part of an integrated transport system, lost its connections with the Hook of Holland, Calais, Boulogne, Fishguard, Rosslare, Dun Laoghaire and Larne along with the Isle of Wight routes, despite the Minister's earlier assurance.

The £66 million paid for Sealink was in marked contrast to its book asset value of £108 million, but who cared about a mere £42 million when political ideology was hungry to be satisfied? This asset stripping of a public body came hot on the heels of the sale of BR's Hoverspeed in February 1984. The hovercraft operation went for a nominal sum to a group of its own managers, who subsequently sold it on to the privatised Sealink for

£5 million. Lessons never being learnt where dogma has overridden reason, the same was allowed more recently with the sale and subsequent resale of all three of the railway rolling stock leasing companies, in which groups of former railway managers became instant multi-millionaires following their snapping up of public assets at giveaway prices and then reselling them at prices nearer to their true value. Within three years of privatisation, for example, Porterbrook had been sold for £300 million more than the taxpayer had received for it, while Angel went for £389 million more.

With the sale of Sealink in 1984, the passenger railway was no longer tied to one cross-Channel operator and, ironically, deals were struck with former rivals Townsend Thoresen to provide connecting arrangements at Dover Priory station. In the old days Townsend coaches had not been allowed to call at Dover Priory (they had tried every so often to poach the 'classic' market but were always rebuffed), but the new spirit of deregulation allowed BR, as much as anyone else, to exploit new opportunities. Through travel promotions with P & O (Townsend's successors) and Sally Line, for example, BR prospered.

British Transport Hotels Ltd too had been broken up in February 1983 and sold. Hotel names such as Gleneagles, North British, Great Western Royal and Charing Cross, some of which had been built by the railways as integral parts of their businesses and which owed their fame to the railway connection, went to the private sector. On the plus side was the abolition of the name of the company, which must have been most uninviting for potential customers.

Later, in 1988, the railway's brand name of Travellers Fare, which had been established in 1973 as part of British Transport Hotels, left public ownership. Until shortly before its sale Travellers Fare had been in charge of both train and station catering – an extremely odd arrangement as these operations have always competed with each other. This appeared to have been overlooked by the Transport Act of 1962 that lumped hotels, station catering and train catering under one roof. Much the same way as the Post Office used to run the telephone system, with inevitable conflicts of interest, so Travellers Fare got itself into a mess. Train catering suffered from a lack of investment, huge pilferage problems and financial fiddles while station catering, which was largely profitable, was taken care of in terms of branding, investment and expansion. Under BTH's stewardship of TF, the successful brands of Casey Jones (eventually sold to Burger King) and Upper Crust were established, while train catering degenerated into Mk I cars with grease stains trickling from the kitchen windows, running in disastrous contrast to their accompanying air-conditioned and quiet Mk II or even Mk III coach sets. On the plus side of this, though, was the undoubted, if perverse, pleasure of swaying around in one of the orange plastic bucket seats in the buffet car with a can of beer while hurtling along the West Coast Main Line at 100mph with the sliding windows open.

The sell-off of TF was, of course, only of the profitable bit – the station catering. InterCity then took over its own on-board catering, while other operators took on contractors. Investment was made in a new generation of catering vehicles, which was a long overdue development and one that was essential if InterCity was to retain or expand its market share in the face of competition from airlines, coaches and the car. However, InterCity's newly formed catering organisation ICOBS (InterCity On Board Services) went over the top in its hype and produced many spurious forecasts and unworkable plans to transform train catering and thus justify the investment. In particular the West Coast Main Line was used to try out new Mk III vehicles, providing a style of catering branded Cuisine 2000. InterCity invested heavily in Cuisine 2000 from late 1986 but by January 1989 the brand had been dropped following bad publicity and the exposure of some of the tactics involved in setting it up. In its first year, though, volume of meals served on the WCML group increased by 70 per cent while the new range of sandwiches, made initially by Telfer's or United Biscuits and including celebrity recommendations such as the Clement Freud range, led to a doubling of sales. Behind the scenes, however, things were not well.

In January 1988 ICOBS splashed out on the recruitment of managers from the hotel and catering industry, mostly paid salaries far in excess of their Travellers Fare predecessors. These new managers formed the bulk of the West Coast team that was intended to transform catering and sleeping-car services. A few existing ICOBS managers and two managers from other parts of BR completed the team. I was one. Trusthouse Forte (THF), a market leader in airline catering, was brought in to prepare food for the restaurant cars and to run the catering stores at Euston, Wolverhampton, Liverpool and Manchester while another firm was awarded the contract to run the operation at Glasgow Central. The contracts were initially worth £3.7 million per year.

Meals, supposedly adhering to ICOBS' stringent specifications of portion size and presentation as defined in a glossy manual, were prepared in THF kitchens under the ill-fated 'cook–chill' system and then taken by road to the various station stores. There, along with all the necessary gear for final cooking and serving, they were loaded on to trains by THF staff. ICOBS crews then unpacked, reheated and served the food in the trust that THF had actually delivered the specified 'modules'. These modules were chilled by the insertion of eutectic plates but the chill soon wore off in a hot kitchen car.

The effect on the morale of the on-board chefs of having to unpack and dish up food prepared by someone else was predictably bad, whilst the gross inefficiencies in terms of portion sizes, wrong deliveries and missing equipment meant that the whole system slid into disrepute. A lot of InterCity management time was taken up over a period of around a year and a half simply overseeing and checking THF, often covering up for their failings. The London *Evening Standard*, having got wise to what was happening, ran an article alleging that InterCity staff had been instructed that shortcomings were to be apologised for but that the failings of the contractor were never to be mentioned. This was true: InterCity and ICOBS took all the blame as it would not have been politically acceptable at the time for staff of a state-owned industry to criticise a private company.

On top of this debacle was the farce of the investment criteria for Cuisine 2000. Investment had been made on the assumption, put forward by ICOBS, that WCML catering could be profitable in its own right, rather than being part of an overall service and therefore subsidised out of fares, as had been the case, is now and is with most railways and airlines. However, profitability could only happen if InterCity could accept that ICOBS would operate only on services that made money for them; a thing that InterCity could not accept because, being a national brand, it needed to offer a uniform service across its entire business. This conflict was never resolved and yet the investment went ahead.

Further to this, the way in which ICOBS had calculated that it could run profitably on any given train was open to doubt. It transpired that costs had been unfairly loaded on to non-Cuisine 2000 services in order to try to show that the return on Cuisine 2000 was greater than was actually the case. In practice Cuisine 2000 cost a fortune to run and as it gradually took over from the non-Cuisine 2000 services, so there were fewer opportunities to offload the cost. So instead of costs falling and thus contributing to a return on investment, it became apparent that the opposite was happening. The figures simply didn't add up: Cuisine 2000 could not do what it was made out to be able to do and the cars had been obtained largely on false pretences. ICOBS' Director, David Sumner and his Financial Controller were unceremoniously removed by the Managing Director of InterCity, Dr John Prideaux in February 1989; THF were given notice to quit (they went quietly in the end, admitting defeat); ICOBS took over the stores management and a handful of long-serving catering managers who had ridden out the storm transformed the operation in terms of hygiene, order and cost control; on-train cooking of meals resumed and staff morale improved. It was a silent 're-nationalisation' at the height of Mrs Thatcher's power. The experiment with private contract catering had been swept under the carpet. Terry Coyle, the new Manager of ICOBS, was quoted in July 1990 as saying, tactfully, that valuable lessons had been learnt by the exercise, adding, however, that 'all in all we were getting a great deal of waste'. In catering terms this means unused food: he did not refer to the money that had been wasted, both in operating Cuisine 2000 and in the lost customer goodwill as it crumbled.

Incidentally, none of the six managers recruited from outside the railway at the time Cuisine 2000 was launched survived until the end: one left during the first week, unable to cope with the concept of a round-the-clock operation spread over 400 miles, while two were dismissed for misconduct. The rest moved back to more peaceful jobs where their kitchens weren't on wheels hundreds of miles away. Similarly, one of the THF store managers at Euston was removed at ICOBS' insistence for incompetence while another was caught (and dismissed) with a car boot full of InterCity wine, which he had taken from the stores of which he was supposed to be in charge. The whole episode was extremely sordid and in all my railway experience I never came across dishonesty and incompetence at management level to the extent I did with ICOBS during the Cuisine 2000 era.

While the way in which ICOBS took back proper control over its stores and restaurant cars after the clear-out of THF and the 'outside' managers was impressive, the organisation and general culture of ICOBS was very primitive. Office facilities were practically non-existent, in terms of actual rooms and desks, but also in terms of IT. At ICOBS' Euston offices, situated in the Stephenson Rooms above the eastern colonnade of the station, there was a huge room full of Clerical Officers who sifted through reams of returns from each catering circuit in a way that reminded me of the early 1970s, adding hugely to the cost of the operation. Along the corridor was a room shared by seven managers. It had two desks, no natural light and served also as a corridor leading to two other offices. The basic philosophy of ICOBS seemed to be that so long as you could charge about like a headless chicken and make a lot of noise you were getting things done. The standard of literacy amongst some ICOBS managers was lamentable and so very little was ever properly recorded. There was little scope for working out strategies, there were no facilities for interviewing staff and there was no respect for anything other than the minute-to-minute tasks, or 'fire fighting' as it was rather proudly called, as if that was to what real managers should aspire.

About the only thing that held the Cuisine 2000 experiment and the WCML catering operation as a whole together was the influence of ICOBS' Business Manager at Euston, 'Billy' Graham, who had been moved from Glasgow to London, charged with implementing Cuisine 2000. Although surrounded on all sides by the grunts and kneejerk reactions of his bosses, peers and subordinates, he retained a firm grasp on the reality of the situation and was somehow able to provide constructive leadership and a rare personal integrity in a sea of confusion. I dare say there were occasions when he regretted not having pursued his original intention of becoming a sports journalist, although he said to me once that train catering, upon which he had initially embarked as a summer holiday job, was 'in his blood'. There were many people I came across on the railway who had never intended to stay but who became absorbed by what they were doing and seemed to think that they needed to see it through.

During the period of Cuisine 2000 I was ICOBS' Sleeping Car Services Manager. However, the amount of management time needed to oversee the deficiencies of Cuisine 2000 meant that I was heavily involved in daytime work, to the detriment of the sleepers, which were, in any case, seen as the poor relations. ICOBS, having little knowledge of, or interest in, the safety and ticketing elements of sleeping car work, had apparently thought that the sleepers were simply a branch of train catering. As such, about their only initial concern was at the low level of catering takings, as if you could wake everyone up every hour through the night to try to make a catering sale.

Responsibility for Sleeping Car Attendants had been transferred at a stroke from Area Managers to ICOBS without there having been anyone in place in ICOBS who knew about sleepers or anyone who could inherit and keep current the necessary paperwork relating to staff safety competence. I had to learn as I went along and this was impeded by being lumped together with the Catering Managers for a while until I was able to demonstrate to Billy that the sleepers needed specialist treatment. However, without office space and other facilities it was difficult to make change in a constructive and lasting way.

InterCity was introducing first-class lounge cars to the Night Scotsman, Night Caledonian, Night Aberdonian and Royal Highlander premier sleeper trains to Edinburgh, Glasgow Central, Aberdeen and Inverness respectively at the time. These cars were very smart, especially the first batch of conversions with loose seating and tables, but as with so many things I came across during my time with ICOBS, they were riddled with problems through things not having been thought through properly: the centralised train fire alarm system meant that an alarm activated in one car sounded throughout the train, or at least half of it, even if this wasn't necessary; the time taken by staff to attend to alarms or to other passenger calls was increased as staff could be anywhere along the train rather than being confined to their own pair of cars as under the old system; there was no temperature control for catering supplies in the lounge cars even though the development of catering sales was one of the reasons for their construction; and, finally, the cars were introduced with the assumption that sleeping-car staff would work together as teams and in this way, rather bizarrely, would be interchangeable with restaurant-car crews. This was a great fallacy for a number of reasons. First, sleeper staff were required to have detailed knowledge of the fire systems and of ticketing, whereas the skills needed by restaurant-car staff were in the entirely different areas of food preparation and table service. It was impracticable to pretend that all staff could have all these skills and keep them up to date to a sufficient level. Secondly, the sleeping-car work entailed long night hours and lodging away from home, and this would certainly not have suited all restaurant-car staff and would have led to horrendous recruitment and training problems if the two sets of staff had actually been merged into one pool.

Inevitably, the people who worked permanent nights had a different approach from the extrovert, bustling outlook required for a busy restaurant car. The best Sleeping Car Attendants were the quiet, somewhat elderly loners, who crept into work without drawing attention to themselves, were firm but polite to their customers and who knew their jobs inside out. For some reason these were mainly Irish, Indian or Pakistani, at least among London staff.

In my opinion these were the true elite of the Euston-based Attendants in the late 1980s and they mostly worked not on the lounge-car trains, which required teamwork, but on the remaining traditional, untitled trains such as the stopping services to Inverness, Fort William, Edinburgh and Stranraer Harbour. The upgrading of the premier, titled trains made these people feel second best and this was a shame as they were the true 'professionals' of the sleeping-car service. However, change needed to be made – InterCity had been told by the Government to break even, a task not set to any other major rail passenger operator in the world.

In order to meet the pressure for reduced costs on the sleepers, I introduced a system for taking half the staff off each lounge car train northbound at Preston each night and southbound at Carlisle. All four titled trains each way called at both points for train crew relief, although the stops were not advertised publicly. The staff taken off then returned home on the corresponding trains in the other direction. This meant that trains were fully manned at the times when passengers were requiring service early in the journey and at the end of it but that in between Preston and Carlisle I had just sufficient staff for fire safety. The result was that we saved on lodging costs during the day as staff were booked into hotels for the day prior to working back the next night. However, it was fraught with difficulties: not least that passengers expected the same Attendant to be there in the morning as had been there the previous evening. In particular, there were numerous embarrassing incidents when the morning Attendant was not of the same sex as the one in the evening, when the passenger had assumed that he or she would be. Incidentally, where second-class berths were both occupied this was on the basis of 'same sex' in each compartment, but even this did not always work. One night a party from Sweden decided to re-allocate themselves in the night on the Night Scotsman and a lady who was not part of the group, having checked in with a Swedish girl in her compartment, awoke to find a young man there. The girl had swapped in order to be with her boyfriend.

Another way of reducing costs was to find cheaper hotels for the Attendants to stay at. I spent a fascinating day walking around that most wonderful of cities, Edinburgh, trying to find somewhere to give us a better deal than the place we were using at the time. Several eyebrows were raised when I asked for prices for accommodation for five people during the day, explaining that they worked at night.

'What are they, then? Hookers?' asked one hotel manager. He didn't get our custom.

Needless to say, there were many eccentric and interesting characters among this group of largely unsupervised travelling nightworkers. Likewise, also perhaps needless to say, there were lots of dubious activities. The Night Aberdonian, in addition to its legitimate traffic of passengers, parcels and mails also often carried fish from Aberdeen and Arbroath to London for sale to one of the Attendant's friends. His activities were curtailed after a passenger wrote in to complain about the smell. Supplies of home-prepared Kashmiri food travelled northwards for delivery to Aberdeen University, where another Attendant's son was studying. Occasionally the father would raid the supplies when I was travelling and we would sit in the lounge car after all the passengers had retired, sampling a beautiful range of authentically cooked dishes that were lavished upon me with typical Asian hospitality. Sometimes I would be given Indian sweets from the specialist shops in the side streets near Euston – this started after I casually remarked that because there were no labels I couldn't tell what they were and therefore wouldn't know what to buy.

Some staff had developed relationships at both ends of the journey. One London-based Attendant resolved his conflicting personal relationships by getting me to transfer him to Inverness so that he could live with and work with the woman he had taken up with there, who was also a Sleeping Car Attendant. A recurring problem was the receipt of letters of complaint alleging unwanted attention from Attendants, who were required to enter compartments to deliver morning tea and biscuits. Attendants were trained not to allow the door to close behind them when they entered, but this meant that they had to rely upon the passenger lowering the bedside table in order for the tray to be placed upon it. If the passenger didn't know how to do this, the Attendant would have to come right into the compartment and lean over the recumbent passenger and the door would close itself.

Ticketing fiddles were possible on the sleepers and some staff may have been doing very nicely out of this. If a passenger turned up just before departure 'on spec' and asked if any berths were free, the resulting revenue could be considerable and would not be expected by a look at the berth allocation list. It could amount to, say, £50 for the fare and another £20 for the berth. An unofficially acquired excess fare book would mean £70 in the Attendant's pocket. Alternatively, and more riskily, a 'cut price, no questions asked' deal with no ticket could be struck for, say, £40. By putting the passenger in a second-class compartment in which the other berth was already occupied, the Attendant would be safe from any Inspector who might board the train and check empty berths against the list. But what if an Inspector checked which berths had been used in the morning, after the passengers had gone, and found twenty used berths when only nineteen had been paid for? The favourite trick was to have spilled some tea or coffee over the sheets of one berth so that the Attendant could say that the legitimate passenger must have accidentally done this and then transferred to the other berth.

Small gains could also be made by selling drinks bought from supermarkets rather than those supplied by InterCity as these would not need to be accounted for. However, the gains from this type of activity were minute in comparison with what could be achieved by dishonest staff on daytime services. While I was working at Euston a Chief Steward who had worked a Sunday afternoon buffet service single-manned was found dead in the train when it reached Willesden depot and ICOBS managers went out to recover the stock, while the Police checked for suspicious circumstances. The Police found none, but the ICOBS managers found they had gained several hundred pounds worth of stock that had never gone through ICOBS' books.

Sometimes there would be management raids just before trains departed as this was when staff sometimes considered it safe to start getting goods out of their personal bags, which could not be legally searched by the management. One afternoon in 1988 when I was on duty the entire catering crew of the 1320 Euston to Manchester Piccadilly (Chief Steward, Senior Steward, Chef and two Stewards) was hauled off by the Police at our instigation and the train went out with no catering at all. All the staff were dismissed after the due process had been gone through.

Euston catering staff also worked the Exhibition Train, which was based at Salisbury but which could go almost anywhere on charter to firms who were trying to impress their customers or staff. Having hired the train and paid for its haulage, most firms liked to make it really worthwhile by splashing out on the catering and vast amounts were often spent on champagne in particular; so much so that it was difficult at times to assess how much was reasonable to expect in revenue from such trains. One Chief Steward had managed to get a tight grip on this train, guaranteeing to be available whenever it went out, transporting the stores down to Salisbury and preparing the train each time. This saved the Euston ICOBS management any hassle in having to try to cover the Exhibition Train workings but one day my colleague, Tony Law, followed the Chief Steward down to Salisbury and found that the substantial and valuable stores from the InterCity depot at Euston were only a fraction of the stock actually on board.

Other charter trains yielded huge returns for BR as a whole and also for ICOBS and possibly also for its staff. Grand National Day was always one of the biggest on the West Coast Main Line with Seagram's and other firms hiring complete trains to Aintree on which booze, tips – and propositions of various sorts – flowed like water. There was never any problem in finding catering staff to work these trains.

10

Shunting and Sorting

A whole book could probably be written about the shambles that went under the name of Rail Express Parcels (REPS) in the 1970s and '80s. This part of the railway's traditional business, coupled as it was with the strangely named Full Loads freight service, was a case study in how not to run an efficient business in a world that had moved on. Eventually the BRB made the courageous, correct, but overdue decision not to allow these gruesome relics to continue any more and the Collection & Delivery part of REPS ended abruptly on 1 July 1981. The 1980 BRB Annual Report timidly stated that the C & D service was 'beginning to undermine the developing parts of the business'. In particular, Red Star, which had been operating for many years as a station-to-station-only service was being impeded in its reputation and development by association with the rest of the railway's parcels operations, which in fact had been losing about £38 million a year on a turnover of little more than that same amount and had been a drain for years, not only financially but also in terms of customer credibility.

The wagonload freight service, of which Full Loads was only a small part, had been transformed rather more gently into Speedlink, while from the ashes of REPS, after a respectable interval with no railway parcels C & D service at all, there grew a more efficiently organised and dynamic Red Star. This came about in a way that would not have been possible had the Board decided to go for a gradual transfer of C & D to Red Star. To succeed in the market place, Red Star needed a clean sheet, untarnished by any inference that it was merely a rehash of REPS. Closure of REPS followed by a period without any C & D operation freed Red Star of this stigma. Besides this, a lot of the staff and management of REPS needed to be cleared out and only sudden closure and redundancy could secure this reliably. In a similar way, Railfreight's new Speedlink Distribution service would have been tarnished by the reputation of the Full Loads service had the latter been a more prominent part of the whole and had it not been made quite clear that it was to go.

The most basic and catastrophic flaw in the REPS business was the fact that it was tied to National Carriers (NCL) for its road Collection and Delivery arrangements by a contract resulting from the passing of the 1968 Transport Act. BR's own road fleet had been hived off to NCL under the terms of the setting up of the road-dominated National Freight Corporation and the 1968 Act forbade BR to run road vehicles for gain. Of course, National Carriers also ran their own Roadline parcels service, which was a competitor of REPS. Thus the only motivation they had for the BR contract was to rip BR off as much as possible, in the knowledge that BR was tied to them by legislation. It was in their direct interests to operate their part of REPS less efficiently than Roadline and the situation was rather like

Despite the branding, BR was bound by law to contract its parcels collection and delivery operations to a rival parcels carrier. A Rail Express Parcels branded road vehicle is seen here in Mansfield, but it is driven by an employee of National Carriers. (Photo: Berisford Jones)

saying that Sainsbury's could only sell food in premises managed by Asda or with stock ordered by Tesco. The people who collected and delivered parcels to and from REPS customers were effectively employed by a rival parcels carrier. So what hope was there?

When the Board's decision to close down the operation was announced, the Managing Director of NCL, Brian Hayward, was quoted as saying, 'Naturally we regret the loss of a big contract, but we have the men, the vehicles and the expertise, and we are going to expand our own business in the field.'

You bet they were, armed as they already were with commercially sensitive knowledge about REPS customers and its prices. They were virtually handed the business on a plate. While the National Freight Corporation may have started out, at least in concept, as 'neither a road-biased nor a rail-biased business' (NFC Annual Report, 1969) it was clearly very soon a road operator with little or no interest in rail.

As well as the restrictive NCL contract, REPS was saddled with a network of trunking trains and depots that was largely left over from an earlier age and which bore little relation to the needs of the 1980s. The depots had poor road access for the delivery vans and little or no automation in their parcels sorting systems. In many cases they were draughty former goods sheds, with poor staff facilities and decaying structures. The highly automated 'hub' and 'satellite' systems being set up by firms such as Lex Wilkinson and Inter County Express (later Federal Express and TNT respectively) were in marked contrast to BR's crumbling, shabby depots, staffed in part by people who had been removed from passenger stations for disciplinary reasons. While the competition operated with professional managers and dedicated staff, REPS was managed as a tiresome sideline by Area Managers whose main interest was the passenger railway. The NFC's first Annual Report (1969) makes the point, in regard to NCL's improved financial performance under NFC management, that it now had specialist managers, rather than the general management style of BR. And yet BR stayed with this generalist approach right through to the mid 1980s, thus ensuring that many of its managers and staff were 'jacks of all trades and masters of none' – a policy that nevertheless made the railway a place of almost infinite variety for people like me who wanted to dodge around and try their hand at different things.

Despite what I have inferred about REPS' management, there were undoubtedly some very good people working there, whose efforts were constrained by lack of investment, the National Carriers contract and the perpetuation of decision-making at senior level by generalist managers. Indeed, many REPS middle managers and sales staff were 'head-hunted', especially by the Australian firm Inter County Express, which had launched a major offensive on the British parcels distribution market in the early 1980s.

Out on the road in their uninspiring Hillman Avengers were REPS salesmen, trying to persuade firms to use REPS and desperately apologising for lost and damaged parcels. Towards the end, when pilferage had become almost a matter of course at some depots, some of these salesmen were in the habit of telling the BT Police when valuable contracts had been won or when individual consignments of high value were passing. One of the places where the problem was greatest was at Bricklayers Arms depot in south London, to such an extent that the British Transport Police had permanent staff there, which was all very well in principle. In practice, however, the police at Bricklayers Arms could not contain the problem of pilferage, some of their own number being directly involved in the stealing. The messages from salesmen, far from helping towards security, were used as tips as to which parcels were worth breaking open. Three BT Police officers from Bricklayers Arms, along with several REPS staff, were sentenced to up to seven years' imprisonment in 1980 for stealing an estimated sixty van loads of parcels as they passed through the depot. Sixty van loads!

As well as a small personal involvement at Bricklayers Arms (or B. Arms or The Brick, as it was variously known), I had the interesting experience of hearing informal confessions from former staff who were transferred to stations upon closure of the Collection & Delivery parcels service. One of these told me about the organisation of the pilferage, how information was obtained, how it was used, how staff managed to be in the right place at the right time and how they avoided detection.

Occasionally the cars of staff would be searched by the resident BT Police as they left duty after each shift. The way round this was to book off sick before the end of the shift if you had stashed stolen goods into your car boot. At one time, the ringleaders would be tipped off about these checks by corrupt police officers, so they could know when to leave early.

Goods stolen were not just for the immediate personal use of the thieves or their families – the quantities were too great for that. There were thriving black market businesses selling the goods on to the streets. Cameras and bottles of drink were among the favourite commodities and most of these came from mail-order parcels, which were easily recognisable by their labels. Christmas hampers offered particularly easy pickings in this respect. The Brick ran on a system rather like a tower brewery, with parcels being hauled to the top floor and then being sorted in stages as they filtered down through a number of floors. Parcels trickled down by lifts on to the various sorting floors, all this handling and movement providing numerous opportunities for tampering as well as for accidental damage.

In an attempt to combat damage and loss, the depot management decided to set up a secure compound in which damaged parcels would have their contents listed and be repackaged within a caged area. The only staff allowed in this area were specially selected people, trusted by the management, but to my certain knowledge one of these was one of the ringleaders of the pilferers (and was known to me, although not at the time) and items were smuggled out of the cage on a regular basis. This same person, upon closure of the Brick and subsequent relocation to a passenger station, ended up within a year being sentenced to eight years in prison for his part in an armed wages robbery at a south-east London meat distribution depot. I was the person who received his letter of resignation, on HMP Brixton headed paper. He had turned to desperate measures after having his easy black market income decimated.

I mentioned that the parcels sorting staff had, in lots of cases, been removed from passenger stations under the disciplinary arrangements; but it was not just the staff. There were certain 'difficult' managers on the railway with whom senior management could not get on. Likewise, there were managers who had been guilty of various misdemeanours. What better place to send them than places such as Bricklayers Arms? One acting manager of the Brick, for example, was renowned for his sexual indiscretions, which eventually, after a number of complaints, made him unsuitable for allocation to passenger station management. So he saw out his time at Bricklayers Arms, which was predominantly a male penal colony, and thus had his activities confined to making unwanted comments to girls on the Old Kent Road bus. Bricklayers Arms, in its last years, had turned into nothing more than a sordid joke.

Parcels trunking trains ran into and out of Bricklayers Arms to and from a variety of places, at each of which parcels were sorted again, or at the very least the vans were remarshalled. BR did not operate a central hub system in which parcels could be sorted at the collection depot, then at an automated hub and finally at the delivery depot. Instead there was a network of places such as Bricklayers Arms with trunking trains linking them all and so a parcel stood the chance of being sorted many times. The costs of land and infrastructure use, handling, haulage and shunting involved were out of all proportion to the value of the traffic and, of course, the additional sorting directly contributed to the incidence of damage and loss. Although the attribution of infrastructure costs and those of other resources was still at a fairly rudimentary stage it was clear even then that a lot of money was going on maintaining resources for an unprofitable and ailing business. For instance, it was clear that REPS was the sole user of the buildings it used, of the trunk parcels trains and of the track and signalling needed to get into and out of its depots. The freight business that had at one time used mostly the same facilities had moved on with the changing pattern of demand, leaving REPS holding the baby.

Bricklayers Arms had always had a precarious history, having originally been built by the London & Croydon and South Eastern Railway companies in 1844 as a passenger station in order that they could avoid payments to the London & Greenwich Railway for the use of platforms at London Bridge. But no one wanted to be dumped halfway along the Old Kent Road and very soon the Brick came to be used as a goods depot only. For many years it thrived, if you judge success merely in terms of volume. Old track diagrams of the Bricklayers Arms branch show numerous dock sidings, which at one time were bustling with activity. I knew a couple of people who had worked there (and at Ewer Street depot) and they told me tales of the antics there during the shunting, loading and unloading of freight traffic. All the freight vehicles in those days had been four-wheelers and therefore relatively light. Crowbars and sheer muscle power were used to rerail vehicles after the frequent shunting mishaps. When the railway ceased to be a 'common carrier' this wagonload traffic fell away and it was then that Bricklayers Arms became the main London parcels sorting depot. Some freight trains still drifted part way along the branch to run round – in later years this was a regular move for aggregates trains running from Brett Marine at Cliffe to Salfords or Purley and for aircraft fuel trains on their way from Grain Refinery and also going to Salfords, for Gatwick Airport.

The lines from North Kent East Junction (South Eastern) and Bricklayers Arms Junction (South Central) to the Brick soon became derelict and vandalised after closure. The Brick itself has now been redeveloped and the grim sorting building is no more, a big-time plan for a Mirror Group rail-served newsprint depot having fallen through. Similarly, plans for an aggregates depot on the branch line failed to materialise. The freight trains that formerly ran round on the branch now simply run via Factory Junction and Clapham Junction, without the need to run round, prompting the question as to why it was ever necessary to run round at Bricklayers Arms, other than perhaps to give some sort of false justification for retaining the branch and to stop the signalman at North Kent West Junction from falling asleep or for looking out for OMO packets. As I mentioned many pages ago, a lot of railway infrastructure was at one time retained for occasional use simply because it had always been there, even if other, more efficient means were available.

Associated with the old REPS network of depots was the equally outdated Full Loads business, which was the rump of a once busy vacuum-braked wagonload transhipment business but which had been overtaken by road haulage and by the development of Speedlink Distribution. For a short time in 1979 I had the dubious pleasure of working at Redhill Full Loads Depot, which, incidentally, was also a REPS C & D depot. As with parcels, freight traffic requiring delivery or collection had to be transhipped to or from National Carriers vehicles, with no opportunity allowed for the railway to shop around either for a keener price or for better, more suitable road vehicles for particular types of traffic. The National Freight Corporation must have been laughing all the way to the bank as it sabotaged its rival and did so with the full backing of the 1968 Transport Act.

Freight traffic of this type at Redhill was extremely light, which wasn't really surprising given the amateurish methods employed in handling it. There was no covered area for loading and unloading and no one seemed to be very well practised in forklift operation. One day a couple of vans arrived from France with palletised Evian water. Shunts at Dover, Ashford and Tonbridge during the painfully slow journey to Redhill, not to mention the shunts on and off the train ferry, had succeeded in wrecking several pallets, whilst the clumsiness of the forklift operator at Redhill resulted in the blades skewering another pallet load. As with the parcels service, the staff employed at the depot were in some cases people who had been reduced in grade and/or transferred from passenger stations for disciplinary reasons. The Freight Supervisor at Redhill had little control over such people. Some were merely serving out their time before being restored to their previous positions, while others were clearly on the slippery slope towards ultimate dismissal.

The railway had always built its vehicles so that they could withstand hard knocks during shunting and the whole philosophy of hump and loose shunting assumed that these knocks would take place. Now this was fine if all you carried was household coal but not so good when customers' goods were packaged for the far more caring methods employed by road haulage. What lorry firm would consider it acceptable to smash its loaded vehicles together at 15mph as a matter of course? And who designs their products and packaging to withstand the impact of a collision between two vehicles each weighing 70 tonnes? Small wonder that damage was high, even under the more controlled and careful attitudes adopted by Speedlink staff in the later years. This inward-looking attitude was typical of the railway up to around 1980. Instead of starting from the question 'what does the customer want and expect?' the premise was more akin to 'this is the railway, so like it or lump it'. For years after other hauliers had adapted themselves to modern attitudes, the railway still wrote to its customers using such 'customer-unfriendly' titles as 'Chief Freight Manager' or 'Sundries Division' or 'Manager, General Merchandise'. All these titles described the particular activities in terms understood within the railway as if that was the main interest, but no effort was made to sound attractive to customers. After all, who wants their products described as sundries or general merchandise? The railway did not learn until the 1980s that for each customer his or her product is the only one.

I visited Temple Mills Yard, near Walthamstow, towards the end of the hump shunting era to see at first hand this calculated mistreatment of freight customers' products. In terms of railway technology the hump yards were fascinating places. Trains from all over London queued up to be accepted into Temple Mills, sometimes for hours on end at busy times. The pilot engines then propelled the wagons, which had been uncoupled from each other, up the slope to the hump. As they tipped over the hump, the operator in the tower above would set the points at the fan below for each wagon, or each raft of wagons, in accordance with the shunting list he had been given so that the wagons would roll into the designated roads for making up outgoing trains. He also remotely operated the retarders that pinched the flanges in order to reduce the speed of the wagons as they careered down the slope. The operator was aided by automatic speed and weight indicators and by secondary retarders further along the slope. Then there were brakesmen who would run alongside the wagons using their brake poles to try to regulate the final speed of the wagons. Nevertheless, the speed at which some of the wagons smashed into each other could never be completely controlled and the first few wagons into a road would have numerous knocks as further wagons were shunted 'on top' during the process. The first vehicle in each road would be the brakevan for the outgoing train and novice Guards were often told that they should remain in their vans while their trains were being made up. A few bruises soon taught them better.

During my visit to Temple Mills I asked the Manager about the shunting of dangerous goods. Surely these were not put over the hump? No, he told me, they were segregated and shunted into their trains individually by the pilot engines. Just as he said that an oil wagon went hurtling down the ramp from the hump, lurching amidst sparks, smoke and dust as the retarders gripped its flanges.

Operating the hump tower was a highly skilled job, needing great dexterity, quick thinking and a high degree of concentration. It was unique to the railway. The 1955 Modernisation Plan had envisaged a whole network of hump yards and some were built, but even at that time the needs of the freight business were changing and the yards were out of date by the time of their construction. As early as 1960 doubts were being expressed about the wisdom of this vast expenditure on fixed equipment in a changing market. G. Freeman Allen, in his book *British Rail After Beeching* (1965) says that 'obliviousness of the way the railways' competitive environment was developing looked most conspicuous in the all-important freight section of the 1955 Modernisation Plan'. The words 'all-important' may seem strange until it is remembered that freight revenue exceeded passenger revenue in those days. The British Transport Commission (and later BR) had recognised that the railways needed drastic action to recover from the ravages of the Second World War and had set about doing this by adapting new technology to old ideas, on the assumption that the position of the railway as the main freight carrier would stay unchanged. In February 1956 the BTC had decided that vacuum braking would be the standard for freight vehicles, despite the fact that passenger vehicles on the same system were nearly all air-braked and that the rest of Europe was also heading towards air braking for freight. Thus a huge number of vacuum-braked wagons were built (more than 30,000 each year for many years) and these, coupled with the associated infrastructure investment, left a lasting legacy of redundant and outdated assets. In fairness, it must be remembered that for decades one of the mainstays of the railway's business had been coal distribution and perhaps nobody envisaged quite the extent to which coal use would decline, taking with it a large chunk of the need for a comprehensive rail distribution network for a product that was, relatively speaking, undamageable and not desperately time-sensitive.

A mammoth hump yard was planned for a site at Swanbourne (between Bletchley and Bicester) and was to be a focal point for freight traffic from a wide area heading into, out of or across London, as well as cross-country traffic. So busy was it expected to be that the flat junction at Bletchley was replaced by massive concrete viaducts to carry the Bedford line over the West Coast Main Line and also to provide a flying junction for traffic from the Wolverton direction. These monstrosities stand to this day as monuments to a freight policy that had failed to take into account the changing market for freight haulage. The railway had still thought that it could get away with running vacuum-braked (or even unbraked) wagons from yard to yard, remarshalling each time, when its competitors were providing a door-to-door service in half the time, with motorways under construction, too. The hump yard policy would undoubtedly have given internal efficiencies but it offered little to the customer. The extent of the national freight network, and the connectional possibilities it provided, was nevertheless impressive in its own right and the planning that went into it was thorough and painstaking, but as with so many aspects of BR, as public attitudes changed and competition developed, it was not enough to have something that was good in its own right or for its own sake – it had to be good enough for the people who had a choice of whether or not to use it. By the time construction of the hump-yard network was under way this need was already becoming apparent. Swanbourne was never finished.

As the years went by, so the railway started experimenting with fast air-braked wagonload freights: first of all was the Bristol–Glasgow overnight

BR invested heavily in hump shunting yards and in fleets of vacuum-braked wagons, which soon became outdated. Tinsley Yard, Sheffield, is seen with its hump control tower. (Photo: Adrian Brennan)

service in 1972. So a new problem was emerging – that of two incompatible wagon fleets. Most trainload freight was running with air brakes by the mid 1970s while wagonload was split between out-of-date vacuum-braked wagons dating from the huge builds of the 1950s and modern air-braked services.

The final demise of the hump yards came with the decisions to abandon the Full Loads service, to set up a new network of fast wagonload services and, most importantly, to go right over to air braking as the standard. This last decision was taken as late as October 1977 and full implementation took many years. I stress the point about air brakes as it meant that new wagons had to be brought into service and at last freight customers could be offered vehicles that looked good, were easy to load and unload, were smoother and faster running and showed that the railway was actually taking some notice of road competition. Many of these wagons were built and owned by firms in Germany and France (VTG, Danzas, Cargowaggon, etc.) and came to this country by means of the train ferry. The fact that these wagons had to be constructed to the British loading gauge was a demonstration of the faith shown by these firms in the new services. The Board itself got things off to a start by building 1,000 new air-braked wagons and the name Speedlink was adopted in order to give some marketing coherence to the new air-braked network.

For a while the vacuum-braked services continued, so that existing contracts could be honoured, but the new Speedlink network of fast trains ran alongside. So, for instance, while the old, short-wheelbase wagons were still trundling along, stopping to be remarshalled at Ashford, Tonbridge and Norwood on their way to Temple Mills hump yard, the new 1050 Dover to Dundee Speedlink service ran non-stop from Dover to Willesden, where its pre-determined sections would be split for their onward journeys in accordance with a connectional timetable that was available to customers as well as staff.

As the vacuum-braked services were phased out so too went the yards such as Acton and Norwood that had largely served as a means of delaying traffic and of incurring additional cost and damage, and were probably only ever necessary because of Regional divides rather than traffic requirements. By 1984 the only vacuum-braked wagons still in use were on a few engineers' trains and on some company block trains, such as the Swanscombe to Bristol cement service I mentioned earlier. The Speedlink network expanded, taking not only wagonload traffic in its own right but also former block traffic in some cases, where it was found to be more economic to do so. For instance, the weekly china clay train from Burngullow to the paper mills at Sittingbourne in Kent was replaced by smaller daily forwardings by Speedlink, thus spreading workload more evenly and using wagon resources more efficiently. Of course, although Speedlink expanded it never handled more than a fraction of the traffic that had been dealt with in years past, but at least it saved that fraction from extinction and was able to build upon it and exploit new opportunities for a freight service more in line with the demands of industry in the second half of the century. The 1976 idea, named Speedlink Mk I, which had been developed by BR's Research Centre at Derby and which consisted of high-speed multiple-unit freight trains, was too revolutionary, though, and was quietly abandoned, although the idea lives on with the Royal Mail's multiple units and with talk of Freight Multiple Units for distribution traffic.

11

The Old and the New

The old freight marshalling system had involved the complete re-forming of trains at nearly every yard, but Speedlink trains were formed in a way that made this unnecessary. Each train had a pre-determined formation, with a section for each calling point. At many places all that happened was that the rear portion, which could in theory be anything from one wagon to the whole train, was detached. Only at Sorting Sidings such as Willesden would trains be taken apart, but then only into the planned sections so that sections from other trains could be added. Shunt moves were therefore reduced in number, with subsequent reductions in delay and damage. Another benefit was that feeder services, or even trunk services, could 'slip' sections directly at customers' sidings without the need for separate trip workings. Strict adherence to the formation patterns was essential, as was correct reporting of the actual train 'consists' to TOPS. Of course, it was information technology such as TOPS that made the whole system possible.

The Speedlink network of the 1980s consisted of trunk trains, feeders and trips. Most trunk trains were well subscribed, conveying a wide range of goods over long distances and with fast timings. Many feeders and trips were well used too, particularly where there were large regular flows such as cement, chemicals, prepared foodstuffs and other predominantly non-seasonal traffic. But the economics of some feeders and trips were questionable, especially where they were brought into use mainly for seasonal flows. In March 1980 BR had let itself loose on a quest for volume of grain traffic without taking proper regard of the true cost. So Railfreight entered into an agreement with Traffic Services Ltd (later part of CAIB) to promote the use of Speedlink for grain traffic under the marketing name Grainflow. The people who had entered into this agreement apparently thought that sufficient volume would be generated on a multiplicity of local trip workings to make them worth running, on the grounds that the trunking revenue would pay for it all. What appeared to have been overlooked was that this sort of volume would only occur a few weeks each year. What was to happen to the resources the rest of the time? How was space on the feeders and trunk trains suddenly to be found for this traffic without reserving space all year round? Did Grainflow really imagine that the Speedlink Network people, who allocated space on trunk trains, would take their sudden glut of traffic in preference to steady flows under long-term contracts? Who was going to pay for the maintenance of track and signalling that was 'Grainflow specific' during the off-season? Such questions were becoming increasingly relevant as cost analysis became sharper.

Another flaw in the Grainflow arrangement was that there was a conflict of interest between its operators. Traffic Services Ltd, as owners of the wagons, simply wanted to get them loaded, it mattered not where. Speedlink Distribution, which was responsible from 1983 for the contract, however, wanted to restrict the loading to places that could be realistically and cheaply served, although this desire only came about after it was realised quite how much things were getting out of hand. Traffic Services had their own salesman, Colin Brown, touring the lanes of East Anglia, Scotland and places between, drumming up loads in obscure places, but his interests were not always in accord with those of the railway. Earlier I mentioned the semi-derelict freight-only branch lines used by the Western Region's milk trains in the mid 1970s. And here we were, in the mid 1980s, and you could still see a Class 31 rumble out of Norwich, with a crew of three, to negotiate its way along the freight-only branch to North Elmham in order to collect two grain wagons it had left there the previous day. The difference now, however, was that the entire cost of that traction, crew, branch maintenance and signalling at Wymondham was charged to Speedlink Distribution. In fairness, the same traction and crew might well have run trips to, say, Wroxham or Diss, on other days, but even so the costs were out of all proportion to the benefit obtained by putting another two or three wagons on the feeder train from Norwich to Whitemoor, especially as the market was highly competitive and so rates were low.

The strange thing about the grain trips was that the lessons from the 'common carrier' period of the vacuum-braked network appeared still not to have been learned. Even as late as 1988, it appeared that parts of the railway still thought they had to be all things to all people. There was a persistent reluctance, even at that late stage, to say 'hold on, this is a business, not a subsidised public service'. Of course it was nice to see freight moving by rail. Of course it was more environmentally friendly. But the cost of keeping little-used lines open for a few tonnes a year, while it had a quaint appeal about it, was a drain on the overall business and was therefore actually impeding worthwhile development that might well have taken a lot more off the roads. By 1991, though, the lesson of Grainflow's early but misguided enthusiasm had been learnt and Grainflow was reduced to a block train from two points in East Anglia to two points in Scotland. All four were on lines used for other traffic, so Grainflow no longer attracted the crippling 'sole user' costs of its earlier days.

From 1986 to 1988 I was involved in this in my capacity of Assistant Development Manager for Speedlink Distribution. This was a relatively short-lived organisation with rather poorly defined objectives. It found itself

'Sole-user' costs of freight-only lines were hurting Speedlink Distribution badly by the late 1980s. 31164 is seen at Dereham with the last train of grain wagons from North Elmham on 19 January 1989. (Photo: Mike Clarke)

progressively being squeezed by financial reality as its status as the poor relation of the Railfreight family became increasingly apparent. It was distinct from Speedlink Network, which ran the trunk and feeder trains and which, as I have said, gave an understandable preference on those trains to regular contract flows from other Railfreight sectors. It was Speedlink Distribution's task to whip up all the bits and pieces of traffic that no one else wanted to be bothered with. Because of the precarious nature of its business, it was rarely able to book regular space on trunk or feeder trains.

On the brighter side, however, were Speedlink Distribution's foodstuffs contracts and its technical development work. It was solely responsible within Railfreight for the movement of foodstuffs and we had one or two really worthwhile contracts. One held by us in the London office was for haulage of Van den Burgh's fish and vegetable oils from Purfleet to Bromborough. This went by trainload and was quite a good earner, running regularly and therefore enabling efficient resource allocation to be made. Similarly, we had contracts for trainload movement of Pedigree pet foods and Kellogg's breakfast cereals, the latter of which we unfortunately lost when Kellogg's switched to 9ft 6in containers, which at the time were too high for the railway loading gauge. Most of our traffic, by contrast to these regular trainloads, was sporadic and included such diverse commodities as paper, timber, whisky, washing machines, yoghurt and sugar beet – to name but a few. A lot of our traffic took many hours of visits and meetings to arrange and then only lasted a few days. Some of it paid fairly well and some not so well, especially after resource costs were taken into account. On the revenue side we did quite well, for instance, out of the one-off movements of valuable timber following the hurricane of October 1987, but the cost of finding places and means of loading it largely negated the revenue benefit.

With regard to innovation, though, we were at the forefront of the drive to develop new loading systems and in the promotion of swap-body techniques. All research needs a sponsor and within Railfreight it was our responsibility to push for these developments, which were essential if Railfreight was to avoid the loss of more contracts such as Kellogg's and be able to create means of attracting new traffic in a changing and increasingly flexible market. One initiative that came to fruition was Minilink, which ran from London to Glasgow. This was a joint venture between Speedlink Distribution and the Swedish firm that had designed the loading system and involved lightweight transfer of small containers from road to rail and vice versa. The huge cost and inflexibility of fixed-transfer container systems such as Freightliner, with its massive gantries, were becoming a burden in the more fluid market of the 1980s. Launched in September 1986, Minilink was followed by Maxilink in 1988 but both failed ultimately, largely because the railway loading gauge meant that the top corners of the containers were angled, so the actual loading capacity was limited. Also, as with so much of our traffic, the amount of effort that had to be put into obtaining each load – management development and selling time, road collection and delivery, and transfer equipment and time meant that the financial benefit was marginal. Nevertheless, useful development work was achieved that would be of benefit when the ageing Freightliner systems were renewed and also in opening up opportunities for future traffic flows that required flexible, lightweight transfer to and from road. The London Minilink depot was beside the West Coast Main Line, opposite Willesden Freightliner depot, and I am sure they were watching with interest our use of a mobile container transfer system. At the time, as again now, they were a separate company.

Development projects aside, the daily workload at Speedlink Distribution was varied and, at times, interesting – if not lucrative. While my colleagues in the bulk-freight departments such as coal, steel, chemicals and aggregates, were signing contracts worth millions over ten or more years and were celebrating the opening of huge new loading and discharge terminals, I would typically be having a pub lunch with a grain trader in a small Lincolnshire market town. We would be discussing the possibility of bringing in portable equipment a couple of times a week just in case he wanted to load to rail. We would just about be able to serve the siding by sharing resources with other similar places, where grain might or might not be loaded, although we wouldn't be able to guarantee the days on which we could serve it. Both of us would have spluttered over our pints of Bateman's had the word 'contract' ever been mentioned.

On the strength of their contract meetings the trainload people would put up investment proposals for new heavy traction or infrastructure improvements and thereby fund the updating of the railway and keep it viable for future business. There was no way we could do this. The very instability of our traffic flows condemned us to using out-of-date equipment with high staffing levels. I used to think how interesting it would have been to have produced figures relating to the staff and management time per forwarded tonne of our traffic in comparison with, say, the traffic of the Trainload Coal Manager at York, which in the late 1980s brought in just under £100 million each year with very little management effort.

One day I could be discussing the details of the layout of a potential private siding in south-east London with a firm of Italian 'white goods' importers and the next I could be in Scotland talking to a farmer about loading seed potatoes or down in Devon, checking the unloading of a trial load of sugar beet from East Anglia. I had regular work at Fort William, King's Lynn, Heathfield (Devon) and Mistley (Essex) amongst other places.

Heathfield was one of my favourite places and I was frequently sent there on a 'panic' mission associated with short-term unloading of sugar beet or grain. To get to Heathfield I would go down on the Night Riviera sleeper train from Paddington to Plymouth, come back up to Newton Abbot and then walk the length of the Heathfield branch, still arriving in time for a mid-morning meeting. I used to marvel at the immaculate state of the track along this supposedly freight-only branch, until I was informed discreetly by the local Civil Engineer that the branch was occasionally used by the Royal Train. Did we pay the track costs, I wondered?

Fort William was also a sleeper job for me. Here we were trying to persuade a local haulier to act as our agent and to take over the former goods shed for the handling of both our and his traffic. It meant that he would assume liability for maintaining this shed and so we could save a few bob there, as by then every building and every inch of track and signalling were charged to whoever used it. On the other side of Scotland I had dealings with two brothers who were farmers and hauliers and who wanted to open a rail depot near Arbroath. We found them a suitable place and opened it at minimal cost, though they hardly ever used it in the end. At the same time I was looking at reopening a grain terminal at Laurencekirk, a remote little town north of Montrose, and at providing a Speedlink service to and from Dundee Docks. Then there were visits to places as diverse as Leith Docks, Craven Arms (Shropshire) and Chichester.

At none of these places could I say for certain that there would be traffic every day, or even at all, while at some there was the possibility of there being too much traffic to handle some days. How could you hope to programme and underwrite resources for this?

At times I was sent off to check trial loads and to smooth out any difficulties with the recipients or agents. Most of our traffic needed handling at both ends by intermediaries and so there was a lot of organisation required. The Act tying us to NCL for road haulage no longer applied and we had regular and occasional hauliers at various places, shopping around as the case arose. I went to Chichester to watch trial consignments of yoghurt being loaded and then to Scotland to see the same loads being delivered. All good stuff, but why we were in the business was a mystery – it needed a special trip from Eastleigh to fetch it from Chichester and was never available more than one wagon at a time. On another occasion, during a particularly snowy night, I travelled to Deanside Transit in Glasgow to check on arrangements for a trial load of malting barley from East Anglia. I got there, albeit a couple of hours late after the sleeper had been diverted via Kilmarnock due to snowdrifts at Beattock Summit, but the load had missed its trunk connection right back at Whitemoor and was now going to arrive twenty-four hours late. I sat in the office of the Deanside Transit Co., warming myself with a cup of coffee before being given a lift back to Glasgow Central. On the way back to London all the train toilets froze up, as did the catering water supplies, so the train was held at Crewe for a good old-fashioned refreshment stop. In addition, the loco had difficulty picking up the traction current from the icy wires over the bleak snowscape of the Scottish summits. So the round trip eventually took around twenty hours and was to no avail.

One freezing Saturday afternoon I stood around in a sugar beet factory at Peterborough watching the loading methods for railborne beet. Perhaps needless to say, these were extremely labour-intensive. With grain and beet, rail was the last resort for loading and therefore had the least hardware allocated to it. Coastal shipping and road haulage had regular movements of these products, while we had the gluts. Then we were suddenly expected to have fleets of wagons and locomotives available. We did our best to take maximum advantage of these sudden orders and to price ourselves so that we could play a part in the regular movements.

After doing quite well with each short notice movement we wanted to be able to say, 'Look, we can do it, let's have a share of the base traffic,' but for some reason we never did.

As you can see, most of the work involved scratching about after a few tonnes, none of which would be on a regular contract. We had rigid Private

Sidings Agreements, however, and one of the things I did, as well as trying to open up new terminals, was to renegotiate old agreements. Basically these agreements laid down who was responsible for which bits of track and signalling and who would pay for their maintenance. They also included clauses about liability and so on. Usually the owner of the siding would pay for the installation of the connection to the running line, with the associated signalling, and would then pay so much per annum for the maintenance of these. Beyond a point identified on a plan accompanying the Agreement, the track and its maintenance would be the sole responsibility of the owner.

Some of the old Agreements were real gems, incorporating archaic descriptions of equipment, constraints upon the behaviour of 'Company servants' and such things as the hours during which locomotive whistles should not be sounded. Many dated from the pre-nationalisation era, while some were even pre-Grouping. Some had horrendous implications for the railway. One such was the Mistley Dock & Railway Agreement. Mistley, in Essex, is an ancient port and it had a twisting 'tramway' (as the Agreement called it) from the mainline station to the quayside. This was sometimes used for grain traffic and there were other potential traffic opportunities. Main line engines were not allowed down the tramway so we had to send an 08 Class pilot engine from Harwich every time there was traffic for Mistley Dock. Upon my making enquiries of the Board's Solicitor, a series of Agreements came to light concerning the construction of the line and imposing requirements upon the Great Eastern Railway in terms of operating the line and keeping it in good repair. There were Agreements with and between various old companies and several individuals over whose land the tramway had been constructed. The local rector had certain rights, amongst others. Just to make sure, I checked with the Solicitor whether we were the legal successors of the Great Eastern and, he said, there was no doubt of that.

During the autumn of 1986, coincidentally at the same time as I was trying to sort out our private siding obligations, the dock company had also been taking a look at the Mistley Dock & Railway Agreement. They wrote to us, making out that we were responsible for part-payment of the rebuilding costs of a portion of the quayside, under the terms of a clause dating from more than 100 years earlier. I spent many happy hours with them, poring over old documents of theirs and then producing, from our archives and those of our Solicitor, documents with which to make counter-claims. It was all strangely amicable, usually taking place in the lounge of a Colchester coaching inn or else in the village restaurant at Mistley. The dock company had brought back a very charming old gentleman from retirement specifically to sort it all out and it was all very civilised. We didn't pay up, though.

One Agreement I unearthed related to a former coal-fired power station at Hardingstone near Northampton that was then in use (very occasionally) as a grain depot, amongst other things. A golden rule of Private Siding Arrangements was that you always made provision for inflation in the charges for track maintenance, but this one did not do this. And who had signed it for the railway? One Robert Reid, who, at the time I was looking at the Agreement, was Chairman of the British Railways Board. Various well-known railway names came to light during my researches into these Agreements, usually with quaint titles such as 'District Freight Superintendent' or 'Goods Agent'. At one time all up-and-coming railway managers were expected to fill positions such as these as part of their management development, a subject I shall come back to when considering management training.

Although charges were specified in the Agreements I was never entirely convinced that we had the accounting mechanisms to raise them, so it may all have been academic anyway. Even in the sharper financial climate of the late 1980s the railway still carried costs that should have either been stripped out or off-charged. The drive towards correct attribution of costs to particular users or even particular traffic flows was a start, but where the flow was discontinued it needed to be seen through to its logical conclusion, i.e. abolition or reallocation of those costs. Here the railway has been (and to some extent still is) appallingly slow. Many connections and loops remained in place even though the traffic to which they were formerly charged had ceased running. Five minutes' walk from where I sit writing this in Canterbury there is a loop being maintained by Network Rail with two sets of points, track and signalling, seven years after the traffic that necessitated and funded its retention stopped running.

Off-charging to outside parties is another area in which the railway was slow to act. Admittedly, when I was with Railfreight, we did charge some project development time to prospective customers when we were undertaking investigative work for them and this was on the understanding that we would refund the charge if suitable traffic flows were to result from our work. In lots of cases, though, many hours were spent on developing schemes that either had little prospect of success or, at best, would result in small revenue gain. The scope for charging for work on a management consultancy basis was much greater than was practised.

One relatively large company I had dealings with was Anglia Agricultural Merchants, whose interests coincided more closely with our own than most. They had ambitions for rail terminals to handle substantial amounts of grain and other agricultural produce, and the locations were on routes already served by Speedlink feeders. Ideal, in the circumstances. The first time I met them was in 1986 at Whittlesea (between Peterborough and March) and I had arrived by train to discuss with them the site they were interested in, checking in first by signing the register in the excellent absolute block GER signalbox. Then, as I was snooping around the yard, a metallic gold Mercedes with darkened windows and the registration AAM 1 swept up beside me. A rear door flew open and I was ordered to get in. Thus was I introduced in fine style to the bigtime barons of grain.

With AAM we came close to achieving a Traffic Agreement, which would have enabled us to programme resources and, possibly, investment. Traffic Agreements worked by reducing the charge for the installation of the siding under the Private Siding Agreement in return for certain guaranteed levels of traffic to or from the siding. It was a sort of sliding scale and was flexibly negotiable, there being no fixed formula. Normally the installation costs would be charged at 'Private Party' rates, which meant that BR made a commercially profitable transaction out of the installation itself, with no consideration being taken of future revenue from the siding. However, if you had a Traffic Agreement, you could, upon your discretion as negotiator, reduce the installation charges towards the 'Internal' rate, which was, supposedly, the real cost. I say 'supposedly' because the charges levied by the various engineering departments were notoriously high. In the hope that we might actually get a decent amount of traffic from AAM we hoped to enter into such a deal with them, but, unfortunately, little came of it, mainly due to uncertainty over the future of the Speedlink network as a whole.

AAM was a good firm to deal with, but others were not so good. In particular, there was a group of 'fly-by-night' characters who drifted about from company to company as advisers or as short-term troubleshooters. A lot of money and time were wasted examining some of their proposals, most of which would have committed us to high resource costs with no lasting benefit – much the same as most of our traffic, really. We wasted a lot of time with one such character who had attached himself to a family haulage firm in Polegate, East Sussex, with promises to revitalise their prospects in partnership with us by reopening part of the Polegate triangle as a private siding. He left them in disgrace after they had seen through his motives and found out about his past. His way of making a living was to dream up grandiose projects and rip off his client while he negotiated for their implementation. Another such character, already well known to us, rang up one day (very little was ever in writing from these people) to say that we must jump to it and install a siding at Denton near Gravesend in order to handle shipping containers as he had the possibility of a break there. Now the North Kent line is riddled with low bridges and tunnels and this was during the time that the small-wheeled bogie was only in its development stage, so containers over 8ft high could not be conveyed. Experience had shown that you needed to carry 8ft, 8ft 6in, 9ft and even 9ft 6in containers to be competitive with road and that is why we had, as part of our technical development work, commissioned the small-wheeled bogie project. In the meantime my boss, Colin Walker, had to say that we couldn't get involved, based upon my knowledge, as former Area Freight Manager, of the North Kent line's restrictions.

The entrepreneurial spirit could only be dampened, however, by Colin's words, 'Let me assure you, Bill, Stephen knows the bridges along that line brick by brick and if he says you can't get containers through, then you can't.'

It turned out that Bill had no real contact with the traffic in any case, much as we had suspected. He appeared next in connection with bulk movement of pet food at Welwyn Garden City, following the bankruptcy of the firm that had previously been agent for the traffic. That flow did materialise, however.

Most of these people had strong links with the road haulage industry but were keen to exploit rail for bulk and longer-distance haulage because they could make a few more bob by doing so. In the main we worked well with hauliers, as indeed we had to bearing in mind that so much of our traffic required collecting and delivering by road. From time to time, though, there have been nasty clashes with the road haulage industry. Back in the 1970s, when I was a Controller on the South Eastern, the railway secured the contract for regular movements of Japanese cars from Queenborough docks. The cars arrived, thousands at a time, in huge vessels and then travelled on open carflat wagons to various destinations in the UK – but had previously been conveyed by road transporters. On several occasions windscreens were smashed and other damage inflicted after the cars had been loaded to rail and then, one weekday afternoon, in broad daylight, a gang of men with sledgehammers smashed up a complete trainload of cars in Queenborough Yard. Shortly after that the importers reverted to road haulage. Rumours abounded at the time of a co-ordinated programme of sabotage by Transport & General Workers Union members and there was certainly a TGWU campaign against the transfer of freight from road to rail at the time.

On another occasion the Freight Sales rep for Kent, Terry Rimes, had persuaded Bowaters paper mill at Northfleet to send their finished reels by rail to the north-west. This traffic had previously been hauled by a well-known lorry firm based in Barrow. Our price was good and the railvans we provided were secure and easy to load so the traffic went by rail for a trial period of a month, being transhipped at Blackburn and delivered by a local haulier who was under contract to us. A few days after the traffic started to roll this firm's depot mysteriously burnt down. Undeterred, we found another firm and managed to keep deliveries to schedule but at the end of the trial month the traffic went back to the original hauliers. Bowaters were quite happy with us and our price but we had been undercut by special terms (and, no doubt, other tactics). We loaded this traffic at Northfleet, incidentally, by obtaining Blue Circle's permission to run a Speedlink trip via their coal unloading circuit. The paper reels were then brought by forklift through a gate from the adjoining mill.

The HQ office of Speedlink Distribution, with Stan Judd as Director, as well as the South of England office, with Colin Walker as Railfreight Manager, were both at 222 Marylebone Road, the former Great Central Railway hotel built in 1899 and also, formerly, the British Railways Board's HQ. By the time I worked there the Board had moved to the revamped Euston House. '222' (sometimes known as 'The Kremlin' or 'The Centre') was gradually being run down and was in a sorry state. We were one of the few offices to be there right up to the last day and it was a strangely haunting feeling to be walking along the empty corridors and up the huge staircase with its stained-glass windows in the knowledge that the railway connection was to be broken that very day. We occupied a shabby corner of this vast, rambling building, which was sold for £15 million for conversion back to a hotel. Upon closure we moved to Watford, where we had plush air-conditioned offices.

At about this same time, however, I became aware of a changing culture within Speedlink Distribution. For one thing, there was a growing realisation that our infrastructure and trip costs were far too high in comparison with the revenue generated. At meeting after meeting to allocate costs between sectors we were being loaded with more. Secondly, it was becoming apparent that nearly all the new installations we were developing would be equally fruitless in terms of the costs they would attract. We had to stop scratching around for the odd few tonnes and have a proper development strategy. This harsh new realism led to an office-based introspection in which we increasingly retired from the limelight and embarked on paper exercises to reduce costs. The actual railway outside became of lesser importance until we reached the stage at which it appeared that Speedlink Distribution had become the Watford office and was no longer the customers, traffic, locos, wagons and staff outside on the ground. As someone who had always thought that railway offices should merely be the support for the railway, I did not like this emerging office mentality, which was also putting paid to my visits to obscure parts of the railway.

But as Speedlink Distribution withdrew itself from the fray, Railfreight Distribution was being born as an amalgamation of Speedlink Network and Freightliner Ltd. The new organisation came into being in 1988 and led to the temporary demise of the independent Freightliner set-up. BR had established Freightliner in 1965 as a Beeching-inspired move to revolutionise the inland transport of container traffic, had lost control of the company in 1968 to the National Freight Corporation, regained it under the 1978 Transport Act and was now merging it with Speedlink Distribution in a move to rationalise the duplication of depot and road transport operations. The 1978 Act had removed the nonsense by which BR was forbidden to run road vehicles for gain, so Freightliner, under BR ownership, could continue to run its road fleet.

There was a political irony in this amalgamation in that Freightliner, being a separately constituted limited company owned by the BRB, was surely a prime candidate for privatisation. Instead, however, it was absorbed back into the railway and lost its identity at the height of the Thatcher Government's privatisation programme. Eventually, of course, it was untangled again.

The continuing examination of costs meant that the Cinderella of the Railfreight business, Speedlink, could no longer survive in the form into which it had grown. Severe rationalisation of the network took place, starting in 1988, and the formal abolition of Speedlink was announced in December 1990. The network was finally dismantled in July 1991, with a large proportion of the traffic being transferred to trainload services, while other pieces were amalgamated into private company wagonload services, most notably operated by the wagon leasing firm Tiger Rail. Other parts inevitably went to road. Another chapter in the stormy history of wagonload freight was drawing to a close as the railway moved towards the concept of 'freight villages', which were to be privately financed and in strategically important places in readiness for the opening of the Channel Tunnel, which was at last a real prospect.

12

Exile on the Marshes

What was the reality of the steel on steel freight railway, as opposed to the 'politics' of resource attribution and HQ organisation? I have spoken already of some of the intricacies and idiosyncrasies of the private sidings, but what about the Sorting Sidings and TOPS offices? Of course, some of these were huge places in what were until recently the industrial heartlands of Britain. Places such as Tinsley (near Sheffield), Tyne Yard (Newcastle), Toton (near Nottingham), Margam (South Wales) and Mossend (Glasgow). Others, though, were more obscure and one such was Hoo Junction. This bleak outpost is situated among the North Kent marshes, made famous by the opening pages of Charles Dickens' *Great Expectations* in which Abel Magwitch awaited transportation in the prison hulk moored in the nearby estuary. Hoo Junction too, had a history as a punishment depot – for people removed from passenger stations.

Most trains from Charing Cross to Gillingham stop at Hoo Junction Staff Halt and a few mysterious characters will either join or leave the front coach.* When I was Area Freight Manager for North Kent, Hoo Junction had acquired the appellation 'Sorting Sidings' in the Freight Timetable and was a relatively minor part of the Speedlink Network. Feeder services ran to and from Willesden, while some trunk trains, mostly on their way to or from the Dover train ferry called to attach or detach portions. Thus we had a 1530 Dover Town Yard to Toton calling at Hoo Junction each afternoon and, in the early hours, the 1605 Tyneside to Paddock Wood of the previous

* 2018 update: No such co-operation exists now between the passenger and freight operators. No trains call at the staff halt.

day. Trips ran from Hoo Junction to Sheerness steel works, Ridham Dock, Sittingbourne paper mills, Maidstone West, Paddock Wood, Swanscombe, Plumstead, etc. Trainload trips, mainly of bitumen, ran into the yard from the Grain branch, which was almost seen as part of Hoo Junction. The branch in the mid 1980s was enjoying an interlude between the heyday of the Grain refinery and the frantic activity of Channel Tunnel construction, during which tunnel building materials were stored on the Isle of Grain and then moved by rail to Shakespeare Cliff. Grain, incidentally, is now the site of Thamesport, and container trains run there following a Government grant to the port operators of £1.8 million in 1991 and following also the successful introduction of the small-wheeled bogie that at last allowed container traffic to pass along the North Kent line. Sea-dredged aggregates trains ran from Brett Marine at Cliffe, which is part way along the branch, and mostly bypassed Hoo Junction, but a few came in to recess or to run round. In addition, there was extensive use of Hoo Junction by engineers' trains.

The Sorting Sidings were staffed by a Supervisor on each shift and a group of Shunters. Freight shunting is dirty, heavy, all-weather work and there seems to be a type of person who absolutely thrives on it. There were several such at Hoo Junction, 'rough diamonds' though they may have been. A basic, sometimes rather crude, camaraderie existed amongst the Shunters and also between them and the Supervisor. I am glad to say that, to some extent, it extended to me. Although I was Area Freight Manager I was provided with a full Station Manager's uniform, which I hardly ever wore as it was impractical for the cold and dirty places I needed to go to. On one occasion, though, I decided to dress up in the full regalia, including my hat with the red badge and 'scrambled eggs' around it. I caused quite a stir at Hoo Junction and, needless to say, received a lot of mickey taking.

It is perhaps easy to think that shunting relies solely on brute force but this is not so: dexterity and quick thinking are needed, too. As well as coupling and uncoupling, a good Shunter is planning the moves in such a way that vehicles barely come to a stand and roads are switched in the nick of time to separate the rakes. The ability to scan the TOPS-generated shunt list quickly and to memorise the required moves helps as well, while close liaison with other Shunters and with the pilot Driver is vital. At Hoo Junction an 08 Class pilot was provided to pull off the wagons and most of the pilot Drivers were 'regulars', which made things easier. One thing about shunting you soon notice is that the methods of giving handsignals to the Driver as shown in the Rule Book are only the start of it. While the Rule Book shows the required movements of the arm, greater clarity is often given to handsignals by holding a rolled up newspaper or a folded Special Traffic Notice. Similarly, after dark, the Rule Book says that the signal to move away is given by a handlamp moved up and down, implying that you should lift and then lower the lamp repeatedly, which is not a very natural or comfortable action. The same effect is given in practice by swinging the lamp from front to back, which is much easier. Shunters and Drivers soon get used to giving and receiving these signals in these more practical forms.

Unusually for a yard so relatively small, there were three entrances to the up yard from the running line so we were afforded a lot of operating flexibility and the Shunters used this to maximum advantage. There were offices and messing facilities for the operating staff and also for the wagon repair staff who were based there. Some of the staff had been removed from passenger stations for disciplinary reasons under the earlier generalist management regimes, but as an independent freight manager I was not prepared to see Hoo Junction being used as a sort of Botany Bay for transported offenders. Not only did sectorisation mean that the businesses had to meet their own costs but also that they could no longer palm off unwanted resources, including human, on to each other any more. Most staff worked well together at Hoo Junction and we had few derailments, collisions or other incidents. Personal accidents were almost unheard of, despite the obvious dangers of having to run alongside moving vehicles and jump on and off the pilot while it was still in motion. Timekeeping of Speedlink services was good as far as we were concerned, although some southbound services would sometimes arrive hours late if they had been caught in the evening rush-hour freight embargo. So most of the time things ticked over pretty smoothly.

The Sheerness steel scrap traffic was one that caused a few problems, however. It moved in private-owner open bulk wagons that could be, and often were, severely overloaded. In particular, one forwarder near Bicester was notorious for overloading and when we complained to the Railfreight Metals people about him, it turned out that he was in breach of contract with them over another matter and his siding connection was severed. The maximum weight for each wagon was meant to be 100 tonnes, but some were known to have gone over the weighbridge at Sheerness at more than

120 tonnes, i.e. more than 30 tonnes per axle. I don't think any line in the country was cleared for axle weights of higher than 25.5 tonnes. Not only did this mean that the wagon suspension system, track and bridges were subject to undue strain but also that, in many cases, the wagons were loaded too high. As the scrap was essentially loose this could be very dangerous as vibration and aerodynamic pressures could build up in movement. On one occasion a tunnel watchman in Strood Tunnel, who revelled in the unlikely name of Fred Glue, had to run for shelter as a scrap wagon went by with metal discs flying from the top of it like lethal frisbees. Watchmen were permanently employed in the unlined former Thames & Medway Canal tunnel to look out for chalk falls.

The overloading and the insecurity of the loads of scrap caused other problems, too. Strange little piles of scrap would appear at strategic places in Hoo Junction yard, possibly deliberately pulled off wagons by certain staff members, or at the very least gathered there by them. These piles would then disappear, usually on a Sunday, when there was no Supervisor booked on duty. I did a 'stakeout' one Sunday and, sure enough, I saw a van collecting piles of scrap. I followed it to an address in Gravesend and reported its destination to the Police, but by the time they arrived it had been emptied and there was no trace of the scrap.

The next day I went down to Hoo Junction and the Shunter who had been on duty on Sunday said to me, 'Guv, you were well out of order calling the cops round.'

I replied, 'I just wanted you to know that I know what's going on.'

From then on we had an 'understanding' of each other, which I would like to think led to a reduction in his illicit activities.

One short-term flow we had was of damaged Army vehicles being brought back from Port Stanley after the Falklands war, going to the repair depot at Donnington. These vehicles were shipped to Ridham Dock and loaded to rail there, being tripped to Hoo Junction for forwarding on the feeders. Some of these were excellent examples of how to secure strange loads. Jeeps with crooked frames, with one wheel in the air so that you couldn't chock it properly; personnel carriers with no ropeholds and so on. Each load had to be examined individually and the skill of the Loading Inspector was put to the test in assessing whether or not each load was safe to go. At about this time, these Inspectors were being pensioned off in a deliberate move to reduce the number of Supervisory graded staff. I spent some time with a couple of them trying to learn about safe loading principles, but most of their expertise was simply intuitive – they just knew instinctively how many ropes to use, how many chocks, how many nails to put in a block of wood on a wagon floor or how many stanchions, and of which size, to contain a load. With their retirement went a lot of vital knowledge and in turn a lot of flexibility in terms of loading capability, and I don't think the Railfreight or Operating hierarchies were sufficiently aware of this loss. Certainly there was no real effort to secure the Inspectors' knowledge for the future and in our Area the little expertise that was transferred was solely due to the recognition by the Area Movements Inspector and myself that we should try to acquire some safe-loading skills while we still could. This we did informally by accompanying Inspectors on visits.

There were many exceptional loads conveyed on the railway, from concrete bridge sections to electrical transformers and from looped undersea cables to nuclear flasks. Some were routine and so did not need individual assessment, while others had to be measured and secured carefully on each occasion. Routing and speed restrictions were sometimes needed, not only for the train conveying the load but also sometimes for trains that passed it. During the Thames Barrier construction we ran trainloads of boulders from Somerset to Angerstein Wharf. Each boulder was a different shape, having simply been blasted out of the quarry, and this meant that each one had to be individually assessed and secured. Near Peckham Rye the railway runs on arches and there are numerous tenants beneath and beside the line, including a beer wholesaler. Arriving for work one morning, the staff there found an enormous rock standing amongst the barrels. At about the same time the contractors at Angerstein Wharf noticed that one boulder was missing and they reported this. Messages went out all along the route from Somerset to south-east London to the effect of 'lost, one enormous boulder. Anyone finding same please notify anxious owner'. Eventually the arch tenants realised that, unless it was a meteorite, the stone could only have come from the railway and it was collected by the contractors. Luckily it hadn't fallen where anyone could have been injured or killed by it, but it went to show how important safe-loading practices were.

Another incident at Hoo Junction was an asbestos scare in 1985. Old mineral wagons had been used for transporting scrap from the demolished

BR was adept at handling out-of-gauge loads. This 16ft-wide bridge girder needed to be loaded off-centre (with counterweights) and required adjacent lines to be blocked for its passage. (Photo: Harold Smith archive)

Fulham power station. The wagons themselves were then being sent for scrap at Queenborough, being life-expired. After a few runs it came to light that the loads were contaminated with blue and white asbestos – both by then recognised as dangerous substances. Analysts came to Hoo Junction from the Southern Region's technical offices at Croydon and confirmed that we should keep everyone away from these wagons and, in accordance with Health & Safety legislation, have them decontaminated. Some were at Hoo Junction while others were already at Queenborough and it was my responsibility to make both lots safe before we could legally hand them over to the contractor who had bought the scrap. We brought the wagons back from Queenborough to Hoo Junction on a special at the dead of night having decided that they would be safer there because Hoo Junction was less accessible to the public, even though it meant moving a contaminated load through the heavily populated Medway towns.

After 'letting my fingers do the walking', I found the numbers of a couple of specialist firms, both of whom for some reason were based in Essex, and they came down to Hoo Junction with me to assess the problem and to give me quotes for the work of making the wagons safe. Our meeting room was the Railway Tavern at Higham and there we discussed the work over pints of Shepherd Neame. The job, if it was to be done properly, would be very expensive but I could get little expression of interest in what was going on from the Area management – I was just told to get on with it. So I arranged for the wagons to be shunted into an isolated part of the down yard and then strange tent-like structures went up around them as space-suited men scraped around inside and came out with sealed bags of waste. The whole exercise took a couple of weeks and the wagons emerged spotlessly clean and painted brilliant white on the inside with special dust-repressing paint. Then they went to be cut up.

The former signalbox at Hoo Junction was in use as a TOPS office and was the main such office for the South-east, having progressively taken over the workload of Tonbridge, Bricklayers Arms, Hither Green, Ashford and Norwood. Dover remained as a security against wagons entering the country off the train ferry without being properly recorded. Because of the workload we had a supervisory Clerical Officer on duty during the day and up to three others on each shift. Shunt lists were generated for the various yards and all wagon and locomotive movements were entered into the TOPS computer. TOPS had come a long way from its trials in the West Country to which I referred earlier and had assumed a greater importance as not only were vehicle movements and maintenance arranged by it but also freight charging could be automatically generated by it. It therefore had to be of the highest integrity in terms of accuracy as freight customers would receive bills based upon it. This use of TOPS, incidentally, enabled teams of Clerks to be done away with and also meant that cash-flow was suddenly jerked forwards as billing could be made 'real-time' and not always retrospectively. The old punchcard systems had been replaced by 'cardless' TOPS, which meant that chattering printers and card racks had become a thing of the past, replaced by a solid-state system. All information was held and processed by the CPU (Central Processing Unit) at Blandford House, Marylebone. TOPS offices, correctly known as Area Freight Offices, were updating, issuing and receiving this information continuously, day and night.

It was part of my job to ensure that the integrity of TOPS information was spot on. Each month I had to make a physical check of every location in the Area where a wagon could possibly be to ensure that the vehicles listed on the printout were actually there. In general the standard of reporting was excellent, but just occasionally a wagon would be shown in the wrong place and a correction would be made. Very rarely there would be a wagon listed that I could not find anywhere, but it would soon turn up elsewhere as someone in another part of the country did their checks.

At Swanscombe there was a fleet of derelict wagons that had once been used for carrying bagged cement. For some reason, Blue Circle, who were the owners, wanted these to remain operational, at least in name, and so they were all shown on TOPS. I dutifully went down to the maze of sidings in the chalk pits and by the Thames to do my first TOPS Integrity Check soon after taking the job on, only to find that most of the painted wagon numbers had worn away and that, in any case, most of the wagons were surrounded by brambles, chalk slurry and mud. In the end I just counted them and the total agreed with that shown on the list, so I was satisfied and thought that would be the end of it. However, nothing at Swanscombe was ever as it seemed and, months later, Blue Circle decided that they wanted some of these wagons moved to Holborough siding near Snodland to be used there for storage purposes. At their considerable expense a string of them was renovated over a period of a couple of weeks to make them fit for running, the track was cleared and then, eventually, they went groaning on their way on a special service paid for by Blue Circle. Two things were never exactly clear – first of all, of course, why on earth Blue Circle went to all this expense but also, secondly, which wagons actually went. I now had two locations with wagons having illegible numbers and had run a train without knowing exactly what was on it – not at all in the spirit of TOPS Integrity. The train list had consisted of any old numbers picked from the TOPS list. The entire operation had been undertaken with some trepidation amongst those of us who recalled a similar move of semi-derelict private wagons one night from the disused Berry Wiggins sidings on the Grain branch and which had ground to a halt on the running line at Hither Green with seized brakes. Luckily the move itself was uneventful on this occasion.

A perennial problem at Hoo Junction (and elsewhere) was the shortage of serviceable tail lamps for freight trains. Most lamps were still of the oil type and had seen better days. As trains came in the lamps would be taken off and left on the ground nearby while shunting proceeded. Sometimes they would then become damaged before they could be collected. Oil trains (and certain others) ran with electric tail lamps, as do all trains now, and these were numbered and lettered with the name of their home depot, which was accountable for their whereabouts. Even so, these would also go astray quite frequently and on occasion it would be touch and go whether a train could run as we searched for a working lamp.

The problem was one of many that were exacerbated by the increasing pace of change on the railway. In this case the number of places willing to repair lamps had diminished to just one, Wolverton Works. The rationalisation of the railway works had concentrated on larger issues than the supply and maintenance of tail lamps. Old systems had gone without new ones being put into place – an all too common occurrence on the railway of the 1980s and '90s.

The management at Wolverton Works were not prepared to allocate full-time staff to the repair of lamps and so stated that a minimum of fifty lamps at a time would have to be sent to them. They would then release fifty good lamps in exchange and would consider it worthwhile to make a special job of repairing the broken ones. This was catastrophic locally as it meant that we had to hold on to broken lamps for longer before we could get them repaired. It also meant, though, that we had to be more careful in the first place, not allowing damage to occur and not leaving lamps unattended in remote sidings to deteriorate or be stolen. But in the meantime we had a problem that was already resulting in trains being cancelled for lack of tail lamps – a ludicrous situation.

One of the lessons of the 1980s was that you could no longer moan about the inadequacies of systems and then sit back and wait for new solutions to be proposed, negotiated and, perhaps, implemented. You had to find your own salvation. So in conjunction with the Ashford Area management I hired a van, drove around all my sidings and yards collecting lamps, went to Ashford to collect theirs and then drove to Wolverton to exchange them. I had just about scraped up the required fifty, some of which were barely recognisable as lamps, but I was far from welcome at Wolverton Works, for whom the fifty rule was intended as a deterrent against having to do any tail-lamp repairs. In the run-up to privatisation they wanted big engineering contracts and didn't want to be seen as a collection of odd-job men tinkering around at traditional workbenches.

I mentioned earlier that derailments were rare but, of course, they did happen from time to time for a variety of reasons. Hand points not being switched quickly enough or not going fully over was a frequent cause, as was track spreading. The track in freight yards was basically not maintained at all, only the points receiving a cursory greasing from time to time. Rotten sleepers would easily give up their hold on rail chairs or would split under strain, causing the wheels to drop down into the 'four-foot' between the rails. Each derailment caused severe delay to freight traffic, which then became blocked in, and the rerailing itself would cause further disruption. In cases where a derailment occurred during shunting, for whatever reason, the effect on staff concerned could be quite devastating. One newly qualified Shunter at Hoo Junction misjudged a move one day and brought the leading end of a train, which was propelling into the yard off the up main line, off the road across the running line. He could not be easily consoled. And neither could the thousands of commuters whose rush-hour service between Gravesend and the Medway Towns was suspended that evening.

At the time I was working in freight in the 1980s we still had steam-powered rerailing cranes, based at Hither Green and Stewarts Lane, and these machines were marvellous to see at work. Likewise, the rerailing gangs were amazing people to watch. They seemed to emerge from nowhere and were sheer experts in their work. The Hither Green steam crane was usually operated by the same man who manipulated its levers and valves with a consummate skill that was always a pleasure to see. At the same time as doing his lifts he was, of course, also stoking the fire and managing the steam pressure. All this was done from a cramped position at the top of the crane's body, with just a metal sheet above him for protection from the weather.

The gangs had a sort of sign language and the Rerailing Supervisor would only need to flutter his hand in a certain way for things to happen. The crane's outriggers would be extended, chocked and packed with large blocks of wood; the jib would be positioned to give the optimum lifting angle for the job in question; and the lifting points of the derailed vehicle would be identified – all with hardly a word being spoken. I used to love watching these unsung 'professionals', even though it was usually at around two in the morning on a bitterly cold night. One day a 100-tonne steel carrier came off the road in Plumstead Yard and I was called out to the rerailing at night with the Hither Green 45-tonne steam crane, although in theory the lift was beyond its capacity. Strictly speaking, to lift one end of a 100-tonne wagon needed a 50-tonne crane with the jib as near vertical as possible. The gang got the rerailing train Driver to position the crane as close to the vehicle as possible so they could get the jib nearly vertical, but even so the cables ran back out under the strain on the first attempt and the wagon, having been lifted a few inches, crashed back down in a cloud of dust. Minor adjustments to the packing of the outriggers and positioning of the lifting chains took place while the crane driver built up maximum steam pressure for a second go. When he was ready, the Rerailing Supervisor gave the signal to try again and indicated that everyone should stand well back. Normally rerailing was done millimetre by millimetre, with calculated precision and care, but on this occasion it was going to have to be quick but still accurate. First the crane driver took up the slack in the chains and cables and then with a flurry of steam and a frantic clanking of flywheels the crane jerked the steel wagon off the ground, the operator quickly interpreting the Supervisor's handsignals regarding the required swing of the jib and positioning the wagon over the track. As he received the signal to lower the wagon, the cables were just starting to run out again under the weight and he was losing control once more, but the positioning had been judged correctly and the wagon crashed down this time with all its wheels on the track. A skilfully manned 45-tonne steam crane, aided by the teamwork of its gang, had lifted a 100-tonne steel carrier and had successfully rerailed it. I remember wondering to what extent a diesel crane would be able to outperform its specification, no matter how skilled the operator. The job finished, the gang packed away all their trappings, stowed the outriggers, secured the jib and climbed aboard their mess coach to go back to the anonymity of their depot at Hither Green. And another British steel export went on its way to France a few hours later.

Incidentally, when the rerailing train was being re-formed on this occasion in readiness for its return to Hither Green, I had the rare pleasure of being able to give the handsignal 'create brake' to the locomotive Driver. This unusual handsignal involved clenching your fist and then moving your forearm up and down vertically in front of your body, and was a movement with the most comically crude connotations. After dark, however, it was a red lamp moved up and down.

As well as rerailing, which was their *raison d'être*, the steam cranes were sometimes used on contract, in particular to the Department of Transport for bridge construction, at the Private Party rates I mentioned a while ago. When the motorway was built under the line near Otford Junction, two railway steam cranes were employed to position the bridge spans.

Perhaps inevitably, Angerstein Wharf had more than its fair share of derailments – and not just the private shunting engine whose tale I told earlier. The 2,200-tonne Marcon aggregates trains were prone to derailment on the tight curve leading from the main line, but fortunately only when empty. On more than one occasion a wagon rode up and over the outer rail and then rerailed itself on the points. After a while you get used to reading the signs of a derailment in terms of score marks on the sleepers and across the rails, cracked rail chairs and damaged points blades, etc. There were several such stories to be read at Angerstein Junction and along the line to the wharf. Eventually the fault was traced to the wagons and adjustments were made. Just as I (and others, of course) could read the signs on the track, the Mechanical and Electrical people could read the signs on the wagons, which told their own story. Being able to match stories always led to a certain satisfaction.

Passenger train derailments, thankfully, were extremely rare, although empty stock derailments occurred in yards occasionally. While I was Area Freight Manager at Dartford we had a passenger train collision at Dartford Junction one morning as a result of a Driver passing a signal at danger. No one was hurt but the disruption was extensive on this section of line, which had an off-peak service of eight trains an hour in each direction, not to mention freight trains. In those days, despite the separation of freight and passenger management at my level, it was still understood that we all worked for the same railway, which is an important distinction from now. So, even though I was the Area Freight Manager, I rang round the bus and coach depots to hire vehicles and dealt with people who had been evacuated from the trains and had been escorted back along the track to the station. Similarly, I would deal with point winding and signal flagging if I happened to be the suitably qualified person closest to hand at the time. With the fragmentation of the railway and its staff first of all into Operating and Retail, then into business sectors and finally into separately owned companies, this sort of versatility is a thing of the past. One imagines smooth-talking franchise staff speaking bland platitudes about 'something on the line being broken' and hurriedly blaming Network Rail, whereas in earlier times station staff would have grunted some form of abuse and then gone down on to the track to wind points or flag a failed signal in order to get the service going again.

13

Winding and Flagging

Rules for the safety of staff working on the track were for a long time fairly rudimentary and people worked in both emergency conditions and routinely with very little protection. It was not until the late 1980s that the concept of training people specifically in Personal Track Safety and of issuing them with PTS certification before they were allowed on the track came into being. Until then, on-track activity and training for it were much more informal, although training records were usually kept. As an Assistant Station Manager and later Area Freight Manager, I was required to help out in emergencies by flagging signals, manually operating level crossings and winding failed points. I also had to ensure that staff were trained in these duties in sufficient numbers. So what sort of incidents necessitated going on to the line?

On a routine visit to Deptford station one day I heard that the evening rush hour was disrupted by a points failure at North Kent East Junction, just nearby. I phoned the Signalman at London Bridge to see if help was needed and he asked me to go to New Cross, join up there with the Station Supervisor and then go to North Kent East to wind the affected points and to handsignal trains past them. One of us was to act as lookout for the other and also report to the Signalman by means of the signalpost telephone, which in this case was by the lineside. The points concerned were in the middle of the six tracks, which are at that point on arches. Each time the Signalman phoned to ask for the points to be wound one of us had to cross three lines (with live conductor rails, of course), wind and clip the points and then return to the relative safety of one of the cutout refuges in the parapet of the viaduct. All around us on all six lines the South Eastern rush hour continued virtually unimpeded. Between five and six o'clock each evening around

100 trains pass this point. By a long way that was the scariest bit of point winding I ever remember having to do.

One Saturday morning when I was on duty at Woolwich Arsenal we had a sudden and unexpectedly heavy fall of snow. The service was severely disrupted as a result of snow compacting in the points around Dartford and I received a call from the Signalman at London Bridge to say that there was a points failure at Charlton as well. Luckily, an up train was just then arriving so I jumped in with the Driver and explained to him that he would be held at Charlton until I could wind the points ahead of him and restore detection for the Signalman. I also needed to collect the points equipment from the Senior Railman's office on the platform at Charlton and the Driver kindly said he would drop me off at that end of the platform before pulling forward properly into the platform, in order to save time. So we stopped, I jumped out and ... nothing. The train had become 'gapped'. This meant that no traction current collector shoes were in contact with the conductor rail and so the train could not move. It was stuck, with just its nose in the platform. This train was a four-car with shoes at front and rear but I recall another incident in which an entire twelve-car train was gapped on the approaches to Cannon Street, none of its twelve shoes in contact with a conductor rail.

The front shoes of my train at Charlton were over a gap in the conductor rail where a foot crossing had once been, while the rear shoes were over a gap by a clipped crossover, so not only did we have a points failure but now we had a train stranded with no 'juice' to its motors. Talk about bad luck. I reported this to the Signalman and also formally relayed to him the Driver's request for assistance from the rear. At that moment, apparently, there was no train our side of Dartford, so we were set for a long wait. In the meantime I collected the point handle, point motor key, clips and scotches and trudged off through the snow to Charlton Junction to wind the specified set of points.

Now at the best of times the perspective of a junction viewed from the ground is different from that of a track plan and so you have to be very careful to ensure that you go to the right points, verifying the point number that is on a plate on one of the sleepers next to the points. When the whole place is covered in snow to just above rail level it's infinitely worse. I couldn't see where any of the points were, let alone their numbers, although I could just see the tops of the conductor rails, which was just as well for my safety as, of course, they were live. By estimating where the points must be and then looking for the telltale gap in the conductor rail I was eventually able to find the right set, after clearing the snow to locate the number. I also cleared the snow from between the rails and the points blades and from around the point motor, and I was then able to wind over the points with the handle, clipping and scotching the points in the new position, as was required by the Rule Book for the passage of a passenger train over facing points. Having reported back to the Signalman that this was done I then returned to the station. There was still no train that side of Dartford, but the Driver had been thinking about his predicament and had come up with a possible solution. We decided to give it a try.

The Driver asked the Guard to sit in the driving cab. He told him to keep his hand on the driving control handle and when he shouted, to open it up and then shut it quickly. All highly irregular, needless to say. The Driver then took the brakes off, collected the electrical short-circuiting bar from the brakevan and got down on to the track by the offside front shoe of the train, which was over the foot crossing gap. I went with him as lookout as we were between the two running lines and with conductor rails a couple of inches either side of us. The metal part of the short-circuiting bar looked just long enough to bridge the gap between the shoe and the ramp of the conductor rail behind it. The down platform had quite a few people on it, who were wondering what we were up to and a group had gathered to watch. The Driver told them to turn away as there would be a risk of flash-blinding. He then positioned the bar on the conductor rail in such a way that the end of it was directly under the shoe.

He and I both turned our faces away as he made contact, shouted 'Now!' to the Guard and the train lurched forward with an almighty electrical flash, a sizzling sound and a smell of burning.

The people on the platform cheered, the Driver bowed to them and I went to tell the Signalman that assistance was no longer required.

'How come?' asked the amazed Signalman, but quickly added 'No, on second thoughts, I don't want to know.'

We'd got the service going again and it was better that nothing was recorded about how we'd done so.

Signal flagging because of signal failure or because of, say, level-crossing failure was quite common, too. We had a lot of level-crossing failures, mainly because of people dodging the lights and colliding with the barriers. This kind of work could be a miserable activity if the weather was bad as the likelihood of finding somewhere to shelter was remote. One morning I found refuge by standing just inside Blackheath Tunnel between trains while flagging a nearby signal. Safety rules meant that you had to be very specific about the message you were relaying from the Signalman to the Driver, but when you'd been saying the same form of words all morning it became almost tempting to say something like, 'Off you go. You know the rest.' Instead, though, each time you had to say, 'You are authorised to pass (signal number whatever) at danger, proceed at caution and obey all other signals.' Drivers were then required to sound the horn and tell the Guard what was happening. Some Drivers expected you to remind them of these two requirements as well before they would move. Sometimes the Signalman would come on the phone in advance to say that a train was nearby and that it could proceed past the signal without being stopped, which, strictly, was not permissible as the verbal authority and warning could not be given. In these circumstances, if you chose to go along with it, you could show a yellow flag before the train had come to a stand at the red light. Some Drivers would take this and carry on but others would stop and register their disapproval, so you stood the risk of causing more delay in an effort to save time. Short cuts with safety procedures were not a good idea in any case, of course. The 'proceed' flag you displayed had to be the colour of the most restrictive 'proceed' aspect capable of being exhibited by the signal you were flagging, which in most cases was a single yellow. However, if you were handsignalling a two-aspect ground signal, such as at a crossover at one end of engineering works, the correct flag to show was green because the signal itself could only show 'stop' or 'go', in effect. Time after time Drivers would dispute this, saying that a yellow should be shown and eventually this was made the case in the interests not of consistency but of eliminating argument. The other important thing to remember was that the flag had to be held not just while the Driver went by but also until the Guard had passed. If you withdrew the flag before the Guard had passed you he had the right to bring the train to a stand, although whether any Guards ever did so I don't know.

On our bit of the North Kent line in the early 1980s we had three lifting-barrier level crossings, operated from two crossing boxes. Charlton Lane and Crabtree Crossings were directly supervised by the boxes bearing their names, while Belvedere crossing had been put on to closed-circuit television (CCTV) control from Crabtree box in 1981, giving the Crossing Keeper there two crossings to work. Sometimes there would be a camera failure, a control failure, or a mechanical breakdown of the lifting-barrier equipment. At other times, as I have said, the damage would be caused by road vehicles. In all cases of damage or failure we would troop out to work the crossing manually. Sometimes this meant pumping the barriers up and down with a handle that you inserted into each barrier motor machine in turn, while at other times it involved dragging pennants across the road in place of the barriers. Every time any of these incidents happened the integrity of the electrical interlocking between the barrier control and signalling systems was broken and so the signals protecting the crossing could only show red and had to be handsignalled. So you needed to call in quite a team of people if you were going to deal with a failure without too much delay to rail and road traffic. Starting it off on your own was a nightmare, though – pumping all four barriers in turn, running to the signal along the line to authorise the Driver to go by and then running back to reopen the crossing each time.

Another emergency track activity on the Southern Region was the operation of hook switches. These were located at certain conductor rail gaps at which the traction current passed instead through a cable. The current could be isolated by opening these switches. In emergency, or in the case of a short circuit, the current would be cut off (or would have tripped out) from one electrical sub-station to the next, which could be a considerable distance away. Upon instructions over the phone from the Electrical Control Operator, the distance of the isolation could then be reduced by the manual operation of hook switches. The ECO could then remotely recharge either side of the more local isolation.

I mentioned in the context of the Charlton 'gapping' how it was necessary for us to turn our faces away to avoid flash-blinding and this was also part of the hook-switch procedure. All stations, depots and trains had, as part of their standard emergency equipment, a hook-switch pole and we made sure that staff were trained to operate the switches. During the 1980s it was part of station staffing policy to have at least one person on duty who was passed out in the Rules applicable to track emergencies. Obviously this no longer applies and most of the stations on which we had staff trained for dealing with emergencies on duty around the clock are now unstaffed for long periods or, in some cases, all the time.

Each hook switch had a number and upon the instruction of the Electrical Control Operator you went on to the track to identify the one to be operated. Every location had an electrical diagram to assist in this. You then hooked the pole into the locking hole and pulled this open first. This released the far end of a hinged plate, along which the current ran. By then putting the hook of the pole into the hole in the end of the plate and pulling, the hinged plate would slide open, breaking contact. It was during this last part of the operation that you had to turn your face away as the current would arc across the gap while the plate was still close to the switch. People were naturally cautious about using these switches at first and would pull gently, but this only made the arcing worse. The thing to do was to yank the thing open as quickly as you could because then there would only be a small flash. Every time hook switches were operated, the name of the person doing it would be recorded at the Electrical Control Room and that person would then be designated 'person in charge of isolation'. Only that person could subsequently close the hook switch again and then only upon the ECO's instruction. In that way one person remained in control of the isolation, as was vital if that same person was the one who needed to be working in contact with the conductor rail.

In the modern world of 25kV overhead electrification, this procedure may seem somewhat antiquated and even makeshift, but it has to be remembered that the Southern was at the forefront, worldwide, of the development of electric traction and that the installation of DC third-rail electrification, as made by the London & South Western Railway from 1913 onwards, had in fact been adopted as the national standard for all railways in Britain in 1920 by the Electrification of Railways Advisory Committee of the Ministry of Transport. The fact that 25kV AC overhead later became the standard should not take away the credit that is due to the LSWR and the Southern Railway for getting on with modernising their railways so early on in what David Henshaw, in his book *The Great Railway Conspiracy*, says 'proved to be the principal modernisation achievement of the railways in the first half of the century'. The way that third-rail DC is now seen as somewhat of an archaic idiosyncrasy, leading to such complications as the need for dual-voltage Thameslink and Eurostar trains as well as Class 92 locomotives, is another illustration of how railway development is necessarily piecemeal and of how the most modern of one age becomes, in turn, the most outdated of another.

But to return to track duties. Station and yard staff, as well as train crews, also had training in the application of Track Circuit Clips, which progressively over the years rose to become the first means of train protection in cases of mishap. While not all lines were track-circuited, these clips gave instant protection on lines that were, as they shorted out the signalling current that runs through the running rails, thus putting the signal in rear at danger automatically. In effect they pretended to the signalling system that a train was occupying the track circuit. An excellent device, except on the Southern, where to apply them to an electrified line you had to fiddle about a couple of inches from the conductor rail. We always taught staff to apply the clip to the rail away from the conductor rail first as the lead between the clips would not then reach the rail itself and in this way the clip could not inadvertently

BR station staff were trained to operate trackside equipment during emergencies or incidents, including opening conductor-rail hook switches. Separation of infrastructure from train running means that Network Rail now has to send staff, possibly from many miles away. In the meantime, trains have to wait. (Photo: Ron Bailes)

be applied to it. Most people thought this was a bit ridiculous – as if anyone would put the clip on 'the juice' – but I think we all knew in our hearts that at moments of stress and, possibly, panic, all sorts of things are possible.

Now the point I made at the beginning of this chapter was that staff safety procedures were scant. In all the cases I have mentioned trains would have, or could have, continued running on the lines concerned or those adjacent and/or the conductor rail would have remained live. It was up to staff on the track and the Drivers of trains to be vigilant and to abide by the Rules. We were responsible for our own safety and for each others'. To this day, despite Personal Track Safety certification, there is probably no other industry in Britain providing a day-to-day service or product that routinely exposes its staff to potential danger to the extent the railway does. But that was half the fun of it.

A lot of safety management is precautionary, of course. You don't wait for things to happen: you try to make sure they don't happen. Training of station and yard staff was seen as a vital part of this in order that everyone had sufficient safety awareness as well as the skills necessary to take charge of an incident until a more senior person arrived. As one of those more senior people I was issued with a delightful armband upon which were the words 'MISHAP CONTROLLER', which always made me feel as if I was a mischief-making Lord of Misrule of medieval times.

As well as training in safety procedures and safety awareness, other precautionary measures on stations and in depots included items of hardware such as Tilley lamps, salt and grit. Every autumn we checked our stocks and distribution of winter supplies, digging out the oil lamps and repairing them as necessary. Just occasionally they were pressed into service, either to light up the track for point winding at night, or, more frequently, for lighting stations during power cuts. Salt and grit were delivered to main stations and then distributed according to the SM's orders. Every station had a supply and was also equipped with ice scrapers and shovels. In times of heavy snowfall you couldn't expect the staff to be able to keep up with the task of ensuring that all platforms were cleared, salted and gritted and so, on the Woolwich line, the SM, other ASM and I would be out there with shovels, too.

It was a matter of pride at that time to ensure that sufficient resources were available to deal with emergencies. If the Signalman called to say he needed a handsignalman, we wanted to be able to get one on site quickly. If a level crossing failed, we wanted to get things moving as soon as we could. If there was a power cut or if the platforms were slippery, we wanted to make things safe as quickly as possible. With staff on most stations at most times, and with those staff properly trained, we were in a good position to be able to meet our objective. Many of us who had the experience of being able to do this view the current situation with some misgiving, I think for two reasons. First, there just aren't the resources, human or otherwise, to carry out all the emergency duties of which we were able. Secondly, and more worryingly, the separation of the railway into a track authority and train operating companies has removed from the TOCs, whose staff work on stations as well as on trains, the immediate concern with track safety. The problem is likely to worsen too, for the reason that in the early years of franchising the railway is still essentially operated 'on the ground' by the people who ran it before and these people, being career railwaymen and women, want to preserve the safety culture. But as they leave and are replaced by managers and staff from other backgrounds who have purely business priorities, so the safety culture will wane and the divide between the TOCs and Network Rail will widen. Safety management has never been 'trendy' and in an environment where it may well clash at times with the achievement of business objectives there is the danger that it will be pushed further into the corner.*

* 2018 update: Sixteen years since this was written the separation of responsibilities between the train operators and Network Rail continues to cause problems, with NR staff having to travel miles by road to resolve infrastructure issues that used to be sorted by local station staff and/or by train crew.

14

Found in Possession ... Out of Hours

Personal accountability of the type mentioned in connection with electrical isolations was an important part of various emergency (and other) procedures. All engineering 'possessions' had a nominated Person in Charge of Possession (PICOP) and the engineering departments had to notify signalling staff in advance of the names of these people. Signalmen were then only authorised to grant possession of the line to the named PICOP, who was then the only person who could authorise train movements into or out of the possession.

Major track replacements, which in fact were fairly routine as the railway was continuously being renewed, were meticulously planned. Most renewals used to take place during a seventy-two-hour possession over the weekend, but increasing use of mechanisation has meant that the time taken can often now be less. Each element of the work had to be planned so as not to impede other parts: for instance, it was no good having diggers 'deep-digging' the trackbed the wrong side of the material train carrying the new track. Co-ordination of the various activities needed careful planning, followed by the PICOP's close control of the site. As well as track lifting, digging, drainage, ballasting, laying track, tamping, lining and destressing, all of which were done by the Civil Engineer's staff and contractors, there would also be signalling staff to disconnect, reconnect and test their equipment, possibly taking advantage of the possession to replace some of it. Also, on third-rail lines, the electrification people would be there to isolate, reconnect and test the traction supply. The Supervisors in charge of these elements of the work had to report to the PICOP to confirm when they could safely start work and to confirm that they had finished and were clear of the line. On occasion there might well be other work going on at the same time as a track renewal – station canopy painting, bridge repairs, embankment grouting, etc., all making the most of the fact that the line was closed. In every case a reporting structure had to be put into place so that the PICOP could retain control of the safety of every aspect of the whole site, which could be many miles long.

The sheer intensity of the heavy engineering work undertaken during such possessions was, and still is, in marked contrast to the drawn-out renewal work carried out on motorways, which goes on even at peak traffic times – or a least the lane closures do. A seventy-two-hour railway possession means seventy-two hours of work, not just of closure.

My first railway job, in 1973, involved attendance at engineers' planning meetings for major possessions. I was then responsible for producing timings for the material trains that would be needed. It was vital to understand from which end of the possession and upon which line each train was to arrive at the site and depart from it and how it might be re-formed on site. Any muddle over this could lead to delay and a possible overrun of the possession time. As an aid in planning and then in monitoring progress on site, each element of work and each event was plotted on a timechart, using a different colour for each area of responsibility or activity. Also to be planned were replacement bus services, the crewing and rolling stock implications of having the line closed and the need to divert freight, news and other services. All major possessions were programmed a long way in advance in order to ensure that the engineers' renewal and maintenance schedules could be fitted in with the need to keep certain routes open at particular times and so that there was, if possible, a diversionary route available. Publicity concerning line closures also had to be issued sufficiently in advance. Speed restrictions always followed a renewal while the track settled in and the number of such restrictions was also part of the planning in order to avoid having a particular route riddled with restrictions to the extent that the timetable couldn't be operated.

The planning meetings that I attended were held at the appropriate Permanent Way Supervisor's office for the site. These were at various locations on the South Eastern Division and were a real eye-opener for me. I had worked previously in the relative gentility of a High Street bank and here I was faced with some very rough and ready characters who didn't mince their words if they thought you were talking nonsense. The Permanent

Way Supervisor would chair the meeting, accompanied usually by the person who would eventually be in charge on site. The Office Clerk would take the minutes and record the plan for the sequence of the work and of the material trains. I would take my own notes so that back at the Divisional office we could quickly assess the likelihood, or otherwise, of providing the resources to meet the plan.

The local Area Inspector would attend to ensure that operating rules regarding the taking and surrender of the possession and also of terminating trains, etc. were properly taken into account. These Inspectors were real diehard railway operators, having spent all their working lives in signalboxes or depots. Some were actually feared and they certainly didn't treat fools gladly. Last of all, the local Station Manager would be there to assess the implications for his stations and to allocate signalling staff, etc. In the relative stability of the early 1970s some of these SMs were true old-timers, too. In my first few months on BR I soon learned that the nitty-gritty of running the railway was carried out in the main by a collection of almost Dickensian characters who would have torn through the 'namby-pamby' atmosphere of my previous place of work like a dose of salts. These were the real railwaymen for whom the railway was everything and who regarded with contempt people who came in from 'outside' to positions of authority, especially if they were doing so solely as a career move. Few such characters survive today and the railway has become to many of its staff and managers just another job. You might work for British Gas one day, Network Rail the next and then go to a city council nowadays, but right up to the 1970s, if you came to work for the railway, you were expected to be loyal.

At the planning meetings, which were usually held in a fog of pipe smoke, the old-timers easily digested in their minds the complications inherent in planning the material trains while the Engineer's Clerk and I tried to record it all on paper so that the plan could be understood by ourselves and others. They would be talking about such things as train 4/1 arriving on the up line at the country end of the possession, re-forming ten hours later with part of train 4/4, which had entered two hours earlier at the London end and crossed from down to up after the up line had been cleared by the bridge gang, while train 4/3 would arrive four hours later at the country end and eventually leave as a combination of itself and trains 4/2 and 4/5 by travelling 'wrong-road' at the London end of the possession. Somehow, no matter how complex, it all worked out and the trains were not required to jump over missing bits of track, skip across bridge spans that had been removed, hop over to the opposite line by magic or leapfrog over each other. Neither were bits of trains, which consisted of all sorts of machines as well as different types of wagons of materials, overlooked or counted twice. Nowadays it would be called 'logistics' and in other industries would probably be planned by computer simulation – in those days it was just railway work and was calculated by a bunch of everyday railwaymen to whom it was second nature.

Most trains going to major possession sites were made up at Hither Green or Ashford Pre-Assembly Depots (PAD) where diggers and other machines were loaded and secured, wagons put into the correct order for the work on site and track materials loaded. In some cases complete junctions were being renewed and they would be assembled at the PADs over the preceding weeks and then dismantled, with the pieces being numbered for reassembly on site. If you were going to take out an important junction you needed to know

Track renewals were meticulously planned and executed. In this scene near Shortlands in 1975, pre-fabricated track panels are being installed. (Photo: Brian Garvin)

that everything you were putting in to replace it would fit. Trains of ballast hoppers usually ran separately from the material trains as did the spoil trains, which were formed of long lines of 'grampus' wagons. On-track machines, such as tampers, would make their own way to and from the site.

All the Civil Engineer's wagon types had the names of sea creatures, which was a rather attractive feature but which seemed a bit odd to me as a newcomer. So the timings I produced would specify loads such as 'five sea-cows and twenty-two grampus' or 'nine whales'. These wagons conveyed ballast or spoil, while salmons, prawns and shrimps carried rails. There were numerous other types too, each with individual characteristics tailored to a particular engineering need, such as a shark, which was an engineer's brakevan fitted with a plough for levelling ballast. As a 19-year-old, standing alongside a bunch of time-served P. Way Engineers and Area Inspectors at a windswept track renewal site and hearing their down-to-earth language interspersed with mention of shrimps and sea-cows, I realised pretty soon that the railway was indeed the 'one-off' industry I had hoped it would be when I joined.

Odd loads of engineering material went on scheduled freight services 'FROR', meaning Free on Rail. This was a sort of inter-departmental courtesy between the engineering departments and the freight people at a time when we all worked for the same railway. Under later Railfreight management this was stopped and the engineers were required to pay the going rate on trains for which there could quite possibly be a surfeit of commercial traffic. These days, of course, every movement is under commercial contract between separately owned companies, with Network Rail or its contractors paying EWS for most engineers' trains. Indeed, the infrastructure contract is one of EWS's biggest now that coal forms such a relatively small part of its business.* Whilst in the early Railfreight days payment from one 'department' to another seemed a rather ridiculous paper-shuffling accountancy exercise, it had the benefit of sharpening awareness of how much track maintenance was really costing and of not diluting the freight revenue. Many times I have mentioned the way in which we didn't

* 2018 update: Several freight companies now compete for haulage of Network Rail's engineering trains. EWS is now known as DB Cargo.

really know how much anything was costing because everything was lumped in together and it was moves such as this that enabled us to start to do so.

For 'ballast' trains, which was a term used for all engineers' trains, we had a primitive system of charging in the early 1970s. Quite how costs were assessed I wouldn't like to say, but each train was charged to a particular account. In another rather quaint custom the accounts were not numbered but bore the names of the Chief Engineers of the relevant departments. Thus at the beginning of the 'ballast pages' of each weekly South Eastern Special Traffic Notice we inserted the words 'All trains Mr Newing's account unless otherwise specified', Mr Newing being the Divisional Civil Engineer. One Christmas a colleague put in a spoof timing for a train from North Pole Junction with the load specified as 'one sleigh'. All hell was let loose when it turned out that a charge against Mr Newing had been raised. North Pole Junction is, of course, a real place in west London, now known mainly for having given its name to the original Eurostar depot.

Several years later, as an Assistant Station Manager, I worked as Bus Supervisor or handsignalman on weekend engineering possessions, raking in a fortune in overtime. On one such occasion, at Dorking West, the bus didn't show but there were so few passengers anyway that I was able to take them on in my car. In the London area things were busier. We usually used London Transport buses or else coaches from a carefully chosen list of reputable firms such as Ebdons of Sidcup. There was little trouble so long as the firm contracted to do the work actually turned up. Sometimes, though, London Transport would sub-contract the work and that could lead to disaster.

When they did the job themselves, they usually supplied an Inspector and all the drivers had schedules to work to. In this way you always knew when the next bus was due and how many buses were meant to be operating. One Sunday at Plumstead in 1982 I remember a handlebar-moustached Inspector not only recording each arrival and departure but also remonstrating with drivers who had lost time. He stood in the road in front of each bus as it arrived, indicating exactly where it was to stop, i.e. about one inch in front of his nose.

That same winter, by contrast, I did a job at Falconwood on the Bexleyheath line where the work lasted on and off for a couple of years while the Rochester Way Relief Road was being built. This involved rerouting the railway, building a new station at Eltham (opened March 1985) and closing the old stations at Eltham Park and Eltham Well Hall. London Transport could not always cover this work and I was unfortunate enough to be on bus supervision on one of the days when they had sub-contracted. The cowboys were out in force that day.

One coach driver had taken a party from London to Worthing, had then come back to do a few trips for us and was then going back to fetch the party. How many driving hours was this? Another said to me that he would stay as long as he was needed, so long as he had a bucket full of water on hand each time he came back to Falconwood as his radiator was leaking. Others just disappeared or appeared without any sort of schedule or notice. I soon learnt to check with each driver whether he or she was going to come back or not. Each vehicle seemed to be from a different firm and each driver was squeezing our work in and around other jobs. Some had to go in convoy because they didn't know the way. Sometimes there was a glut of vehicles and at other times a dearth and, needless to say, these fluctuations did not coincide with our needs. Chaos!

When you worked in this way at different places each time you sometimes forgot where you were. Having done some bus jobs at Falconwood I was later booked up as a handsignalman at Kidbrooke, which was at the other end of this same major work. As nobody turned up to man the station I did the announcing there as well as the handsignalling. It was pointed out to me by a passenger that I was announcing, 'Falconwood, this is Falconwood. All change please for a special bus service to Kidbrooke.' For how many trains I had been saying this I never knew. Even at the best of times, if you had a string of stations under your control, you could momentarily forget which one you were at. People would come up to me and ask me the time of the next train and my first reaction would be to look up at the station name sign to remind myself where I actually was.

Another source of hefty weekend overtime payment was on-train revenue protection. At one time we decided to have a purge on fare dodgers on Saturdays and Sundays in the Dartford Area but could not enlist the support of the Travelling Ticket Inspectors to do this. Therefore we did it ourselves. I worked in a team of three and as we joined each non-corridor coach we did so simultaneously by three consecutive doors, with the late George Foster, who was a very large man indeed, bellowing, 'Have your tickets ready, please!' Once we had checked each seating bay we would leapfrog past each other to the next unchecked bay and so do each coach in no time. The aim was to move along one coach at each station, but where fares had to be taken this was not always possible.

At that time the Southern's suburban stock still had a lot of single non-corridor compartments, which were a boon to fare dodgers (and others – you never knew what you might find). Historically, these compartments were not entered by Inspectors because of the inability to escape if things turned nasty. Indeed, in their last years in service these units had a red stripe painted above the doors of the single compartments to warn passengers who might be concerned about their personal safety. We, however, thought that we weren't going to let people deliberately avoid us by using these compartments and so we joined three neighbouring single compartments each time and checked for each others' presence at every station. We caught a lot of very surprised people that way. Overall, though, we were surprised at how few tickets we needed to issue. While we covered our own overtime costs we did not bring in much towards the £18 million that was estimated by Southern Region management to be out there. Of course, this was all several years ahead of the Penalty Fares Act that increased the stakes for fare dodgers and also did away with ticket barrier staff. One of the first £10 penalties on the South Eastern was extracted from the pocket of Michael Howard, MP, at the time Home Secretary.

At weekends and at night local managers, such as myself, would do 'out of hours' visits to stations, depots, boxes, etc. in order to check that the correct staff were there and that they were doing their jobs properly. In the Dartford Area we were supposed to visit not just our own places but each others'. This meant that as Area Freight Manager, as I had become, I could still keep my hand in with passenger stations and, of course, get a share of the overtime, which seemed to be important at the time. Another advantage was that I wasn't known on lots of the stations so the surprise element of a visit was that much greater.

15

Passing Times and Pulling Cords

The Special Traffic Section at Beckenham, in which I worked during my early days, did not only produce timings for engineers' trains. We also produced runnings for a variety of self-propelled on-track machines. Most runnings were for tampers and liners, which at the time were mostly separate machines and were made exclusively by Plasser, who had their British depot at Ealing. There were some larger, newer machines that tamped the ballast, consolidated it and also lined the rails. The runnings for these were easier to produce as they had higher top speeds and could be relied upon to operate track circuits. With the smaller ones you had to show stops in the timings for the Conductor Driver or the machine's own operator to contact the Signalman in order to confirm where the machine was, even in track circuit block areas. Incidentally, in this age of radio communication between Drivers and Signalmen the need to stop to contact the Signalman may sound odd but it had the advantage over radio of eliminating any doubt as to exactly where the call was coming from. Each call made from a signalpost telephone to a power box would have the number of the signal indicated in the box, whereas a radio call could be coming from anywhere and a slip of the tongue over a number could go unnoticed. The use of signalpost telephones also made sure that Drivers were not driving at the same time as talking. Radio has undoubted safety benefits but it has to be used carefully and only for certain purposes, as it is more open to the making of mistakes than is a closed system.

If the machine's journey was under 15 miles the machine operator was allowed to drive without being accompanied by a Conductor Driver and most operators had quite extensive route knowledge of the Division. The hours they worked were very long, though, and whether it was really safe for them to be moving their machines along the running line after having worked all night on a site is doubtful.

Other machines for which I produced timings included the Matisa Track Recorder, the water cannon and an ultrasonic test train. The Matisa was a strange little machine with flimsy outriggers that rode on small wheels ahead of the main body of the machine. These sensitive outriggers measured the difference in height of the rails relative to each other and relative to what the difference should have been. Where the difference was beyond the specified tolerance the machine squirted paint on to the track. In that way the gangers knew which bits to pack. It was altogether a lightweight machine and when you rode on it and a train went by it was rather like being in a rowing boat as a supertanker goes by. The person in charge of the Matisa at the time, 1973, was a tiny Scotsman named Jim Cairney. Jim had a very high voice and his shrill telephone greeting of 'Hilloo' was much mimicked.

The water cannon was one of many attempts to deal with the autumn leaf-fall problem, a battle that still rages with the Train Operating Companies accusing Network Rail of doing too little – Antoine Hurel of the French-owned Connex Rail, for example, was at a loss to understand why the British don't just cut down all the trees and be done with it. The water cannon involved high-pressure water jetting on to the rails to clear the soggy mess of leaves. It was a conversion of an old two-car suburban electric unit and was booked to run up and down sensitive areas both day and night. I rode on it from Dover Marine to Faversham one night. The cab was really quite basic and I remember the Driver saying, 'Imagine having to run round the houses for eight hours in this thing.' The operator rode further back near the tanks and at the designated blackspots the Driver slowed down while he operated the pressure jets.

My only ride on the ultrasonic test train was more eventful. This train was a converted Derby lightweight DMU with a glass floor in the test coach, beneath which was a test bogie that took ultrasonic readings from the rails and analysed them for flaws or developing breaks. On a journey from Ramsgate to Ashford one winter's evening I was riding in the test coach. One of the staff had just put the kettle on the stove when he and the kettle were suddenly sent flying across the coach as the test bogie beneath us got itself caught on a wooden conductor rail guard board on the sharp curve leading into Ashford station. The test bogie rode up and derailed under the train, short-circuiting the traction current as it did so. It mangled itself and a length of guard board as well as displacing the conductor rail. We ground to a halt and the rest of the night was spent disentangling the test gear so that the unit could move off. The test train had fallen victim to Southern electrification.

There were numerous other special vehicles and trains from time to time: de-icers, viaduct inspection gantry trains, tunnel inspection trains, the Speno rail grinder (lots of sparks in the night), TRAMMs (Track Relaying and Maintenance Machines), vegetation flayers, cable layers, etc. Long-welded rail trains were a regular feature as most track renewals were done with welded rails rather than jointed. These trains ran as Exceptional Loads and carried stacks of 600ft rails. You realise how flexible steel rail is when you see such a train snaking through points, the continuous rails bending on the wagons as it does so. But conversely you realise how strong the finished track must be under the train as it withstands the lateral pressure and this brings home the importance of stressing the rails after laying. In effect, stressing stretches them to take out the slack and without this a ride on the railway would be extremely rough, as it is in sidings and on light railways where the rails are simply laid and not 'stretched' properly.

All the machines and trains had to have timings prepared for them in order that crews could be properly diagrammed for them, to ensure that they could get to and from site without delaying other work and to make sure that they did not cause disruption to timetabled services. Each Division (and, after they had gone, each Region) had its own Special Traffic Section that worked out these timings, as well as those for engineering possessions, special and altered freights, special boat trains, excursion trains, stock movements, etc. The Southern, because of the intensity of its timetable services, was the only Region to provide detailed point-to-point timings for all special movements. The other less busy Regions often simply gave a starting time and left it to Signalmen to regulate the moves the best they could. At Beckenham in 1973 there were twelve of us in the section and at times we had to work overtime to cope with the workload.

On-track machines were timed at a maximum of 20mph so it was not easy to find 'pathways' for them, especially those that could not be relied upon to operate track circuits. Ballast trains were timed at an average of 30mph and this wasn't much easier. Basically, to provide a timing for a ballast train you took the junction-to-junction distance from the Working Timetable, doubled it and added a bit. That then became the number of minutes you needed to find and you looked for a gap of that size between timetabled trains. Graphical representation of the timetable was also used as gaps more easily show up on a time–space graph. By starting at the known pinch points and then working backwards from them you hoped to find a path. After a while the distances became familiar, as did the signalling capacity of the line and you got to know the pattern of paths that was available. So then the timetable would change and we'd have to start all over again. All information was taken from the Working Timetable (WTT) which showed calling points for all booked trains and also their passing times over every junction. 'Q' paths were also shown and these were for use if necessary, such as for additional boat trains. In addition, the WTT was in two parts – Mandatory and Conditional, the first to cover trains that had to run and the second to provide pre-planned pathways for certain freight trains that ran according to customers' demand. Our timings had to take account of both parts, so a lot of cross-checking was necessary, especially on a railway such as the South Eastern that was riddled with flat junctions over which conflicting timings could easily be made. Passing times over junctions were the most critical and formed the basis of each train timing. From the public point of view the first important time after departure of, say, the 1640 Victoria to Ramsgate would have been Bromley South at 1656, but from a timing point of view the Bromley South time has lesser relevance; the important times are the passing times at Factory Junction, Shepherds Lane, Herne Hill, Beckenham Junction and Shortlands Junction because it is at these places that you have to ensure no conflicting moves are timed.

Timings were cross-checked to see that no two were foul of each other and then the whole lot went to the printers for the draft Special Traffic Notice to be produced. This happened each week and there was always a last-minute rush to get timings or alterations in. The weekly draft was sent out to all interested parties throughout the Division for comment and they sent in or phoned through their remarks as necessary. Station Managers took this responsibility with differing amounts of zeal and it was usually the same few who contacted us week in and week out to point out that such and such a train was one minute foul of such another one or that the box at some place would not be open at the time we'd shown a train to pass. I stood by each week for the calls from Mr Rooney at Swanley and Mr Bond at Shepherdswell.

Amendments would then be made and the 'final' would go off for printing. All train crews, Station Managers, Supervisors, Signalmen, Regulators, Controllers, depots and station staff would receive a copy so that everyone not only knew what was going on but also so that they could make the arrangements appropriate for dealing with the special or altered movements. Train crew Supervisors would check the notice against the altered train crew workings sent to them by the Diagram office to see that everything was covered. Individual crew names could then be allocated to the special diagrams. Station Managers would ensure that notices were displayed to the public, that additional staff were booked on duty or that signalbox hours were extended to cover special movements. Carriage depot Supervisors would make sure that extra coaches or trains could be made available as specified. Every day and night was different in some way on the railway and arrangements had to be made accordingly.

The Special Traffic Notice reflected the planning for the short term, but after the printing deadline had passed the responsibility for planning became a shift-by-shift matter for the Divisional Control. This was known as UCA (Under Control Arrangements). Asking for a train UCA was a risky way of doing things as there might not be resources available at the time to do the job or the Control might simply be too busy dealing with other matters to give your request consideration.

Other weekly, or even daily, publications included amended train crew and rolling-stock diagrams and the P/EW notice, later known as the Weekly Operating Notice and still in use as such by Network Rail. The P/EW gave details of temporary speed restrictions, engineering possessions and alterations to track, signalling and safety procedures. This in turn could be amended by a daily sheet issued from the Rules Section. It was, of course, vital that all amendments were recorded carefully and, especially in the case of new or altered speed restrictions, that crews were notified properly. Motive Power Supervisors (later Train Crew Supervisors) were responsible for posting details of such alterations at train crew signing-on points and every train crew duty had time built in for reading such information.

The need to make sure that train crews had up-to-date information each time they booked on was one of the arguments for large, centralised crew depots at which proper facilities could be provided. Another argument was the desirability of having each crew member seen by a responsible person as they signed on, so that their fitness for duty could be assessed. The question of unsupervised booking on by train crews was raised by Col J.R.H. Robertson in his Inquiry into the fatal derailment of the 2005 Margate to Kentish Town excursion train at Eltham Well Hall on 11 June 1972, which he found was caused by Hither Green Driver R. Wilsdon being unfit through drink. Although Col Robertson did not specifically recommend that all Drivers (whom he somewhat quaintly described as 'a fine body of men') sign on with a Supervisor, it became official railway policy to aim towards this, but even twenty years on there were still depots on the former Southern Region, where the accident happened, which were unsupervised and some may exist to this day. In the early 1990s I was working for Network SouthEast's South Central Division and plans were being drawn up for a replacement station at Tattenham Corner, to include the perpetuation of an unsupervised Drivers' depot. Despite this, many small depots, such as Maidstone Barracks and Plumstead, have been abolished and staff transferred to places where they sign on under supervision.

While centralisation of crew depots undoubtedly resulted in closer control over information to crews and better assessment of their fitness, the counter argument was always one of cost. Centralising meant building in additional unproductive time in many cases. For instance, if the depot I mentioned at Tattenham Corner were to close, additional empty stock running from, say, Selhurst would be needed to start up the branch service each morning. It is for this reason that the railway was slow to act upon its own stated objective. Freight operators see operations being conducted from fewer, though possibly different, depots than at present but whether the passenger Train Operating Companies will want to incur empty running costs is not so likely and the issue of supervised signing-on has largely been conveniently forgotten.

Even with supervision mistakes occur and an example of this was the Railfreight Distribution train derailment at Maidstone East in 1993. The Driver of this train was found to have been drinking before taking duty at Dover, which is a supervised depot. In the 1970s and '80s it was well known that certain Hither Green crews, while waiting at Thame in Oxfordshire for their oil trains to be unloaded, would nip off to the town centre for a drink, while Drivers and Secondmen would sometimes take turns to go for a drink while they were meant to be jointly working their trains around the merry-go-round circuit at Northfleet Cement Works. Remember too that Driver Wilsdon had been one of their colleagues at Hither Green and that his Secondman, who survived the crash at Eltham Well Hall, was by that time Driver Stokes – also of Hither Green.

Notices may be posted and they may be read. They may be signed for. But the information they give may still not be acted upon. One morning in 1978 I was travelling home on the 0720 Charing Cross to Maidstone West. A temporary speed restriction of 20mph had been in force for some time on the down line in Polhill Tunnel due to 'condition of track', the most common cause of restrictions. During the previous day the Permanent Way Supervisor at Orpington had decided to reduce the permissible speed to 10mph, which was an unusual thing to do but was necessitated, in his opinion, by the deteriorating state of the track. The 20mph restriction had been published in the weekly notice for a couple of weeks and was indicated on the track by a warning board one mile in advance and a commencement board at the start of the restriction, as was normal practice. The further reduction had been made in time to go on a daily amendment to the weekly notice and this had been issued to all crew depots. In the meantime the '20' board had been switched for a '10' board and the 'speed' (or 'slack' as it would have been called on some parts of the railway) was 'banged', i.e. Drivers were additionally warned of the reduction by detonators placed on the line. Banging continued until it was confirmed that the notice of the reduction had been properly issued and so, by the time the 0720 Charing Cross came along there were no detonators. Automatic Warning System (AWS) ramps to indicate speed restrictions had not been introduced at that time, so everything depended upon the vigilance of Drivers.

The Dover Driver of the 0720 CX not only forgot there was a 'speed' but also ignored the warning board and had failed to remember the notice telling him of the further reduction to 10mph. We hit the 'speed' at around 70mph on the downhill gradient inside the tunnel. Coming home off nights, I was fairly dozy but no one could have slept through what happened next. The train was flung violently from side to side and up and down. There was a repeated thumping sound, which naturally made me think that the coach I was in was 'off the road' and was banging along the sleepers. The train showed no sign of slowing down, the Driver evidently having decided to ride it out on the basis that his driving coach was not derailed, but eight coaches back I thought we were in for a disaster so I reached up in the lurching coach and grabbed the communication cord. The swaying train eventually came to a stand with the cab just out of the tunnel. The Driver, thinking by now that part of his train was off the road and that the train had been brought to a stand by the tearing apart of brake jumpers, rushed across to a signalpost telephone on the up line and raised the alert. The Signalman at Orpington sent 'Obstruction Danger' to Sevenoaks so that traffic would be stopped on both lines and also notified Divisional Control, who initiated the major passenger train emergency procedures. A passenger train derailed in a tunnel is almost as bad as you can get.

In the meantime, the Driver and Guard were walking along the train to see what had happened. Amazingly, no part of the train was in fact derailed, although subsequently the Permanent Way staff found evidence that could have been indicative of a derailing and self-rerailing in the tunnel. The Guard reset the 'butterfly' valve on the coach I was in (this red-painted valve on the outside of the train was turned by the pulling of the cord and so indicated in which coach the cord had been pulled) and the crew rejoined the train, the Driver having reported that, after all, all was well.

All was far from well, however, as the rolling stock had been severely knocked about, the track could have been further damaged and the Driver had failed in a most dangerous way to adhere to the Rules. No one did anything about it that day, though, much to my amazement when I took duty again that night as Area 3 Controller. I was surprised to find out that the incident had been dismissed as soon as the Driver had reported that it was a false alarm. He had not, apparently, made any reference to having run over the 10mph 'speed' at 70mph or to the fact that the cord had been pulled by a passenger who considered the train to be derailed. I duly put in a report and an inquiry ensued. In the meantime we traced the rolling stock and had it stopped for examination.

Part of the inquiry concerned the length of time taken for the train to stop after I had pulled the cord and I was taken to some stock berthed in the bay platform at Beckenham Junction to demonstrate my cord-pulling technique. All I remembered from the actual incident was that I had red lines across my hand where I had been hanging on to the chain and that the valve outside was fully turned so I don't think I could have pulled it any harder. The implication, of course, was that the train was going much faster than the Driver was making out and therefore took longer to stop.

Whenever the emergency cord is pulled the train crew, as well as sorting out the emergency, have to take the name and address of the person who initiated the action. Sometimes this is not possible, for instance on a football special with a whole coachful of people fooling around. At other times it is best just to ignore the incident – such as when a Japanese tourist on a Folkestone Harbour to Victoria boat train thought the red chain would be a convenient place to hang his umbrella.

Years later I had my second cord-pulling experience. I was travelling on the 2325 Euston to Edinburgh as far as Milton Keynes Central, having just finished work at Euston. This was quite a rowdy train at times, with a lively crowd in the Mk I buffet. On this particular night I heard a commotion in the coach adjoining the buffet and saw a man hanging out of an open doorway, either trying to jump out or to close the door. The buffet stewardess, a stocky little Scot called Linda, had followed me and she grabbed the man by the belt of his trousers with one hand while hanging on to the frame of an internal door with the other. I went into the coach and grabbed the cord. The door concerned was on the offside, next to the up main line. Being a relatively heavy mixture of sleeping cars, vans and day coaches, our speed was only about 75mph, but an up InterCity train could have passed at up to 100mph on the adjacent line. Without a shadow of a doubt the man would have been killed if this had happened – and Linda could have been dragged out with him. Luckily, though, we came to a stand before anything passed, the man was brought back into the coach and the crew had the up line blocked while they checked the outside of the train and closed the door. We never established exactly what the man thought he was doing as his condition didn't permit any rational discussion, but I was able to keep my hand in with cord-pulling. Of course, in the same way as provision of AWS ramps for speed restrictions now makes my earlier incident impossible, so does the introduction of central door locking make the second impossible. Slowly but surely the railway has become a safer place in some respects, while in others safety slips away.

16

Sit, Sleep or Stand?

The part-seating, part-sleeper trains of the sort to which I referred in the last chapter were not really a desirable proposition for InterCity's Anglo–Scottish services in an era of first-class lounge cars and the move upmarket that this encompassed. Invariably there was rowdiness and heavy drinking going on somewhere in the seating coaches and this was considered a threat to the security and peace of mind of those who had paid to travel in the sleepers. In an effort to give some respectability to the overnight seating market, InterCity had introduced in May 1982 a fleet of declassified former first-class coaches with subdued lighting under the marketing name 'Nightrider'. But things didn't improve and the image of InterCity Sleepers was being tarnished by the noise, the drunkenness, the intermediate station stops and the general ambience, which was progressively being seen as rather seedy. Under the Managing Directorship of Dr John Prideaux it was decided in 1988 to pull out of the overnight Anglo–Scottish seating market entirely, although for some reason a seating coach lingered on for a few years, on a reservations-only basis, on the Night Caledonian, only finally going when that train was amalgamated with the Night Scotsman under the new stewardship of the privatised Scotrail.

In May 1992, Stagecoach Holdings, seeing InterCity's move away from overnight seating as an opportunity to break into railway operations, hired a couple of seating coaches and put them on the Night Aberdonian each night, marketing this as the way to go rather than by coach. This was hailed as a precursor of a burgeoning private sector interest in rail passenger operations in the run up to privatisation. Stagecoach had their own livery and their coaches were staffed by Stagecoach personnel who served snacks and drinks 'at seat'. Six months later, though, Stagecoach handed the operation back to InterCity, merely retaining a block booking of seats and by May 1993 they had pulled out altogether. Those who had trumpeted the private sector enterprise only a year earlier were strangely silent. Stagecoach did, of course, eventually get into the market in a big way with the award of the South West Trains franchise and, scandalously in the view of some, the purchase of the controlling share of Porterbrook Ltd, the rolling stock leasing firm that curiously just so happened to be the main provider of stock to ... South West Trains.

Before the move upmarket had been made by InterCity on its overnight services, the night seating trains were a real adventure. One night I caught a train from York to Aberdeen during the oil exploration boom there of the 1970s. The train consisted of Mk I TSO and FK (Tourist Second Open and First-Class Compartment) stock, all dimly lit and all of which had seen better days. Every seat was taken and there were people lying on the floor in the corridors and vestibules. Luggage was everywhere and there were large groups of burly men completely smashed out of their heads swearing, shouting and throwing cans to each other. These were the oil riggers on their way to Aberdeen where they would simply hang around in gangs waiting to be called out to the rigs. When we arrived at Aberdeen these gangs piled into the station buffet, which was one of the unofficial calling-on places for the rigs and which also served a cooked breakfast. There was a diminutive Scottish lady of about 50 in charge behind the counter and I thought she would be overwhelmed by the onslaught, but not a bit of it. This was obviously a daily event for her and she knew exactly what to do.

Above the din of swearing and the crashing about of drunken bodies her voice rose – 'Stop that language and put away those cans.'

There was a sudden hush and the riggers, now as meek as lambs, put away their drink and sat talking quietly amongst themselves.

All over the system until the late 1980s there were trains like that trundling about every night and the journey opportunities they offered, in conjunction with day trains, were tremendous. At towns and cities the length and breadth of the country you could pile out of the pubs at closing time and get a train either to London or somewhere else. The stock used, though, was always the oldest and tattiest, and detracted from InterCity's marketing image. As late as 1980 I remember catching a train from Loughborough to St Pancras at about midnight that was hauled by a Class 25 and was steam-heated. Even some of the late night (as opposed to overnight) trains were formed of the dregs of the fleet. When working at Euston in the late 1980s I was a 'regular' on the 2340 Euston to Wolverhampton service and until October 1989 this was formed of Mk I and Mk II stock with a scruffy Mk I buffet, although by that time virtually all other 'EBWs' (Euston/Birmingham/Wolverhampton) were formed of complete Mk III sets. The dim lighting, scratched interior woodwork and rattling doors of the 2340 were in keeping with the general seediness of many of its regular passengers – pub strippers and so on. There was a rather dodgy character who was part of the buffet car coterie on this train and it was rumoured that he could 'arrange' something for you if you were interested. I was even tipped off that two female InterCity On Board Services employees, both known to me, were part of a ring offering certain personal favours on the 2340. When the Mk III set eventually arrived the train was transformed, showing that the railway can dictate to some extent the kind of clientele it wants by the type of train it provides.

It is perhaps remarkable that so many overnight (and other) trains survived for so long, well into the period during which InterCity was required to pay its own way – possibly the only national passenger railway in the world to do so. The InterCity trains that ran a few times a day to places such as Grimsby, Blackpool North and Shrewsbury were cut back, while the daily InterCity service from the North-west to Dover vanished, almost unnoticed. So too went such gems as the summer Saturdays-only service from Euston to Pwllheli, of all places, which ran right up to 1989. Some of these trains continued running after InterCity had broken even, only being discontinued subsequently because they were considered by the Franchising Director to be insufficiently attractive for privately owned franchisees. Those same franchisees, of course, then received a Government subsidy even though InterCity had run without subsidy from 1988 until its demise.

As well as the overnight seating trains there were other strange legacies from the past that managed to survive surprisingly long. In addition to InterCity's Anglo–Scottish sleeper routes, there were, right up until 1990, sleeper services operated by Scotrail that ran from Edinburgh and Glasgow Queen Street to Inverness and Aberdeen (and vice versa). Towards the end of their time, when InterCity put up its sleeper prices, the Scottish sleepers remained at the old price. They were running around barely used and accompanied by rundown day coaches, whereas InterCity had moved upmarket to the era of smart lounge-car trains. Some sleeping-car Attendants at Aberdeen and Inverness worked solely on these internal trains and so never left Scotland. They probably also hardly ever saw a passenger. I joined the Inverness to Edinburgh sleeper one night at Aviemore and was the only passenger. The Attendant was a rather elderly lady from Inverness.

This meant that until May 1990, two years after subsidy was withdrawn, there were still three sleeping car services most nights from and to Inverness: the Royal Highlander lounge car service to and from Euston; a stopping sleeper/seating service to and from Euston via Birmingham and the internal service to and from Glasgow/Edinburgh. How all three contrived to last so long under the harsh financial regime is difficult to imagine. By 1993 the only survivor was the Royal Highlander, which also conveyed Motorail traffic. This concentration on to one high-quality service each night with its consequent cost savings must have more than outweighed the loss of revenue from the other two trains, as well as raising the profile of the InterCity brand name and tidying up the image of the Scotrail brand.

In the first steps towards financial self-sufficiency and eventual privatisation, the Motorail network lost its peripheral destinations, too. The somewhat strangely located Motorail terminals at Ely, Stirling and Brockenhurst were early victims, dating from the time when cars were conveyed on open flat wagons rather than the later enclosed vans, with the consequent horrors of smashed windscreens. Incidentally, I recall an incident when I was working at Beckenham Control when the Stirling to Brockenhurst and Dover Motorail was wrongly split at Kensington Olympia and the Brockenhurst cars went to Dover and the Dover cars to Brockenhurst. There were a lot of very angry holiday makers at both places that morning.

When the list of services to be offered for franchise was compiled, Motorail was not included, it being considered by the Government-appointed Franchising Director that the service was not sufficiently attractive for a private operator. So on that basis Motorail was discontinued. Likewise, it was thought that the sleepers, slimmed down as they already had been, would not attract private sector interest and the Anglo–Scottish sleepers were reduced to just two departures per night from Euston with the Night Scotsman and Night Caledonian running as one train until splitting at Carstairs with a similar arrangement for the Night Aberdonian, West Highlander and Royal Highlander, which split at Edinburgh. Two trains with sleeping cars going to

In the last years of InterCity we ran sleeping car trains to/from Euston and twelve destinations in England, Wales and Scotland. To make the operation palatable to the private sector this was reduced to just five. The cross-country sleepers went, too. Here the northbound *Royal Highlander* from Euston crosses Culloden Moor on its morning approach to Inverness. (Photo: Bob Avery)

five destinations, whereas we had seven departures per night with cars going to eleven destinations as recently as 1989 when I was working at Euston. The remaining trains, marketed as The Caledonian Sleepers, are now run throughout by Scotrail.* Incidentally, it was an Anglo–Scottish sleeper train that had the distinction of being the last departure to be run by BR, being the 2355 Edinburgh to Euston Night Scotsman of 31 March 1997. The train was seen away from Edinburgh Waverley by the Chairman of the BRB, John Welsby and, five minutes later as it rumbled through Haymarket, it passed into the hands of the private sector. At the same time as the London-to-Scotland sleepers were reduced in readiness for privatisation, the cross-country Poole and Plymouth to Glasgow and Edinburgh sleeper was discontinued, leaving

* 2018 update: Caledonian Sleepers are now run by Serco on behalf of the Scottish Executive.

the Night Riviera from London to Penzance as the only other sleeper to remain running other than the Caledonian Sleepers.

Only a handful of sleeper cars are required now and even after the lounge-car rationalisation of services fewer than 100 were required. Yet only in 1979 the Mk III sleeper fleet received its investment authority and the build was 236 cars. They were to be built at a total cost of £39 million to replace the ageing Mk I fleet. The findings of the Inquiry into the deaths at Taunton on board a Mk I sleeper train that caught fire resulted in an overspend of £5 million as additional safeguards were built in at short notice. But why were so many built? I think possibly because in 1979 InterCity was just a marketing name and not a coherent business organisation. With the organisation of its sleeper services dispersed between the Board and four Regional managements it is perhaps understandable that a true assessment of needs would be difficult. By 1987 ten of the cars had been transferred to the Danish State Railways and others went to the Land Cruise sets, while until 1990 others dawdled around the country on slow Anglo–Scottish or cross-country services and on internal Scotrail services, looking as if they were needed but not paying their way. Many of these cars are now simply in store at places such as Bicester, with GNER announcing in the spring of 1997 that it was to lease ten redundant sleepers, sadly not for a new East Coast overnight service, but for conversion to day use.** Similarly, two more were to be picked off for conversion to luxury vehicles for the Royal Scotsman, operated by the Great Scottish & Western Railway Company. The building of 236 cars was a classic case of over-investment resulting from confused organisation, which surely could not happen nowadays. No? Well what about the fleet of horrendously expensive sleeping cars built in the mid 1990s at the instigation of European Passenger Services Ltd for night services from London and elsewhere (including, incredibly, Plymouth and Swansea) to the Continent and which now stand idle, the plan having been largely abandoned by Eurostar's new owners? They ran a few trials through the Tunnel but now stand alongside their predecessors in store, 139 of them at a cost of £1 million each. Sometimes lessons are learned and sometimes not.

** 2018 update: This never happened but a few Mk III sleeper cars run on excursion trains operated by Direct Rail Services.

17

Spotting the Enthusiasts

Despite the drastic reduction in overnight passenger trains that took place in the run-up to privatisation there is still a lot going on at night on the railway. The West Coast Main Line, for instance, is full of activity at three in the morning. There are Travelling Post Office trains, Freightliners, steel coil and plate trains, chemical trains, coal trains, EWS Enterprise wagonload trains, DRS freights, etc., as well as the remaining sleepers. Further south, freight trains operated by EWS International and the SNCF are running in flights nightly through the Channel Tunnel as Britain's railways gradually become absorbed into the vast Continental system – at least so far as freight users are concerned. Up to twenty-five such trains run each day from and to places as diverse as Exeter to Sezzadio, Evian to Neasden, Garston to Genk and Milan to Wembley. With many manufacturing processes limited to day work, the rapid transport of components or finished products at night makes good use of resources and some freight trains are part of a production line, delivering parts, etc. for the next stage in the process. Now that the nonsense of splitting the bulk freight railway into three separate companies (Transrail, Loadhaul and Mainline), on the premise that a national freight railway would be too big to sell off, has been remedied by the purchase of all three by EWS, a cohesive freight strategy can once more be developed. This strategy appears to be, in the main, expansionist and so we can look forward to more freight going by rail, hopefully at cheaper prices as EWS drives its costs further down. With EWS's takeover of Railfreight Distribution now accomplished as well, the scope for pooling resources has increased and the rigid divide that has existed for so long in Britain between trainload and wagonload will disappear as EWS develops both – a move started by Transrail with its Enterprise wagonload service, under Julian Worth's management.*

As well as the expansion sought by EWS, Freightliner and Direct Rail Services have also, in 1997, stated their intentions to seek out new traffic and have expanded their traction fleets accordingly. The lucrative container market from the Irish ports to the Continent, of which only around 10 per cent currently passes through Britain by rail, is there for the picking now that direct rail haulage from, say, Holyhead to Turin is available, while Direct Rail Services, a subsidiary of BNFL, is seeking contracts for the movement of freight further afield than just its original stamping ground of the Cumbrian coast.**

Who sees all this, though? So much moves at night that the ordinary rail user is not aware of quite how much really does go on. It always used to strike me in the 1970s and '80s that the Sidcup loop line, which was the epitome of a busy suburban commuter railway in the rush hours, was also the prime freight route at night for North Kent cement, oil, coal, steel and aggregates trains and yet none of this was seen by the thousands of commuters.

There are, however, the diehard railway enthusiasts for whom the prospect of a bleak winter's night on the end of the platform at Crewe, for example, is full of interest. For others, it is all in a night's work. As Sleeping Car Services Manager for ICOBS, based at Euston, I spent a lot of my time between 1988 and 1990 riding around at night, changing trains mainly at Preston, Carlisle or Crewe, noting the variety of activity as I did so.

The Royal Train was a regular feature overnight on the West Coast Main Line, either working empty to or from its home at Wolverton or running in service to or from Euston. Platform 1 was always used for a 'Royal' at Euston because of the road access at the side. For hours ahead of departure the whole area would be sealed off and searched, and although for security reasons the

* 2018 update: TPO trains are no more and the freight companies mentioned in this chapter have been joined by several others, but without the 'cohesive freight strategy' I foresaw in 2002. EWS is now known as DB Cargo and has progressively lost market share. Freight usage of the Channel Tunnel has declined and wagonload services have gone.

** 2018 update: DRS is now a subsidiary of the Nuclear Decommissioning Authority and is very much a national operator.

fact that a Royal was running was not widely broadcast, you could always tell from the re-platforming of other services on the daily station working sheets.

One evening we had two conflicting Royal events. Asking around informally, the story unfolded to me that the Queen's office had booked the Royal Train, followed by a request for the train to be used at the same time, but for a different journey, by the Princess Royal. I needn't say who took precedence. HM the Queen left in the Royal Train from platform 1 while Princess Anne and her daughter, Zara, had to travel on the Night Aberdonian from platform 3. Makeshift security arrangements had to be put into place at short notice. I helped to reallocate sleeping berths so that three consecutive compartments were made available, but, for security reasons, I wasn't allowed to tell the people who had booked them why we were moving them. The two Royals, mother and daughter, had decided that they wanted to share, so we had to convert the middle berth hurriedly back from a first-class configuration (single berth) to standard class (two berth). Detectives then travelled in the neighbouring berths, which stayed as first-class. So as not to draw attention to themselves, the Royal party came in by road through the parcels deck above the station and down the narrow ramp near the open end of the platform, which was all very well but for the fact that the limousine was too big to turn at the bottom of the ramp. So the chauffeur had to reverse along the edge of the narrowing platform with the Royals still aboard. A far from ideal arrangement, and one which, inevitably, succeeded in drawing to them the attention they had sought to avoid. By the time they got away, the Royal Train would have been serenely cruising through Rugby; the cameras, tape recorders and notepads of the 'gricers' no doubt doing overtime as it did so.

Railway enthusiasts were in some ways the bane of the railway but in other ways its saviour. Their activities have led to a public perception that the railway is not a serious industry in the way that mining or steel production are. If you start talking about railways you automatically attract the label 'anorak' even though you may be a railway manager, environmental campaigner or business analyst wanting to talk about serious issues. The image of the spotter is to blame for this. That's the downside.

On the positive side, BR did well out of the loyalty that enthusiasm for the railway as a 'concept' engendered amongst the great many railway staff who were, openly or otherwise, railway enthusiasts. In my first job, at Beckenham in 1973, I worked in a room along with Malcolm Burton, Chairman of the Locomotive Club of Great Britain, and the eccentric Chris Gammell, already established as a railway photographer and author of railway books. For them, and for so many other people working for the railway, there was the belief that the railway, despite the foibles of Government, ownership or current management, was in itself a good thing. It is difficult to imagine such an underlying faith existing in other areas of employment – do bank staff, for instance, enthuse over the very concept of banking? Many such people, unfortunately, have felt betrayed by the fragmentation of a great industry and by the bringing in of 'outsiders' to whom the railway is just another branch of a supermarket.

As people from other industries come along, some only for short spells, the loyalty to the railway diminishes. For many railway people it is a smack in the face to be expected, overnight, to become loyal servants of a French water company or, worse still, of an established bus and coach operator, when for so long the railway was an industry in its own right. As it tries to emulate high-street retailing practices or the public relations activities of double-glazing firms, so the railway becomes less of a one-off industry and merges more and more with the blandness and predictability of so many of our household names. The seeming variety of the bright new liveries, far from creating individuality, has meant that the overall industry has lost its status and has become a collection of bits and pieces to be traded off between people for whom it is just another part of a money-making process.

The change, superficially attractive as it may seem to some, is not just cosmetic and is not just financial. There are other implications, most notably, of course, for safety. Despite the accidents such as Clapham and Purley, which marred BR's later years, the notion of safety was part of an ingrained culture that dominated railway work and drove so many professional railway people. Under the business sectorisation of the 1980s and the franchising of the '90s, the unglamorous work of these people, many of whom are enthusiasts of the railway (as opposed to railway enthusiasts), is being marginalised: they are being forced into the background so that prominence can be given to the more obviously commercially attractive activities.

Safety has become something that is discussed discreetly behind closed doors rather than being something that every railway manager recognises as being his or her lifeblood. Until the early 1980s, most railway managers considered themselves to be operators first and foremost and were proud of this, even if they had subsequently moved on to other things. A sound background in operational management was a prerequisite for higher management and in this way a safety consciousness permeated all levels of management decision-making. Of course, it also slowed down the decision-making process and in the heady days of the 1980s this became increasingly unacceptable, while in the 1990s it took a crash such as the one at Southall in September 1997, in which it appears that the single-manned cab had its AWS isolated, to awaken people to the conflicting interests of expediency and safety. In earlier times no train would have been allowed to have started its journey with the AWS isolated and all trains timed to run at more than 100mph would have had two Drivers.

One implication of the concept that to be a railway manager was to have different (and commercially unattractive) priorities from those of, say, a manager who might work for a bookstore chain one week and a department store the next, was that it was difficult for railway managers to get jobs outside the industry and, until the 1980s, for 'outsiders' to get in. Now as I have said, most railway managers did not want to leave anyway, the railway being in their blood, while most outsiders saw the railway as an unexciting, stifling industry and so, in all probability, didn't want to get in. In this way the railway became isolated from the financial and trading realities of the world in which it was, supposedly, competing. So the sharper practices of the more recently appointed railway managers have to be balanced against the safety-dominated and relatively commercially complacent attitudes of earlier times. The actual survival of the railway depended on this balance being struck under a Government of the 1980s that would quite happily have virtually closed down the railway as it did the mining and steel industries. The balance was struck, albeit precariously, by BR's fortuitous appointments to the post of Chairman as commercial awareness and, eventually, privatisation loomed.

The Chairmanship of Sir Peter Parker from September 1976 brought the concepts of business management into the railway and also elevated the railway's profile in public relations terms. Looking back through newspaper records of the time, it is most noticeable how much more prominent the BRB Chairman became in the public eye during Sir Peter's incumbency, culminating in his famous address to the nation on television. His lack of specific railway knowledge was countered by that of his Chief Executive, Robert Reid, and BR was incredibly fortunate in having him, as Sir Robert, for the next Chairman, from September 1983 until March 1990. Sir Robert combined the realism of being a lifelong railwayman with a politically acceptable attitude for a Conservative Government. In this way the deliberately confrontational management styles imposed on the steel and coal industries by the Thatcher Government were avoided on the railway. It is my belief that the railway today would be only a fraction of the size it was in 1983 if it had not been for the appointment of Sir Robert to the post of Chairman and if, instead, someone such as Sir Ian MacGregor had been unleashed on the railway. Thus the storm was ridden out, a balance was struck and the railway survived – not just as a rump, but as an industry still sufficiently large to need splitting into more than seventy different parts to make it palatable to the private sector. Having got this far, the second Sir Robert Reid was able to see through the mechanics of how this should be done, while it was left to John Welsby to undo the actual nuts and bolts. But the concept of the railway as a good thing, to repeat my earlier phrase, had been saved by their predecessor's love for, and belief in, the industry.

Although the railway has done well in some ways out of the loyalty of many of its staff, who might have expected better pay and conditions elsewhere, their very enthusiasm for the railway has meant that some changes were unnecessarily slow in coming about. No railway enthusiast likes to see freight yards closing even if he or she (yes, some are she) knows that in reality it means that goods are getting to their destinations more quickly and more profitably and therefore with more chance of reinvestment and, in turn, more chance of staying on the railway. There has at times been too much inherent belief in the railway, which has led some people to think that any railway activity is better than none, even if parts of that activity are dragging others down with them. Some very senior managers have certainly had a blindness to the reasonable expectations of the railway's customers in the modern age, possibly daring to think that Joe Punter will forgive the railway because underneath it all he loves it, remembering his childhood train set, whereas in all likelihood he resents the way the railway treats him. I well remember escorting an extremely senior InterCity manager along platform 3 at Euston to see the boarding of the Night Aberdonian one evening in 1989, while Royal Mail vans were screeching about, reversing across the platform and racing up and down next to InterCity's customers as they loaded the Travelling Post Office train at platform 2. I did not think this was acceptable, bearing in mind how much these people had paid for their tickets and I had been trying to get the platforming changed for some time. Here was my chance to enlist the help of someone senior, who would surely realise that his customers would be drawing comparisons between the treatment we gave them and that received from the airlines who were our direct competitors in the Anglo–Scottish first-class market. But no, he appeared to be of the school of thought that believed that as long as the railway was, or looked, busy then everything was OK.

Lower down the management chain there were people who would do all sorts of things to keep the railway going or to keep themselves in practice with operating activities. This too was a mixed blessing: on the one hand it meant that there was always a wealth of expertise ready to dive into when things went wrong, but against that it also meant that very many staff were not pulling their weight because they knew that all they had to do was to call in the guv'nor and he would come running along with shunting pole in hand or announcing voice at the ready. Here again, as with so many things on the railway, a balance had to be struck between the conflicting interests of getting people to accept responsibility, getting incidents sorted out quickly and, most contentiously for some, getting personal satisfaction out of having done a good old practical job oneself. Many potential senior managers chose to remain instead at lower levels of the chain in order to stay in touch with the 'real' railway and many of those who moved on looked back with a certain fondness and pride at their operating days, myself included. It may have been grim at the time, but it was a real job.

Enthusiasts are a source of revenue too, and there is a wealth of (mainly) derogatory names within railway circles for such groups, depending upon which part of the country you come from. As with any fanatical body, expense seems to be of little object: people will travel hundreds of miles to travel behind or to see a dying class of locomotive. When I was Assistant Traction Controller on the Western we were withdrawing the diesel–hydraulic Class 52 'Westerns' and there were hordes of enthusiasts out every day of the week desperately trying to get a last ride behind each machine before it was taken out of service. Much despair was occasioned when 1055 *Western Advocate* was written off following a fatal light-engine

Regional independence being put to rest: the swansong of the Western class diesel-hydraulics was a series of enthusiasts' specials in 1977. Here the double-headed *Western Tribute* leaves Paddington. (Photo: Author)

collision at Worcester Tunnel Junction in January 1976. Most of the fans thought they had several months to go before they needed to get their last ride in behind that one. The 'Western' spotters, some of whom worked for the railway, had got hold of the Traction Controller's outside telephone number at Paddington. This line really needed to be kept clear because of the atrocious state of the Western's internal telephone system at the time. Some of the enthusiasts were quite devious, putting on good impressions of being, say, shed staff at Plymouth Laira depot concerned about the maintenance of certain engines and therefore needing to know their whereabouts. Eventually some Controllers became fed up with these calls and so would deliberately mislead the callers. Several enthusiasts must have traipsed off down to St Erth to see an engine on a milk trip when in fact it was on a Paddington to Birmingham passenger train.

The interest in this fleet of locomotives wasn't just for the machines themselves but also because they were a symbol of the independence of the Western Region and thus harked back to the individualism of the Great

Western – a name steeped in history and which, of course, was revived by InterCity and has now been adopted by its successor on the Paddington routes. The Western's numbers and names were all on cast plates as if to assert the permanence of the Western Region. Why, I wonder, during the modernisation and supposed standardisation of the late 1950s and early '60s, had the Western been allowed to develop and build its own unique type of diesel locomotive and then name them all so ostentatiously after its own greatness? The first in the series was named *Western Enterprise*, surely in defiance of the British Railways Board, while others had names such as *Western Challenger* and *Western Gauntlet*, the second to last being *Western Glory*. They had done so also in the 1950s with the Warship diesels, of course (and there were the Hymeks, for what it's worth). To quote A.J. Pearson, in his book *Man of the Rail*, the Western 'had its own special way of doing things; it was distinctive'. He goes on to say that there were 'tough debates' over its policy of hydraulic transmission for diesel locomotives when the rest of the railway was opting for electric transmission. In fact, in the year the 'Westerns' were introduced (1961), the Board finally got its way and electric transmission for diesel locos became the standard for all engines built subsequently. The 'Westerns' were splendid engines, though, with a pleasing element of care taken in the design of their external appearance, over which, perhaps remarkably, the Western Region had collaborated with an industrial designer appointed by the BTC Design Panel. They were also practical in service during a time of considerable unreliability amongst diesel traction on BR. They had two Maybach power units each, so if one failed in service the loco could still limp home on the other one. In the mid 1970s the rate of loco failure in traffic on the Western Region was alarmingly high: summer Saturdays in the West Country were a nightmare with the timetable stretched just beyond the theoretical capacity of the single track sections of the main line by additional holiday trains, compounded by engine failures. The most common cause of failure was overheating, which would cause automatic shutdown and blowing of the fire bottles. During the hot summers of 1975 and 1976 I sometimes covered the post of Passenger Controller at Paddington Control, where we kept a list every day of delays caused to Class 1 trains by engine failure. On occasion the list could amount to twenty-odd trains in one day, an atrocious record and one upon which the notorious Class 50s featured most prominently.

The disaster-prone Class 50 fleet had its own following, though. These unreliable machines were inherited by the Western in 1974 after the completion of electrification of the LMR's West Coast Main Line from Preston to Glasgow. Being of limited number they were an ideal group for enthusing over in that you could theoretically hope to see each one or ride behind it without having to take years doing so. How, in practice, enthusiasts managed to ride behind some of them, though, I don't really know, bearing in mind that they were out of service for so much of the time. 50005 and 50050 were our most notorious 'rogue' engines on the Western in the mid 1970s, almost guaranteed to fail in service. The Class 50 was, however, the Western's fastest engine at the time, being the only BR diesel designed to run at 100mph. Having been chased off the LMR by the Preston to Glasgow electrification, they were subsequently pushed off on to the Waterloo to Exeter route with the advent of InterCity 125 on the Western. Their introduction on the Waterloo line was heralded as the start of a new era for that line, with posters advertising the new traction and the improved timings it offered. Strangely, though, the illustration on the poster looked more like a Class 31, which was hardly an advertisement for speed. But very soon the Class 50 fleet was having to be baled out by Class 47s and Class 33s as its reputation for unreliability continued, eventually leading to a crisis for the line west of Basingstoke that was only resolved by the bold decision, of a type that could only have been taken under the stewardship of Network SouthEast, to build the South Western Turbos, complete with a new maintenance depot at Salisbury. The irony is that if the Class 50s had not been quite so unreliable the West of England route could well still be muddling along instead of having received its biggest revamp ever.

An aspect of railway enthusiasm that took up a lot of management time was the transfer of lines to private operators. In 1990–91 I was involved in formulating agreements for private operations along our track formation between Birchden Junction and Eridge, near Tunbridge Wells. The organisation concerned, which delighted in the mockingly self-disparaging name of TWERPS (Tunbridge Wells and Eridge Railway Preservation Society), wanted to share our trackbed by using the redundant down line while we continued operations over the former up line, which had been converted a couple of years earlier for single-line working of the Oxted to Uckfield service. The questions about liability for accidents and about

50005 was one of the worst offenders at the Western Region 'Rogue Control' in 1975. It somehow survived into Network SouthEast days and is seen here at Exeter St Davids on a Waterloo train. (Photo: Phil Wood)

responsibility for the maintenance of bridges, earthworks, level crossings, fencing and the track itself were almost endless. The BRB also had a statutory requirement to ensure that Health & Safety at Work measures were met on its property, but how was this to be ensured with a largely unregulated enthusiasts' body running the trains? In the course of several meetings with TWERPS and the Board's Solicitor it became apparent that there would need to be a Running Rights Agreement, a Light Railway Order, leasing agreements, rentals, indemnities, proofs of insurance, etc. The whole thing was a nightmare of paperwork and made me wonder at the time how on earth the forthcoming arrangements between Network Rail and the TOCs were to be thrashed out. In retrospect I can only assume that a lot of the precautions that we considered we were bound to adopt were quietly swept under the carpet in the interests of political expediency. But whatever the national issues, the Spa Valley Railway is now up and running.

One major worry was the fact that another operator's vehicles would be running alongside our own. In the event of a derailment that fouled the other line, who would be responsible? How could we be sure that their vehicles were fit to run? What obligations did we have to see that they were fit each and every time they ran? However you looked at it, it seemed that responsibility came back to the Board for every eventuality. Only a few years previously there had been an incident at Hope in Derbyshire in which a privately owned wagon on a private exchange siding had become foul of the adjoining running line and all Areas had been required to submit details of any places where such incidents might occur. There were a great many, of course, not least the sidings at Swanscombe mentioned earlier. Coupled with the realisation of this hazard was the knowledge that we would soon need to share trackbed with such schemes as the Croydon Tramlink and that this would involve 'heavy' and 'light' vehicles running alongside each other, each with hugely differing impact resistance. The legal implications of joint operation were tortuous in the extreme and most of them involved safety. The TWERPS/Spa Valley project was an interesting one, however, as it enabled us to offload the costs of maintaining Eridge station on to them and thus ensured the preservation of the attractive station buildings and long canopies there. It also brought more business to the poorly used Uckfield line. To have hammered it out was a useful precedent in many respects.

Another money-making activity for the railway has been the running of enthusiasts' trains over freight-only lines, with or without unusual traction. Every so often an excursion would be booked down the line from Hoo Junction to Grain while I was Area Freight Manager, including one hauled by a Class 50 (it didn't break down). The Grain Crossing Keeper, who was also the Shunter there, would be booked on specially to receive the train under the token block signalling system. On these occasions he was always armed with a supply of platform tickets for Grain station, which had closed many years before. These tickets were of dubious origin and Brian would go along the train when it stopped at the derelict platform, selling them to the enthusiasts.

A lot of preparation had to go into such excursions, mainly in terms of ensuring that facing points were clipped. This was one of the greatest differences between a passenger line and a freight-only line in operating terms: no passenger train was allowed over facing points without those points being secured by a locking device (usually automatic these days) or being manually secured by a point clip and scotch. In the case of the Grain branch I went down by road ahead of the train at the Signalman's instruction to ensure that facing points were secured and proper indications put in place to show to the Driver that this was so.

The ultimate enthusiasts' special, remains, of course, steam-hauled and in regard to steam the railway's policy has been decidedly patchy. During the 1980s there were regular steam excursions at express speeds from Marylebone as well as trips along the North Wales Coast and Mallaig lines, while in other areas such activities were frowned upon. Much of it seemed to be according to the whim of the managers of the lines concerned, rather than being a national policy. At the start of the 1990s, the South Eastern Division of Network SouthEast had a pro-steam policy under the Directorship of Geoff Harrison-Mee and, as well as allowing steam-hauled charter trains

Corporate consistency had fallen apart by 1991. 34027 *Taw Valley* arrives at Folkestone Harbour with the Golden Arrow special, but the neighbouring South Central Division forbade steam running. (Photo: Author)

to run, it organised its own steam events. By contrast, the adjoining South Central Division, under Chris Jago, would not consider steam running. The current operators of both former Divisions do not involve themselves in steam running but, having no direct control over the infrastructure in the way that Messrs Harrison-Mee and Jago had in earlier times, are in no position to stop Network Rail from allowing steam-hauled charters to operate – and they still do.

During the 'dark' years when steam was meant to be forgotten, the Merchant Navy Class 35028 *Clan Line* was allowed to run under its own power from Ashford to Hereford and several of us who were 'in the know' went along to see it off. This happened under the cover of dark one night in 1974 and the loco was severely restricted in speed under a lot of the overbridges on the South Eastern main line. During steam days the track had dipped under these bridges to allow for the additional height of the locomotive chimneys, but following electrification the track had been levelled in an attempt to give a smoother ride. Those reading this who are familiar with the South Eastern will appreciate my use of the word 'attempt'. Back on that night in 1974, *Clan Line* had a slow run, proceeding cautiously under these bridges in accordance with a very detailed 'Exceptional Load' specification in the Special Traffic Notice. Years later, however, as a result of a massive bridge rebuilding programme for Channel Tunnel freight trains, steam traction is able once more to run at line speed along this same stretch. One evening in June 1992 there were two express steam trains from Ashford to London to mark the end of a weekend of steam haulage on the Ashford to Hastings line, one of the engines being *Clan Line*'s little sister, the West Country Class 34027 *Taw Valley*. I stood with about thirty other people on the platform at Pluckley, reputedly Britain's most haunted village, to see these ghosts from a former age rush through at express speed, whistles screaming and exhaust being driven down in clouds over the platform and all around us by the arch of the overbridge.

For many years the reason for the ban on steam traction on the former Southern Region had been because it was thought that such events would encourage people to trespass on the electrified line. There had been near-misses at an Open Day at Eastleigh in 1973 in which people had been seen actually standing on the conductor rail (but not earthing the current) in order to get better photographs. These people did a massive disservice to their own cause as their actions resulted in a ban on steam on electrified lines until the early 1990s. It took the abolition of the Southern Region and the creation of more autonomous Divisional management to lift the ban. As with so many aspects of the railway, the long memories of the old days were being consigned to retirement, with the incoming management beginning to realise that, if they wanted to, they could reinvent the wheel in their own shape without having to take on board the lessons from the past.

18

Footing the Bill

The rolling stock for special trains is, of course, as with all other stock, now privately owned – as are the steam engines occasionally used to haul it. These always were, following their purchase for preservation. The days when BR had its own excursion fleet are now firmly in the past, although Waterman Railways and, more recently, Eversholt Leasing have kept coaches for charter use. Efficient utilisation of rolling stock does not allow for sidings, land and maintenance facilities to be used for holding strings of coaches that will only be used occasionally, but until at least the 1970s there were many such sets and they were the dregs of the fleet. They were used for enthusiasts' trains, charter bookings and holiday relief services, and in this way the railway was able to demonstrate convincingly to its most occasional (and therefore, possibly, its most impressionable) users that it was insensitive and anachronistic. Some of the excursion sets were in a shocking state: as late as 1974 a colleague of mine had been on duty at Newton Abbot station one Saturday when a relief train made up of former LMSR stock rolled in, still in a much faded maroon livery. As he closed one of the doors, the exterior door panel fell in. As well as being held for excursion work, large numbers of vehicles were at one time retained for seasonal peaks. Geoffrey Freeman Allen, in his book *British Railways Today and Tomorrow* (1959) cites a typical Christmas week special train programme of the mid 1950s at Euston that involved the use of 161 vehicles drawn from the sidings at Verney Junction 'for which there had probably been little or no employment since the summer'.

Some stock, whether excursion or ordinary, had special facilities for different eventualities – 'ambulance windows' for loading people on stretchers, or even in coffins, straight into compartments, for example. The

General Appendix to the Rule Book contained, amongst a great many other things, details of precautions to be taken when transporting corpses and I recall seeing, in 1975, the former Great Western Railway coffin-carrying barrow still in use at Paddington station. Strangely enough, on the same day I also saw the surviving LNER wooden-bodied buffet car, which was still in service at the time on the Western. There were occasions on the railway when you wondered which age you were living in.

In the late 1970s there was a spate of loco-hauled charter trains taking pilgrims from the Midlands to Dover on their way to Lourdes. One night we had several such trains passing the windows of the Beckenham Control office, almost in convoy, which went to show how many resources were still kept at that time for occasional use, their costs being hidden in the general mass of expenditure, long before the days when each business sector had to underwrite every resource attributed to it.

Even after resource attribution, some sets were retained but these were few and far between. Most notable were the Land Cruise sets operated by InterCity, which consisted mainly of upgraded Mk I coaches but also included Mk III sleepers. They were best recognised by their white-painted roofs. Land Cruises ran until 1991, mainly from London, and went mostly to the Highlands of Scotland, providing sightseeing opportunities and a rail 'adventure' for tourists. While the income from these was high they were nevertheless seasonal and so a lot of idle time was inherent in their retention. Traction and crews had to be found in 'marginal time', a commodity that was being increasingly eradicated as costs were driven down, and I doubt if the Land Cruises met their true, year-round costs. When I was in charge of the Euston Sleeping Car Attendants in the late 1980s we were expected to provide Attendants for Land Cruises during the summer, just when our own staff holiday commitment peaked. Traditionally, the complement of staff had been maintained at an artificially high level in order to meet this requirement but this meant, of course, that InterCity Sleepers were cross-subsidising the Land Cruises. In order to sharpen the awareness of the Land Cruise management I negotiated for two staff to be charged full time to Land Cruises during the seasons of 1989 and 1990, but they would still spring little surprises on us, such as requiring two cruises to run at the same time, thus needing four Attendants. As InterCity got to grips more and more with its costs, the true price of Land Cruises became apparent and they came to be operated with a smaller fleet and with haulage shared with the West Highlander sleeper train.

Having moved in 1988 from Railfreight, where every traffic flow was charged with the cost of each inch of track and each horsepower of traction dedicated to it, I found the attribution of staff costs in InterCity rather amateurish, which was surprising given the financial performance required of InterCity. In Railfreight terminology the process started with the principle of 'freight avoidability', which meant that the cost of providing or of maintaining a particular resource would be saved were it not for freight use. Beyond this, though, 'avoidability' went right down to the actual traffic flows that used the resource so that you could balance these specific costs against the benefit of the revenue derived. This applied to traction and train crews as well as to track and land and was possibly taken to obsessive extremes, being the death knell for many seasonal and irregular freight flows. However, if I had started talking within ICOBS about Sleeping Car Attendants being 'Land Cruise avoidable' no one would have understood me. To put freight avoidability in context, we did have the ability to underwrite poorly used or unused resources if we considered there might be a future opportunity and I well remember a long and argumentative telephone conversation with the Regional Freight Manager's office at Waterloo in 1987 concerning the retention of the connection to Crabtree Sidings on the North Kent line, which we thought might be used for substantial trainload traffic to and from Erith Oil Works – 'might, might, might – that's all we ever hear from you,' was the response of the RFM's representative, who was responsible for maintaining records of who was underwriting what.

Nevertheless, InterCity was tightening its overall control of costs and revenue, as it had to do to meet the Government's requirement that it be financially self-supporting from 1989, even if allocation within its own organisation was not as precise as Railfreight's. One step towards proper accountability was the creation of Senior Conductors in 1989 and the assumption by InterCity of their separated wage costs. New uniforms and special training were given to those selected from the ranks of Guards at strategically chosen depots up and down the country and these people were to work exclusively for InterCity, whereas train crew depots had previously mainly been multi-functional in order to give flexibility and economies of scale. Selection to the grade of Senior Conductor was supposedly made entirely on the basis of suitability but at some depots, such as Wolverhampton, it was certainly made strictly upon seniority, which was the largely discredited system of promoting a person purely on the grounds that he or she had longer service within the relevant grade than someone else had. So even in the changing world of the late 1980s, InterCity couldn't quite shrug off the restrictive practices of the past. But it was a start.

Some Senior Conductors were confused about their new role: they had smart new InterCity uniforms, they carried portable phones so they could make arrangements for customers in cases of disruption and they had greater discretion regarding such things as holding their trains for connections and authorising the provision of free refreshments during delays, but at the same time they were still, for the time being at least, answerable to the old depot management. So on the one hand they would receive glossy letters from Dr Prideaux, the Managing Director of InterCity, encouraging them to make use of their new discretionary powers to the benefit of InterCity's customers, while on the other hand they would still receive the good old 'please explain ...' letters from local management accusing them of having delayed trains. Eventually the policy settled down and Senior Conductors became one of the most visible advertisements for a properly integrated and identifiable national transport product – just in time for it to be broken up.

One year earlier than was required by Government edict, InterCity amazed the pundits and broke through into operating profit. The 'small surplus' that was rumoured to have been achieved in the year 1988–89 turned out to be an operating profit of £153m. Britain's Government had expected (and BR had delivered) something unheard of anywhere else in the world: a high-quality express railway system that needed no Government support. This achievement reinforced InterCity's perceived position as BR's 'flagship' service, obscuring the fact that Railfreight had been unsupported by subsidy since 1979. InterCity's success also, of course, accelerated progress towards its eventual demise as the predators started to hover with more interest, especially as it became clear that they, unlike InterCity, could expect and did indeed receive Government subsidy. At a seminar in a hotel near Marble Arch we were told by Dr Prideaux that the success had been largely due to the fact that the East Coast and Great Western services were so profitable that they had carried the rest, thus giving an overall surplus nationally. It is interesting to note that the franchise holders of these two service groups, GNER and First Great Western, received Government subsidy, as well as all the others.

Identification of staff and other resources with their brand activity was an important part of what was called 'sectorisation'. Senior Conductors were able to identify with InterCity and thus to see it as a separate product. Similarly, but less publicly, Red Star began to appoint its own staff to its renamed Parcels Points rather than having them come from a pool of indifferent Station Managers' staff. There were four reasons for this policy: first, the promotion of strong branding to the public; secondly, the planting of the idea in the minds of staff that they were a valued part of a branded business; thirdly, the identification and control of the true costs of the brand and, fourthly, of course, the ability to present each brand as a purchasable entity. Traditionally the railway had left it to local management to deploy resources as they thought best, crossing the boundaries of the different activities. As sectorisation began to take hold in the mid 1980s this was followed by 'contracts' under which Area Managers undertook to provide certain services, such as staffing, for the businesses at agreed prices and with monitorable criteria such as quality and safety as well as cost. As with many other things, this was a stepping stone towards the eventual direct employment of staff by the businesses and now, of course, by the franchisees or owners.

All this was a far cry from the flexibility that had been so desperately sought by railway management and that was, after much industrial relations upheaval, introduced in 1968 under the Pay & Efficiency Agreement. Under that regime, a Leading Railman, say, could be expected to see away passenger trains during the rush hour, then sweep the platform and then man the parcels office, also dealing with any on-track incidents that may occur. While this led to huge increases in productivity and the elimination, through amalgamation, of many under-utilised posts it also resulted in a lack of interest in, or pride for, any particular activity. The same person, possibly later working for Red Star, would receive information about financial and volume performance and targets, both for his own Parcels Point and for Red Star in general. In the past, when all station and depot activities were lumped together under a Station Manager or Area Manager, even that manager would have had scant resource to such information, let alone his or her staff. Taking business involvement right through to every member of staff undoubtedly increased interest and responsibility for those who were happy with their allocation and gave 'brand loyalty' in a way that the old versatility could never have achieved. Against this, though, is the demise of the do-anything, go-anywhere railwayman who was competent (but probably not much more than that) to man the ticket barrier, wind points, work the crossing box, uncouple trains, do the cleaning and announce the trains. For many railway staff and management, myself included, the variety was the appeal of railway work.

The separation of the businesses from each other also made it more difficult for displaced staff to be found continuing employment. At one time, for instance when I was Assistant Station Manager at Maidstone West in 1979, when we closed the parcels depot the staff employed there were first in line for any suitable vacancies elsewhere in the Area. A great many people survived numerous such displacements, relatively painlessly moving to new jobs within the overall BR umbrella. It happened to me several times, but when I was no longer required by InterCity in 1990, no effort could be made by InterCity to place me with, for example, Network SouthEast or Railfreight and neither would those organisations have been under any obligation to take me, even if they had a suitable vacancy just across the road. I was left to find my own salvation and each business had to bear its own redundancy costs, a policy that eventually went to ridiculous extremes with BR staff receiving large sums to leave the railway, only to start the next Monday with a firm offering the railway the same services they had been providing 'in-house' the week before, but at inflated prices, all in the drive towards privatisation.

I mentioned a short while ago the system under which Area Managers provided resources under 'contract' to the businesses. This started while I was Area Freight Manager at Dartford in 1985. On the Southern Region, in the days when there was still a Chief (later Regional) Freight Manager, we had all seemed to be part of the same organisation, with the same objectives. With the advent of Railfreight, however, local operators became 'contractors' and Railfreight became the hirer. I remember an acrimonious meeting that was held in the intimidating environment of the Southern Board Room at Waterloo but which had been arranged by Railfreight Construction, at which I and other Area operators sat along one side of the table, while Aidan Nelson from Railfreight and the actual customers sat along the other. The

Railfreight representatives had assumed the role of some sort of intermediate customer as if they weren't really part of the railway any more, let alone were answerable for any of its failings.

The allegations that Areas were not providing the quality of service required by Railfreight under the terms of the new contracts started to come in thick and fast. Some accusations were difficult to refute while others were clearly unreasonable. Over a period of months, for example, there was criticism about the behaviour of Drivers on nights at Northfleet cement works. It was alleged that they were failing to respond properly to the creep signal instructions given by the cement loaders. These signals told the Driver either to proceed at regulated slow speed, stop or set back, as appropriate to loading requirements, but the system was designed with the intention of allowing continuous loading at slow speed without the train having to stop. So the 'stop' and 'set back' instructions should only very rarely have been necessary.

I went to Northfleet, unannounced, on Midsummer's Night 1985 and watched from behind a pillar as the 0324 Northfleet to Dunstable service was loaded. The creep signals were going on and off like Christmas tree lights, which was decidedly unseasonal. How any Driver could keep up with all the changing instructions was beyond me. I timed and recorded all the changes of signal aspect and sent the log to the Railfreight Construction office in London. Blue Circle then admitted that they had problems with their loading gear and the accusations died down. There had often been difficulties with the loading at Northfleet (one night they dropped several tonnes of cement down the roof exhaust outlets of a Class 33 as it went under the chute, necessitating a complete strip down and rebuild), and I think BCI simply wanted to test how gullible the new Railfreight organisation was and whether they could get the blame for delays shifted from them to us. This was a favourite trick of Blue Circle – I recall another occasion when a discharged coal train was held at Northfleet one morning awaiting a path back to the LMR. An irate Works Manager rang me to say that the Driver had left his train across three internal works roads and was therefore bringing the place to a standstill.

'What's more, the bastard's now stuffing a free breakfast down his gob in our canteen,' continued the Works Manager indignantly, this possibly being the main point of contention.

Upon arrival I found out that the Works Supervisor had told the Driver he could leave his train there and had suggested that he might as well have breakfast while he was waiting. This sort of silly incident was just the sort of thing that the new Railfreight sectors liked to level at us as an example of our operating indiscipline. After a while, though, things settled down and good working relationships were established between customers, Railfreight and, as service providers or 'contractors', the Areas.

It was Railfreight that led the way with separate identification of resources. Railfreight's bold, modern locomotive livery designs by Roundel Design Group signified the division of the freight traction fleet into distinct commodity-based business sectors. Each machine was not only allocated to Trainload Coal or Speedlink Network, for example, but was painted in that sector's livery and was diagrammed to work exclusively for that sector whenever possible. The liveries were designed to express the essence of each sector's main commodity and were important in making a break from railway tradition and isolationism. They were industrial designs, meant to show that Railfreight was a vital part of Britain's industrial processes and not just a part of BR. In design terms they put Railfreight at the forefront of British industry, winning the Design and Art Directors Award and being finalists in the BBC Design Award. The concept was a complete package too, covering not just the locomotives but signing, stationery and publicity materials. This was at a time when BR spent more on design than any other organisation in Great Britain.

The liveries were unveiled in a spectacular ceremony at Ripple Lane in east London in October 1987, during which locos emerged in a staggered formation on parallel sidings amidst the smoke of fireworks and the sound of a brass band. Within ten years, though, the freight liveries had changed twice more – first to the varied liveries of Transrail, Loadhaul, Mainline, Freightliner and Railfreight Distribution and finally to the maroon and gold of EWS along with the new independent colour schemes of Freightliner, Direct Rail Services, etc. Of all the subsequent liveries, only the black and orange of Loadhaul, with its bold assertion of power, anywhere near approached the innovation and sense of purpose inherent in the 1987 Railfreight Roundel designs.

From a practical point of view the livery relaunch in 1987 was nonsense, though. For the first time you not only had to find traction that matched the requirements of the route, the Driver's knowledge and the weight of the train but that was now also of the right colour. Needless to say, many freight trains ran with engines of the wrong livery – no self-respecting Locomotive Controller or Train Crew Supervisor would cancel a train for the sole reason that there wasn't an engine of the correct livery when others were available to do the job. However, in some cases the cross-suitability of locomotives was deliberately sabotaged in order to make it more difficult for locos to be used on other sectors' work. Some Railfreight locos had their train heating equipment removed and/or were restricted in speed so as to be of little use on passenger services. Historically, freight trains had been cancelled if a passenger train needed the resources and this sometimes happened on a regular basis, with the same freight customer's traffic being repeatedly delayed for twenty-four hours in order to save a thirty-minute wait for some passengers. With separately managed resources, paid for exclusively by each business, this was no longer acceptable and each sector had, for the first time, to make sure that it really did have sufficient resources to match its needs. No one could ride on anyone else's back any more, other than by hiring – which is now, of course, quite commonplace – with Virgin Trains in particular buying in traction from other operators on a regular basis.

Once the fleets had been divided and each sector was meeting the running and maintenance costs of its locomotives, the sectors started to look more closely at why and where they had their fleets and their Drivers' depots. To a large extent the old depots were not well placed for the traffic flows of the 1980s and beyond. Under the generalist, Regional approach there had been a drift away from the long-established depot at Hither Green, for instance, towards Stewarts Lane. Some maintenance was transferred, as was fuelling and breakdown work. However, from the point of view of Railfreight Construction, who had heavy traction requirements in North Kent and who had assumed 'ownership' of most of the Stewarts Lane engines, this was not such a good idea. If anything, they wanted to move nearer to the aggregates and cement terminals of North Kent and not further away into south London. All over the country similar reassessments were being made and new options were being examined for the location of depots. In practice, however, the extent of the changes was limited by cost and by the lasting perpetuation of old working and industrial-relations practices. Even the most profitable sectors, such as Trainload Coal, flinched at the horrendous in-house BR costs quoted to them for the establishment of new sheds, along with fuelling, maintenance and staff relocation costs. The new operators, being more able to shop around, will doubtless make more progress in their stated aim of having freight operations based at more appropriate locations. This includes not just crew and locomotive depots, but now, with the acquisition of Railfreight Distribution, the location of shunting yards.

When Railfreight Construction were looking at the possibility of breaking away from both Stewarts Lane and Hither Green and of setting up their own new depot I tried to 'sell' them the idea of Hoo Junction as this was only a few minutes away from Northfleet, Cliffe and Halling, where their traffic came from. As things were at the time, such a move would have been administratively beneficial as the Area organisation at Dartford meant that, although I was a specialist freight manager for North Kent, there was no control within the Area over freight train crews, these being based outside the Area, mainly at Gillingham and Hither Green. The Area boundaries had been established on the basis of passenger traffic flows, once again highlighting the weakness of what I have repeatedly called 'generalist' management. To have had freight crews and locos on the doorstep would have been an excellent move from a local management point of view, but therein was the downfall of my argument. The local management structure was, of course, only transient and to have based a case for heavy investment in buildings and plant upon the premise that the Area structure would last would have been most foolish. Nevertheless, a train crew depot was later established at Hoo Junction, but for different reasons – and after the Areas had long gone.

Area management itself on the Southern Region had been set up at huge cost in terms of buildings, and the short time that these buildings were actually in use verges upon the scandalous. At Dartford, the Area empire grew and grew as responsibilities were transferred to it from the dying Divisional tier above and the increasingly impotent Station management below. At considerable expense a new building was provided in 1985 for the Permanent Way Maintenance Engineer and his staff as the main building became needed in its entirety by the Area Manager, but only a year later the Area ceased to exist as an administrative unit and the main building stood idle, Dartford being swallowed up by the Areas at London Bridge and Thanet. Similar buildings to the one at Dartford stand to this day underutilised at

Gillingham, Dover, Basingstoke, Orpington, etc. – all specifically built for the Area management of the 1970s and '80s.

What all this emphasises is the sheer arbitrariness of a geographically based management structure for the railway for anything other than the most local of control. An individual Station Manager can make a realistic go of, say, ten or so smallish staffed stations along with one or two larger ones and these can be managed as a sensible group along a line of route or on routes radiating from a main point. This is, of course, how station management has always been, although the responsibilities within that structure have changed. At any level above this, however, almost any combination can be tried and possibly has been. Small Areas, large Areas, Divisions, Districts, Territories, Regions – call them what you will, they are endlessly divisible or mergeable depending upon the emphasis of the time upon the need to appear 'local' or the need to save money.

The Scottish Region of BR (and later Scotrail) traditionally led the way in cutting out unnecessary layers of management, but it was Network SouthEast that abolished Areas completely, making its Station Managers report directly to renewed Divisions that were sufficiently large to have some stability. They also corresponded more sensibly with the operating and marketing requirements of the routes they covered, which is broadly to say that they perpetuated the old boundaries created when the railways were built. While this enabled manageable units to be identified, it did mean that new service opportunities that crossed boundaries may not have been easily spotted, a problem largely perpetuated by the franchising system. So there was and still is no easy answer to the question of whether the railway should be managed geographically, by line of route or by function and the only conclusion I can offer is that whatever system is in use at the time this is being read, it will not be permanent.

Many railway people have gained from the short lives of some of these organisations, using them as stepping stones on their way to higher things in the confident knowledge that they wouldn't be anywhere long enough to become answerable for anything. On the Southern there was a nucleus of 'old boy' Area Managers who stayed put, took the flak and got things done slowly, but there was also a group of much younger Area Managers who had dodged about the country and simply wanted to make their names known in higher circles. At one time the ultimate position for such 'climbers' was that of Personal Assistant to the Chairman of the BRB. Occupants of this post were usually selected from the ranks of young Area Managers and much of the work involved representing the Chairman at meetings and at social engagements – making sure, of course, that at the same time one's own name became known to Government ministers, top civil servants, the press, etc. At other times, though, the Personal Assistants lived up (or down) to their nickname of 'Chairman's bag carrier'. I couldn't help smiling to myself one evening at Euston in 1988 when I watched Sir Robert leaving The Clansman and chatting to the staff as he passed by. His Assistant, who had been my boss at Dartford a few years earlier, was scurrying along behind with the suitcases and briefcases.

Another chap I knew, who had been a Management Trainee with Freightliner, ended up as Personal Assistant to their Chairman, Cyril Bleasdale and, it seemed, had a more relaxed time of it. He had been with the Chairman so many times to his exclusive London club that he was admitted, so he said, without question one night when out on a 'crawl' with his friends, all of whom he signed in, equally without question.

19

Holding the Purse Strings

Towards the end of the last chapter I used the phrase 'increasingly impotent Station management'. What did I mean by that? Well, this was another irony in the intricacies of management control on BR in the 1980s and '90s. At the same time as Station Managers had their objectives more clearly defined in the direction of retail management, so their overall control, authority and status were reduced. So while on the one hand they knew more clearly what they were meant to be doing and, importantly, why – and had more information with which to do it, on the other hand they became increasingly surrounded by a railway over which they had less control.

From their origins in the nineteenth century and right up until the 1980s, Station Masters or Managers had been responsible for all stations, yards, signalboxes, etc. on their 'patch', including the staff. At some places they even had control over local Permanent Way gangs. They also held the purse strings in regard to hours worked and payment of wages. Gradually, with computerisation of paybills, with creation of the retail culture and with sectorisation, their control was eroded, until the Station Manager of the last years of BR and now of the TOCs is a lounge-suited salesperson who would be equally at home in charge of a department at Debenhams. Gone is the responsibility for signalling and shunting staff. Gone is the responsibility for parcels and freight. Where these activities still exist on stations they are separately managed and, as with station catering, may be on the stations as tenants rather than as an integral part of the operation of the station. Indeed, with some franchises being for only a few years, the Station Manager him or herself is probably no more than a tenant in effect.

Control of the purse strings was a vital tool in the assertion of Station Managers' authority and that of their Assistants. No single item has as much sway over staff 'on the ground' than knowing that their immediate boss can penalise or reward them financially. Although both tasks were time-consuming chores in the 1970s and early '80s, the rostering of staff and the control we had over their timesheets as Assistant Station Managers lent enormous power to us.

On the Southern Region most station groups had a Station Manager and two Assistants, who alternated between early and late turns, week about. Some smaller groups had just a Station Manager who was of a grade between most ASMs and the SMs of the larger groups, thus providing a well-structured career progression from ASM to SM of a small group and then to SM of a large group. This structure was yet another thing that was lost in the reorganisations of the 1980s and '90s, leading to a lot of dead-end jobs of the same grade being created.

When you were the late-turn ASM you were also on call during the night and at the weekend, working the Saturday of that same weekend. On Friday afternoon and Saturday morning the ASM would, amongst other things, be collecting, checking and certifying the staff's timesheets, without which they could not be paid. Having also produced that week's roster towards the end of the previous week whilst working early turn, the same ASM had close control over every hour claimed for payment, from its original allocation to the individual staff member through to its certification for payment.

In this way, ASMs were able to reward co-operative staff by, say, giving them first option for overtime, punish others by withholding it or by rostering them to unpopular jobs and, if thought desirable, leave particular shifts uncovered in order to save money. This meant as well, of course, that there was scope for personal vendettas and victimisation and while this was not a good thing in itself it certainly added to the ASM's perceived authority in the eyes of the staff. Within the overall paybill budget, close control of rostering and of pay in this way even gave room for adding hours that had not in fact been worked to the timesheets of staff who had done a particularly good job or who had helped out in some way. In 1983 the rostering and paybills on the Southern were transferred to the Areas that were staffed by Clerical Officers who had no such discretionary powers, so while the integrity improved the direct management control was eroded. Remote voices on the telephone began to arrange staffing hours and a lot of goodwill was lost, taking with it a chunk of useful management power along with a chunk of abused management power.

Another powerful management tool at station level until the early 1980s was the maintenance of staff files. Before the administration was reallocated to the Areas, each Southern SM held the file concerning each staff member. Many hours were whiled away by me in my early days at Woolwich Arsenal reading about the chequered history of the many diverse characters I had to deal with. Knowing their length of service, their employment background, their disciplinary and personal records made it much easier to deal with them as individuals, although, of course, it didn't beat talking to them.

The formal disciplinary procedures were carried out at station-management level too until the Areas took this over as well. Station Managers and their Assistants hired, fired, reduced staff in grade, promoted, suspended from duty and transferred staff from job to job. The 'Form One', which was the basic disciplinary notice, was notoriously issued by some SMs like the proverbial confetti. A hearing ensued at which the accused person could be represented by a union rep. After taking this representation into account, the SM, who was, of course, also the person who had initiated the charge, pronounced the punishment, which was perversely referred to as an 'award'. This was then confirmed by the issue of a 'Form Two', everything being recorded on the culprit's file. There was an appeal procedure as a safeguard against abuse and there were certain offences that could not be heard in the first place by an SM – these included such things as physical attacks on the SM and drunkenness on duty and were heard in those days at Divisional level, as were the appeals. Many disciplinary hearings took a great deal of preparation and were very time-consuming, not just for the SM but in terms of the amount of time needed for the release from duty of the accused, the representative and, sometimes, of witnesses. However, proper record keeping and fair behaviour on the part of the SM could result in a case being built up over several incidents towards a dismissal that could not be challenged, even though each incident might not be all that serious in its own right.

Some offences could attract immediate, or summary, dismissal without there even being a hearing. Being caught red-handed with your hand in the till or being witnessed in the act of destroying railway property or of assault were such offences, all of which examples I came across in various forms. Usually, though, the person concerned would be suspended pending an inquiry.

So what sort of things were people up to on the railway, to merit the invoking of the formal disciplinary procedures? Most concerned personal timekeeping and unauthorised absence from duty, and were pretty routine but others were more interesting. One night a Railman at Erith went on the rampage with his mates and smashed up part of the station when I was on call, strewing the remains of what had been a very solid old-fashioned ticket collector's box on the track. The Police were called by local residents, the service was suspended until the wreckage could be cleared and the Railman was summarily dismissed whilst 'helping the Police with their inquiries' at Belvedere Police Station.

Years later, one of my Euston Sleeping Car Attendants had an altercation with the Rt Hon. Jack Straw, MP, who was later, of course, the Home Secretary but at the time was the Opposition spokesman for Education. This took place on board the late lamented Barrow-in-Furness to Euston sleeper, the argument nearly coming to blows. It was witnessed by the Headmaster of St Bees public school, who felt moved to write to InterCity management in support of Mr Straw, despite the cavernous gap in their political beliefs regarding education, a point he felt it necessary to emphasise in his letter. We had to show the red card to the pugilistic Attendant.

Another Attendant, based at Liverpool (also no longer served by sleepers), was caught defrauding the railway on ticket revenue, resulting in the black cap being donned once more. All over the railway, despite the protection offered by the employment laws, there were dismissals; dozens every day. Then again, there were transfers and reductions in grade. Many pages ago I made mention of the drunken Leading Railman at Charlton who showed us all up by appearing on the bridge to cheer Prince Charles on his way to Scotland. This same man was on duty one evening when I had cause to ring Charlton in order to pass on some train-running information that had been received on the teleprinter at Woolwich Arsenal. My call was taken by an (in)distinctly slurring Leading Railman, out of whom I could get no sense. I went to ask the Station Manager to accompany me to Charlton as in such circumstances we always tried to have a witness present. Upon arrival at Charlton we found the station basically neglected with the Leading Railman hiding in the office on the platform. The SM challenged him, to be met with a torrent of personal abuse. Eventually the abuse turned to physical threats and the SM had to leap on a departing train for his own safety, leaving me to calm the enraged man who, by this time, was charging around the station swearing and shaking his fist. All this was going on at the height of the evening peak, when down trains discharge a couple of hundred people at Charlton every fifteen minutes or so.

I persuaded the Railman to leave the station and to cool off a bit.

As I walked and he staggered along the street he turned to me and said, 'Guv, now we're off the station, tell me, everything I said about that bastard was true, wasn't it?'

On or off the premises, though, you obviously can't allow yourself to be drawn in that way. The man was sent up to the Division for his disciplinary hearing, at which I was the prime witness, and, with impeccable irony, the Divisional Movements Manager reduced him in grade and transferred him to Woolwich Arsenal so that he would have to work every day under the nose of the SM he had so thoroughly denigrated. He also went for 'drying out' treatment at Bexley Hospital.

Another time, also at Charlton, I had to remove a Booking Clerk who had been given overtime specially to deal with football traffic and had sloped off to the pub during the match. He was unfit for duty when he returned and had to be dealt with in full view of hundreds of passengers, which was most unsatisfactory. He was banned from overtime working for a while as punishment. Years later I recall a belligerent InterCity chef from Manchester who was refusing to work correctly and had been booked off by me with instructions that he was to return to Manchester as a passenger on the next train and report to his manager there. He refused to leave the Euston office and was blocking the door, leaving me eventually with no option but to call the station police to remove him and to put him on the train.

Cases such as these were not at all unusual and I think they are representative of the types of incidents that were taking place day in and day out all over the railway. It must be remembered that most railway staff worked unsupervised, such as Drivers alone in their cabs, Signalman alone in their boxes, Booking Clerks alone in their offices, etc. and so there was a great emphasis on personal responsibility and also a great scope for abusing the freedom that came with it. Not all people can cope with this and many need a work environment in which they are being watched, as they would be in a factory or a large shop. This was one more aspect that made the running of the railway different from so many other jobs.

When I was first appointed to a job involving what was then called 'man management', I was given a useful tip by the Divisional Movements Manager who made the appointment, John Elliott. He told me that most staff will respect the position of their manager, but that the manager's job will be that much easier if he or she can also get them to respect the person as well. This worked in both directions, of course and, for instance, when it came to holding hearings and doling out dismissals and other punishments it was certainly a lot easier and less acrimonious if you knew you had been fair and had given the person the respect due to them as an individual, regardless of how they had behaved as an employee. Such respect, if it could be won, was invariably mutual.

All the time this was going on, though, as I have said, the power of Station Managers and their Assistants was being worn away. Rostering and paybills went to the Areas; disciplinary procedures went to the new 'functional' operating, passenger and personnel managers at the Areas. Also to go were the Negotiation and Consultation Procedures that had previously been conducted by SMs. Each station group had a Local Departmental Committee (LDC) of elected representatives and regular meetings were held to discuss staffing levels, new rosters, introduction of new equipment and many other things. Some items had to be agreed before they could be implemented and hence were termed 'negotiable', while others could be imposed or else were just for discussion. These were 'consultative'. The whole procedure was laid down in the 'Machinery of Negotiation for Railway Staff', dated 28 May 1956. This was a classic of the type of catch-all procedure that was painstakingly arrived at by unions and management at a time when everything had to be discussed between them. The booklet containing the 'Machinery' was forty pages long and was the bible for negotiators at all levels and on both sides.

At some places the LDCs were notoriously militant (many Drivers' LDCs fell into this category) and nearly all negotiable items would fail to reach agreement and have to be referred up to the next stage of the Machinery for resolution. These days, of course, many such items would not even be discussed in the first place. As with all levels and aspects of industrial relations, the balance swung decidedly towards the management during the 1980s and early '90s, and whilst this meant that worthwhile ideas were not held up so much, it also meant that some pretty crass schemes became implemented without the benefit of proper discussion with those who would have to operate them. The cab layout of a new multiple-unit design for Network SouthEast, for example, which at one time would have been endlessly tested and evaluated, turned out not to allow the Driver proper means of looking back out of the side window at the same time as Drivers were being expected to see themselves away from platforms, thus making the side window more important than ever. This was an instance in which the solution to one problem, that of old rolling stock, created its own new problem, but the underlying cause was the advent of a more authoritarian and, sometimes even arrogant style of management in the very late 1980s that lacked the continuity of experience.

Another example in which managers flew off at tangents, without being checked as they would have been in earlier times, was the introduction of Penalty Fares and of Driver Only Operation. What organisation, other than the railway would have, unattended and out of doors in places notorious for vandalism, two ticket machines and a collection of mirrors, cameras and monitors? And yet this was what was installed on whole groups of stations throughout Network SouthEast. Two separate machines were needed for Penalty Fares, which surely must have been the result of muddled planning, typified perhaps by the fact that at the same time as NSE Divisions were pushing on towards the abolition of ticket barrier control and the introduction of Penalty Fares, NSE HQ was in discussion with a firm who wanted to sell automatic ticket barrier machines. I briefly held the position of Planning Manager for the South London Lines of NSE in 1991 and was called to a meeting at Victoria at the instigation of HQ to discuss this equipment, while at the same time we were buying the equipment needed for Penalty Fares and designing the new 'open' platform access for Victoria.

From the early 1970s until it was made illegal in the early 1980s, the railway had operated a closed-shop agreement in which every employee had to belong to a trade union. This arrangement, as well as the Machinery, was explained to new managers as being in the interests of management. It meant that once you had struggled through the negotiation procedures and had eventually emerged with an agreement (either nationally with the union executives or Regionally with the Sectional Councils or locally with the LDCs) it then applied to everyone, because everyone was represented by the union. Thus it was enforceable automatically on every employee and, even if agreement had to be wrung out of the union, they would still support its implementation as to do otherwise would reduce their credibility as negotiators. After all, if they didn't support it, why had they signed it? Such was the management argument in favour of the Machinery and of the closed shop, as expounded to us at training seminars.

There were many union activists on the railway at all levels. Some stirred up discontent while others were greatly respected and were informally consulted by the management before the proper procedures started. Some of these were like elder statesmen and managers half their age would bow to their expertise and wisdom. Whether militant or constructive, they all put a lot of their own unpaid time into their activities. Basically, in most places, there was a good day-to-day local relationship with the union reps, whatever big issues they were falling out over nationally. During stoppages it was always a bit solemn notifying some of the more respected reps that you had withheld their pay, as the consistent union line at all levels was that stoppages were the last resort and were to be resolved as quickly as possible. The Government of the day, along with some sections of the media, sought to create union stereotypes, portraying these people as ogres, whereas in fact they were just ordinary people with families and hobbies like anyone else who, most of the time, just got on with their jobs.

In some cases, though, the LDC members were feared by the management and also, to some extent, by those they represented. The Slade Green Drivers' and Guards' LDCs were dominated by a handful of hard-liners who kept being re-elected. The Drivers' LDC insisted on more than one meeting each week, as well as site visits for various purposes on other days. Some of them hardly ever drove a train. Every Thursday they were booked off driving turns in order to provide 'scrutiny' of the following week's rosters. They had so many local agreements, some going back many years, that they could usually find something that had to be changed before they would agree to the publication of the duties. Their aim above all else, which was also that of their union ASLEF, was to ensure that the maximum number of driving jobs was maintained. They constantly strove to persuade management that the establishment numbers needed to be increased and the ploys used were many. Even obtaining agreement to another two minutes' walking time allowance between sidings and depot, for example, could ultimately lead to another Driver being needed somewhere, once all the extra minutes for the whole depot had been calculated. It was widely regarded as a joke among other grades that Drivers seemed to need twice as much time to walk anywhere as anyone else did, but the management kept falling for it. One restrictive practice at Slade Green was that two Drivers were needed before a special could be run, leading to the scandalous situation one night when some passengers were stranded at Dartford and rolling stock, Guard and Driver were available to run a special to get them home but the Driver refused to work without a second Driver. The Drivers did themselves no favours in the eyes of other staff or passengers by this sort of behaviour. Neither were they protecting their own livelihoods in the long run.

The Chairman of the Slade Green Drivers' LDC was also a magistrate at Gravesend and considered himself to be untouchable. On one occasion when I was covering the job of the Area Operations Manager at Dartford for a couple of weeks this Driver went missing on duty, resulting in the cancellation of a train on the Maidstone West line, which only had an hourly service. There seemed to me to be a cast-iron disciplinary case but the rigmarole I had to go through with the Area Manager before I was allowed to proceed was ridiculous. As he was an LDC member, ASLEF HQ had to be primed that an investigation was taking place first. Then, when I had prepared what was essentially a very straightforward case, the Area Manager sat on it until the Area Operations Manager came back from leave, after which they jointly decided to let the matter drop. So, after all, he was right in thinking he was untouchable. This same Driver, not long before, had refused to shunt his train from one platform to the other at Maidstone West one day when the service was disrupted because his diagram did not include the word 'shunt'. So a following train had to remain outside the station for twenty minutes while he sat in his cab doing nothing until his booked departure time.

The BRB and NUR ran joint industrial relations courses in the days when co-operation through negotiation was still the fashion. The NUR had bought Frant Place, near Tunbridge Wells (in the heart of Torydom) in 1974 for use as a residential school and I went there in 1982 and wallowed in the NUR's luxurious hospitality for a week. It was run as a high-class hotel, the manager having only recently moved from such an establishment in Paris. The cuisine was superb as was every aspect of the NUR's care for us.

Managers and union representatives learned about the intent, interpretation and implementation of the 1956 Machinery together, with instructors drawn from both sides. We ate together, went to the pub together and generally existed in a pleasing state of harmonious equality. Incidentally, there were two pubs in Frant and it was explained to us that when it became known that the NUR had bought Frant Place, the snootier of the two became a focal point of resistance in which it was made clear that the union riff-raff would not be tolerated. The landlord of the other pub was more than pleased to welcome people who were visiting from all parts of the country and his regulars apparently enjoyed the variety that this brought to their lives.

A London Bridge Guard, who happened to live along our stretch of the North Kent line, came back from one of these courses, fired with enthusiasm, and decided to set himself up as a sort of unofficial spokesman for the staff at Abbey Wood station. He found out that we were using split turns, i.e. four hours on, four hours off and then four more on in order to cover the rush hours. Although the people working these turns were paid twelve flat hours per day, he thought this was an outrage in terms of the spread of hours demanded. After he had come to see me about this, I went to Abbey Wood to consult the staff, suggesting to them that we really should be looking for another way of doing it, but knowing all along that it suited us and them. Following my visit they soon told the interfering Guard to shut up – twelve hours' pay for eight hours' work was just fine by them.

The NUR was keen to be involved in staff welfare matters, but with mixed results. We had a retirement 'do' in the function room of a particularly gruesome pub in Plumstead in 1981 and over 100 well-wishers attended it. About five staff had left within a few weeks of each other and they were there with their wives to be presented with retirement gifts by the Area Manager, John Norman. Mr Norman gave a very gracious presentation speech, the essence of which was the wholly appropriate wishing of good luck to the retired staff and their wives. This was followed by a speech from Jimmy Knapp, who at that time was the Southern Region organiser for the union. His speech was wholly inappropriate, being essentially a rallying call for opposition to the Board's latest pay offer. The retired couples were not impressed.

20

Red Posts, Pubs and Sightseeing

Schemes such as Driver Only Operation and Penalty Fares, which were good ideas in essence, were largely the brainchildren of managers who quickly moved from post to post and who wanted to leave their mark as they went along. At one time you couldn't really hope to be able to leave your mark individually because of the nightmare of negotiation and consultation required before change could be contemplated. Thus any decision that was made would be as a result of numerous committee meetings and the individual inspiration behind the idea would be lost through dilution. At the forefront of the move towards a more assertive approach in the 1980s, Government requirements notwithstanding, was Chris Green with the establishment first of Scotrail (1985) and then of Network SouthEast in 1986. Of course, from the cynic's point of view, the setting up of these organisations may have been no more than a politically motivated rush to make the railway more attractive to its eventual private operators, who have now inherited the benefits without having paid the costs, but whether that is true or not there were at least positive developments taking place at long last.

The small details that marked the launch of NSE were devastating in terms of the way in which Chris Green demonstrated that swathes could in fact be cut through the bureaucracy. By this I mean the red painting of all the station lamp posts and the re-signing of the chosen few 'flagship' stations.

Completely ignoring the cyclical painting gangs with their complicated schedules, restrictive practices and slow working methods, other gangs appeared from nowhere and did all the work in a fraction of the time the normal gangs would have taken. It was even rumoured that at one station on the Bexleyheath line the routine painting gang broke for lunch and came back to find the station transformed into NSE colours. To those in other industries it may not sound much, but on the railway it was a profound 'culture shock' to see that someone could simply decide that something was to be done and it would be, especially on the passenger railway. Likewise, the choice of the lamp posts may not seem much but it was a simple, clever idea: a practical move that could be demonstrated on every station quickly, thus defining both the new NSE area and its management philosophy simultaneously.

In the Dartford Area we knew that Chris Green had come back to London from Scotland in January 1986 after having successfully established Scotrail not only as a marketable product but also as a cohesive organisation. We knew also that he was forming plans for changes in the management and marketing structure of the London suburban services, but no one at Area

The launch of Network SouthEast gave a much-needed boost to morale, along with a bold statement of identity and purpose. Here a 4-VEP unit leads a 4-CEP unit through Beckenham Junction, while a 4-EPB unit waits in the bay platform. All three are in NSE livery, as is the station. (Photo: Tony Watson)

level knew the form these would take until one day, at very short notice, we had a management briefing with the Area Manager. He had been told to tell us the basic concepts of NSE and to give details of the launch, which was to be on the following Monday. So secret was the scheme that he was reluctant even to tell us the name 'Network SouthEast' until persuaded to do so by the Area Operations Manager. Then it all happened around us in the space of a few days.

There had been a half-hearted attempt to make the London area suburban services into one unit a few years previously but it lacked any identity. David Kirby, after spending several years with Sealink UK Ltd, had become General Manager of the Southern Region and was also made Director, London & South East in 1981 in an effort to co-ordinate things, but there was little positive strategy visible to those of us 'on the ground' or to our passengers. Sir David Serpell's report on the future of the railways was commissioned in May 1982 and recommended contraction. The ugly word 'bustitution' was coined in order to give new impetus to the discredited theory that by specifying substitute bus services, railway closures could be more easily accepted. The stance at that time seemed to be one of apology and withdrawal rather than one of action. Marylebone was put up for closure and even some railway managers started talking about the supposed benefits of express busways in place of some railways, echoing sycophantically the anti-railway noises that were emerging from the Prime Minister's advisers. (Busways, despite the 1980s hype, were in fact far from a new idea, it having been proposed in 1911 that the river bridges leading to Charing Cross and Blackfriars could be converted for bus use.) The short-lived and ill-conceived 'Jaffa cake' livery of grey, brown and orange made its appearance during this regime, but nobody really knew what it signified, if anything. But despite the lack of direction within the railway, the Serpell Report was mistimed – the public and politicians could see all around them the effects on the environment and on society of an unbridled rush towards car dependency in a way that was not foreseen during the previous major era of cuts. Stan Abbott, in his Foreword to David Henshaw's *The Great Railway Conspiracy*, makes the point also that when Dr Beeching assessed the future network needs he failed first to tackle the effect that dealing with overstaffing would have made to the viability of the railway. This time, though, there were people such as Sir Robert Reid and Chris Green in charge: people who even an anti-railway Government could trust to do just that, prepared as they now were with the meaningful costing practices that were so lamentably lacking right up until the early 1980s. So Serpell and bustitution faded from the Government's armoury.

Closures and busways vanished from the railway vocabulary with the setting up of NSE. Instead, lines reopened (Corby and Bicester) and new stations sprang up on many lines – Winnersh Triangle and Welham Green, for example. Even a new railway was built – to Stansted Airport – and, of course, the Thameslink project got off the ground at last. In fairness, it has to be said that NSE was able to ride on the back of the false economic boom of the 1980s and so money was available for pumping into new rolling stock, station refurbishments, electrification and resignalling. Later, as the boom receded, I worked for a while for NSE's South Central Division and while we managed to get the big schemes through, such as East Croydon rebuilding and the construction of Victoria Island, we were at the same time having to put many smaller stations on minimum maintenance, removing canopies and closing buildings in order to save cost. We still hoped for the return of the good times, though – and there were positive occasions such as the relaunch of the South London Line all-day service, which echoed the heyday of NSE. For some time the Victoria to London Bridge service had only run in the rush hour but we revamped it in conjunction with the London Borough of Southwark. Stations were renovated, access and signing were improved and a half-hourly service was introduced with new rolling stock. In May 1991 we invited the Minister for Public Transport, Roger Freeman, and the local MP, Simon Hughes, to the launching ceremony, along with the press. After a tour of the line on a special train we adjourned to the Phoenix & Firkin at Denmark Hill for lunch. It was good publicity but in the scale of things it was small-time stuff in comparison with the big ideas of the late 1980s.* I remember the horror on people's faces when the Minister asked why we didn't have a high-level station at the point where the South London Line crosses the South Eastern at Brixton. He told us he wanted the idea investigated. Now of course we'd have loved to have had a station there and the idea certainly wasn't original,

* 2018 update: The line described is now part of the orbital route operated by London Overground under the auspices of the London Mayor.

but just who would have been able to have come up with the money to construct a station on top of one that was already elevated above the busy streets of Brixton? By 1991 that sort of dream had passed. Nevertheless, I had to go to a site meeting with the Civil Engineers to have the likely costs and problems of construction explained to me so that a reply could be sent to the Minister. Similarly, Millwall Football Club wanted us to build a new station near South Bermondsey in order to fulfil a condition of their planning consent for relocation of The Den. I went to several meetings with them and while we found a suitable site we simply couldn't afford to chip in with any of the costs and The Den was eventually rebuilt without its own station. But this was all in the later era of recession.

With the new style of management epitomised by the launch of NSE in 1986 and its continuing expansion in the boom years arose the immediacy of decision-making that had been lacking for so long and that then characterised the way in which change was able to accelerate into the 1990s. For many of the old Station Managers and Area Managers, though, this was all too much. Lots of them had been used to sitting around letting things tick over, with the overriding idea that their jobs consisted of simply running what was there and not of thinking of, and implementing, new ideas. Many of them were very good at ensuring that efficiencies were realised but only within a continuing framework of stability that, in some cases, bordered on complacency.

Towards the end of the pre-NSE era this complacency was sometimes frightful to behold and at other times comical. Relief Station Managers on the Southern would drift in to cover leave or vacancies and then spend all day telling tall stories about the 1950s and '60s. When they were not required to cover a post they would congregate as 'supernumeraries' at main stations, getting in the way of anyone who was actually trying to do some work and then sloping off to the pub. In the mid 1980s the Area Manager at Dartford and his collection of cronies adopted the clever tactic of having 'WTT' meetings, which was meant to sound as if they were discussing the Working Timetable. In reality it meant that they were off to the Wat Tyler Tavern. One day they came back even worse for wear than usual and carried on chatting in the Area Manager's office, which was next door to mine. After a while one of them came out to swap his chair for one with arms, saying to me, 'I need one with arms, otherwise I'll fall off.'

Another day the Area Manager himself fell over on the stairs after a WTT meeting, being assisted to his feet by a member of train crew who was making a rare visit to the office. And we were meant to be responsible managers, setting an example of how to run a safety-critical transport system.

During a short spell as Assistant Station Manager at Maidstone West in 1979 I worked with an SM who went for a drink every lunchtime and expected his Assistant to come along, too. We toured the Kentish lanes and visited some lovely pubs so that I could be regaled with tales of signalling adventures and other scrapes over a couple of pints. I did wonder sometimes, though, whether Cyril was pulling my leg with some of the things he told me – did the P. Way department really build a conservatory on to the SM's house out of redundant railway materials and at no cost to Cyril, and was there really a finished car being loaded on to a train at Dagenham Dock with two doors on one side and only one on the other? While these tales were being told the stations and signalboxes were left to run themselves and we were completely out of contact, pagers not then having been introduced, let alone mobile phones.

One lunchtime when we were unusually pressed for time we went into the pub right outside Maidstone West station and I pointed out to Cyril that some of the station staff were also there.

'Oh, that's OK,' he said, 'so long as they're in the public bar and we're in the saloon. Then we can pretend we haven't seen them and they can pretend they haven't seen us.'

So much did I come to assume in 1979 that this sort of thing was acceptable that I went off for a drink on Saturdays when the SM was off duty. The Senior Railman and I would take turns to announce and despatch the trains at lunchtime so that we could each have the maximum time in the BR Staff Association bar across the road. One day, the Chief Booking Clerk, who had himself been an SM at one time and had been removed for some wrongdoing, emerged from the Staff Association and fell flat on his face in the station car park. He was on duty at the time. Meanwhile, on Thursdays, the local Permanent Way Supervisor would 'hold court' at the Staff Association bar, all his gangers breaking open their pay packets and spending most of the afternoon drinking.

Further along the line, the staff at Strood, which has three platforms, would talk of going over to 'Platform 4' between trains for a quick pint in the Steam

Packet. How different from the Woolwich days of a few years later when such behaviour could have led to instant dismissal for station staff, although the Permanent Way department continued to be unavailable for work on pay days for a long time to come.

For a long while one particular person had held the post of SM at Paddock Wood, apparently simply by being affable. He said to me, as a 'new boy' on the adjoining section of line in 1979, that the most important things for me to know were my Operating Rules, finishing by telling me that if there was something I wasn't sure about 'then don't ask me ... I know bugger all about it'. Similarly, when in 1982 the Woolwich Arsenal station management area was extended to take over the Greenwich line, two of us went, by appointment, to visit the Relief Station Manager who was covering Greenwich until the new organisation came in. We wanted to find out about the stations, the staff and any other useful information that would make the transition go smoothly.

First he made us a cup of tea while he told us how his sons were getting on at university and then said, 'Right, you want to know all about Greenwich – follow me!'

We saw the *Cutty Sark*, the Maritime Museum and the market. Returning to the office at about half past four the SM declared that it was time for him to be going home.

'Can you just tell us a bit about the line, though?' we naively asked him.

'Oh, don't worry about that. It'll all fall into place after a while,' said Gordon as he shepherded us out of the door.

And he was right, really: you can't hope to be told everything. You have to dive in and find out for yourself.

These Relief Station Managers were a law unto themselves in the early 1980s. Many were very senior in years and decidedly eccentric. Some could be extremely strict, but only after you'd drawn their attention to a miscreant. One of the most notorious on the South Eastern was 'Jackboot' Girling, who came along to Woolwich for a fortnight in 1983. I found him a most charming and understanding man, but having referred a persistent absentee to him, I was amazed to see this same person emerging from the SM's office twenty minutes later, pale and shaking. Another Relief SM, Len Ray, who always wore a silk handkerchief in his top pocket, would fire off requests for reports from errant staff, followed by Form 1s, like a machine gun in the first few minutes each day. Then he would sit back and take it easy for the rest of the day.

One Relief SM used to like coming to Woolwich Arsenal because he could slide unnoticed (or so he thought) out of the platform door to the SM's office, a door that nobody else ever used as they preferred to pass through the ASM's office when coming or going. Jim would then jump on the 1240 train, travelling to Lewisham where he had lunch each day with his lady friend. I don't know whether he thought that no one knew this; in fact we all did, to the extent that the Senior Railman would look out for Jim as he shot out of the side door and on to the train.

He would then ring me if I happened to be in the ASM's office with the simple message, '1240's gone, Guv.'

It became quite a joke between us.

When I was appointed to the post of Assistant Station Manager at Woolwich Arsenal in 1981 I found that the person covering the job, and with whom I 'doubled' for a couple of weeks, was a Relief Station Manager from Hastings. This chap, 'Tony' Hancock, travelled each day even though the early turn was supposed to start at 0700. Far from running across the footbridge at London Bridge to catch the first available Woolwich line train, which might just have got him to work by 0740, he would stay on the up Hastings train in order to have a cup of tea in the staff canteen at Charing Cross before eventually taking the train to Woolwich.

Then there were Relief Station Managers who liked being given two jobs on the same day. Relief Booking Clerks also operated this fiddle. What happened was that they would be given one early-turn job and one late turn by the Divisional Staffing Office, as the only means of covering both. Arriving late for the early turn at, say, Elmers End, they would tell the staff that they couldn't stay long because they had to be at, say, Sidcup later on. So, leaving Elmers End early and taking a long lunch break, they would eventually arrive late at Sidcup moaning about the workload at Elmers End that had detained them. Of course, all this was too exhausting for them and they would have to leave long before the end of the late turn. Nobody supervised these Relief staff. The Staffing Office at Beckenham seemed to take the view that so long as there was a name against each job needing cover then everything was OK. They certainly didn't want to upset these people as it might become difficult to win their co-operation in future. So everyone had an easy life.

The Network SouthEast culture, coupled with the abolition of the Divisional Staffing offices, did away with this lack of accountability and in a very short time nearly all the perpetrators had taken early retirement. The Wat Tyler Tavern had to look elsewhere for its trade, as did the Staff Association bars and the Charing Cross staff canteen. The WTT meetings were almost at the end of the chapter for drinking, as far as managers were concerned. By 1990 I think it would be fair to say that no railway manager would drink on duty, the example being set right from the top with a ban on alcohol at meetings and at office parties, unless these were held off the premises.

As the drive against drink became tighter we had to try to catch people who looked likely 'boozers', rather than just waiting for incidents to occur. One dark evening two of us did a 'stakeout' at Slade Green station and depot as it was rumoured that the Senior Railman on the station and the Depot Supervisor were nipping over the road to the railway club while on duty. I remember Karl and I hid behind a VW camper and peered through the windows to see what the Senior Railman was doing in the club. We saw him raising a full pint glass to his mouth so we waited and challenged him when he came out.

'Apple juice, Guv,' he said (in a pint glass?) and we couldn't prove otherwise, so we just cautioned him for being missing from his post.

These days, of course, the matter would be dealt with by breath-testing, but this was when such equipment was only available to the Police and, in any case, staff would not have been compelled to co-operate.

Creeping surreptitiously around the depot, we failed to catch the Supervisor misbehaving at all. We did notice, however, that two other people were slinking around in the shadows and, being concerned for the security of equipment and trains, we eventually challenged them. It turned out that they had been about to do the same to us. They were Mechanical & Electrical Engineer's management, out to catch fitters who were rumoured to be slipping out to the railway club while on duty. We gave up spying as a bad job, went to see the Supervisor and got him to take us right round the depot so that we could check that everyone who was meant to be there actually was and that they were fit for duty. From the carriage washing-machine operator to the permanent nightshift carriage-cleaning ladies, from the lowest Shunter to the Supervisor himself, everyone was working industriously and soberly. In the various mess rooms (Shunters, men cleaners and lady cleaners) the cupboards contained only tea and coffee. And yet, as we knew full well, in a place as large and complex as Slade Green depot you could hide almost anything if you really wanted to.

In the 1980s, the depot at Slade Green consisted of two sheds. The running shed was an operations responsibility while the maintenance shed was under the control of the M&EE manager.

The demands of the M&EE were always and automatically deemed unreasonable by the running shed staff and there was a constant war of attrition between the two departments, with the running Supervisor saying, 'Don't they realise we've got a service to run?' and the maintenance Supervisor saying, 'Don't they know we've got a fleet to maintain?'

Despite this, though, most units managed to get in and out according to the work programme and a great many special shunts and other movements were made each day and night to accommodate M&EE requests at the same time as meeting the traffic requirement for anything up to twenty departures each morning and evening rush hour, each of eight or ten coaches.

The running shed, in which interior cleaning and other minor servicing took place, had an amazingly dangerous traction system that was outlawed during my time in the Area. With fitters and cleaners working in, around and under the units it was obviously unsafe to have live conductor rails in the shed, so in their place there was an overhead trolley wire. To make this work you pulled the hanging trolley cable along to the required position above the end of the train to be moved and then connected the end of the cable to the power jumper on the end of the train. A good idea in principle, but the frightening thing was that the hanging cable was live at all times. After the trolley system was abandoned the safer but more time-consuming method of using a tractor unit whose front shoe was still on the third-rail outside the shed was adopted.

In the maintenance shed the heavier work was undertaken, including stripping motors, removing asbestos and implementing 'mods'. These modifications included such things as installing headlights, converting luggage racks from string to metal, etc. and were done to pre-determined programmes, some of which, such as the asbestos removal, took years to complete, the fleet being so huge. Incidentally, the replacement of string-net luggage racks by metal ones was not just a policy decision. For years there had been one person whose job it was to re-tie damaged nets and there was no problem for as long as he was there. But then he retired and with him went the expertise. Only then was it realised just how fiddly it all was.

Slade Green was also the collision damage repair depot for the Southern Region and so some pretty sorry sights were sometimes seen trundling their way there. One such was a Hastings unit, built in 1957 and which had been derailed at Appledore, tipping on to its side. This arrived in the shed for repair and the Foreman set a gang to work cutting away the damaged bodywork, the standard practice being that you kept on cutting until you reached sound metal for the repair to be based upon. Having become involved with other work, the Foreman then realised that he hadn't heard from the gang for a while. He went back to them to find that they were still cutting, a long way back from the damaged section, vainly seeking sound metal. Although these particular units were later withdrawn from service following the long-awaited Hastings electrification there are still, in the twenty-first century, diesel multiple units of the same era running on the former Southern Region with severely corroded bodywork. In 1991 I saw correspondence from the Depot Engineer at Selhurst in which he stated his opinion that if an Uckfield or Ashford–Hastings line unit was in even a minor buffer-stop collision, the frame would stop but the body would sheer off and keep moving. These same units are still in service with Connex South Central.*

By the time the Selhurst Depot Engineer wrote his letter, another positive change had been made by Network SouthEast – the Depot Engineers, along with engineers from other disciplines, were part of the Divisional Directors' teams running the Divisions, being involved in the making of decisions concerning commercial and financial activities as well as their own specialities. NSE broke down the antagonism between departments (such as at Slade Green) that had existed for so long and ushered in a new era of collective responsibility in which everyone could see directly the effect their actions would have on the end product. Under privatisation, of course, many of these same people are now up to three or four companies removed from the end product.

* 2018 update: These units have long since been withdrawn, although Pacer units with poor crashworthiness remain in operation.

21

Officers and Gentlemen

Hand in hand with the more sober attitude towards management was the gradual 'depersonalisation' of the railway. In keeping with this trend the Managing Directors of InterCity and Network SouthEast during the time I was working for those organisations were the meek-looking Dr John Prideaux and the apparently modest Chris Green, who was followed at NSE by the unheard of John Nelson. Despite this, though, Dr Prideaux and Chris Green transformed the finances, investment strategies, marketing and, perhaps most importantly in a time of great sensitivity, public and political perception of their businesses. But they did so with none of the showmanship and panache of some of the railway characters such as Malcolm Southgate or Peter Rayner, both of whom bruised their way through controversy with wit and charisma. Incidentally, both these two survived right through the age of mediocrity with Malcolm Southgate being on the board of Eurostar (UK) Ltd and Peter Rayner very much active as a railway safety campaigner and anti-privatiser.

Malcolm Southgate (who joined BR after graduating from Corpus Christi, Cambridge and was reputedly the youngest ever Station Manager at King's Cross) was Divisional Manager at Beckenham when I signed up in 1973 and was thus the first railway 'character' in any position of authority to come to my notice. He was very much of the school who got on through a combination of force of character and sheer enthusiasm for the railway. He was greatly respected by the staff. In the days when there was still a Divisional 'spirit', we had an annual charity walk on the South Eastern: in 1973 we set off from the now closed Wye racecourse with Mr Southgate and his chums in the lead after he had given us a rousing send-off. A mile or so later, however, his group was seen disappearing up a side turning. At the same time as the rest of us were losing copious amounts of fluid through sweating, Mr Southgate and his friends were doing their best to compensate by absorbing copious amounts of fluid. They emerged in time to arrive at the finishing line at what seemed to be a respectable mid-field time.

Excursion trains, marketed under the name Merrymaker, were also a feature at that time and the Divisional Manager was often to be seen on these trains, regaling staff and customers alike with witty stories and buying numerous rounds of drinks. Similarly, several people I knew were dragged into the bar at Victoria while waiting for a train home in order to have drinks poured down them by Mr Southgate.

Malcolm Southgate went on to become General Manager of BR's biggest Region, the LMR and later to occupy a series of Directorships at the Board, including those of the Policy Unit and the Channel Tunnel departments. To many of us, people like him gave a refreshing and comforting link of continuity in an industry that was changing faster than it, or we, could really cope with.

Very much of this same school of managers was Peter Rayner, the controversial Divisional Operating Superintendent at Manchester who had to leave his job because of his outspoken criticism of the Woodhead line closure and a full account of whose life and times can be read in his book *On and Off the Rails*. After serving a spell in the backrooms he re-emerged as the last Divisional Manager at Beckenham and was able to wind down the Division with none of the acrimony created by his predecessor, Bob Poynter, who, it was thought, would in fact be the last DM. Peter Rayner's blustering good humour left everyone laughing, even at their own demise. He had little time for the shallow exploits of those who thought that changing the name of something would change the substance and he was decidedly politically 'incorrect' during the 1980s, describing himself to me at a Divisional closure party as a 'moderate socialist' and having been one of the first members of the now defunct Social Democratic Party. He had the habit of 'testing' people whom he was meeting for the first time by asking things such as their opinions regarding the killing of Blair Peach at the National Front rally in 1979. I think your future standing with him depended to a large extent upon how you answered these questions. There was no place for him in the blandness of the 1990s, even though by that time he was Regional Operations Manager of the LMR. He left at about the time the Regions were finally disbanded, again in a sea of controversy, his infamous letter to the Region's Area Managers having been leaked to the press. The London *Evening Standard* and *The Times* reported this at length in August 1990, quoting his words on the pending reorganisation: 'We are ditching an understood, geographically logical organisation for a confused, geographically extraordinary organisation solely to make ultimate privatisation easier and to enable subsequent asset-stripping ... Safety is threatened ... Only blindly arrogant, politically motivated, personally ambitious people can believe in it.'

A Board spokesman was duly wheeled out to say, 'His view is emphatically not shared by the Board.'

The reorganisation in dispute was the trendily but meaninglessly entitled Organisation for Quality, or 'O for Q' as the buzzword became.

During Peter Rayner's days at Beckenham we were in the throes of the 'contracts' between ourselves at Area level and the emerging businesses, which I have mentioned earlier. Along with this was a new railway phrase: 'operations audit'. We were to be formally audited periodically to check that we were carrying out our safety and operational procedures correctly, as well as giving good value to the businesses. Our first such audit, in 1985, was to be conducted by the Divisional Manager and his Divisional Movements Manager, David Burton, and was to be an introduction to the principles of audit in order to prime us for the type of things that would be expected of us later, including the sorts of records we would need to keep. Messrs Rayner and Burton spent the afternoon discussing matters with John Norman, our Area Manager and then hosted an evening session for all the Area management in a Gravesend hotel. Serious stuff though it was, it was one of the most hilarious evenings I have ever spent, all because of Peter Rayner's spontaneous wit and humour.

Later on, as Regional Operations Manager at Crewe, Peter Rayner had little patience with the inefficiencies of InterCity On Board Services (ICOBS), for whom I was by that time working. On one occasion he boarded a train to find that there was no buffet Steward, even though supplies had been loaded. These supplies were blocking a doorway, a persistent pet hate of the Region's operating managers. His solution was to pick up the boxes of sandwiches, Danish pastries, etc. and to walk through the train giving them all away. Another time when he was dining on a train from Euston to Manchester, but alighting at Stafford, he had asked for the bill in plenty of time but the Chief Steward failed to turn up with it before the train drew into Stafford station.

The train was delayed there while the Chief Steward tried to get Mr Rayner to return to the train to pay up – 'You can't leave without paying!'

'Yes I can and I bloody well have!' – and he had.

There was a somewhat acrimonious row in correspondence between the ROM and ICOBS after this, but in the end the bill was settled.

There were plenty of other forceful characters in senior positions, too. In 1974 I was working as an Assistant Controller at Waterloo HQ Control. One winter's afternoon the door flew open and a rather scruffy man with screwed up shirt sleeves and a tatty sleeveless jumper burst into the room. I thought he was possibly a Permanent Way ganger who had got lost in the corridors. Ignoring the normal preliminary courtesy of greeting the Deputy Chief Controller (as the person in charge on each shift), he started shouting at the Locomotive Controller. Before the Loco Controller could explain himself, the whirlwind had taken itself back out of the room.

'That was our boss,' the DCC explained to me, 'the Chief Operating Manager, George Weeden.'

This fiery character, with his no-nonsense style and intimate knowledge of what made a busy railway tick, would seem ludicrous in this age of smart suits and of the understanding of 'concepts' in place of hard experience. When the front cover of the Working publications read 'By Order, G.A. Weeden, Chief Operating Manager', you knew it really was by order.

On the Southern's South Western Division there was another such character as Divisional Manager around 1980. Bernard Whitehall had a reputation for being short-tempered. The story went that during a visit to Woking yard one day he spotted a small building that he had not been shown around and which had the appearance of being a Shunters' lobby or something of that sort. Marching into this building he started berating the man inside about the appalling state of the interior.

'Get these f****** papers tidied up and make sure the bloody floor is swept,' was the gist of his rebuke before he rushed on to deliver similar harangues elsewhere, leaving the tenant coal merchant to wonder what had hit him.

Meanwhile, on the Central Division there was a different kind of eccentric in the position of Divisional Manager. In 1979 I was taken on as a Management Trainee (more about that later) and allocated to the Central. My colleague, Susan Carey, and I were required to report to Mr Mackmurdie at Essex House, Croydon. Mackmurdie was an ex-London Midland Region manager who, it was rumoured, despised the Southern and all who worked there. He sat us down on two very low chairs on one side of his desk while he appeared to be sitting on a very high chair on his side. His secretary came in with a tray bearing one cup and saucer, a milk jug and a teapot, all made of bone china. As he poured his tea he peered over his reading glasses down at us, explaining his so-called 'open door' policy of management. Maybe he didn't realise how incongruous this seemed to us or how intimidating and distant he appeared to be.

This same man, it turned out, rather bizarrely, was a collector of regional variations of rugby songs. He travelled around the country noting different versions in different parts of Britain and researching their origins. He was interested in football, too. One day a major signalling failure had made hundreds of Brighton and Hove Albion fans late for a match at Crystal Palace. As a regular attendee of their home matches, Mackmurdie arranged with the club for him to come on to the pitch before the start of the next match to broadcast an apology to the fans. Or so the story around the Division went. His courage was obviously not as delicate as his tea set.

Individualism expressed itself at all levels until the time came when everyone was expected to conform to the business ideals of the image-makers of the 1980s. I have already mentioned the affectations of certain office workers in the days when the railway still had huge teams of Clerical Officers wading through vast heaps of correspondence. Each person expressed, quite freely and often controversially, their political and other beliefs. They dressed with personal eccentricity or scruffiness and they had their own catchphrases and mannerisms that would elicit cries of derision or loud cheers each time they were pronounced or displayed. There were routines that were repeated at certain times each day, very few of which had any relevance to the work of the office. Even in those large, smoky rooms of the 1970s open-plan era there were very few nondescript people, despite the fact that they were basically nine-to-five Clerks. PCs, mainframes, electronic mailing and disc storage of information have their own quirks, of course, but not in such an entertaining way as their predecessors – the real people of the clumsy, inefficient, obstructive, frustrating but never dull railway of the past.

One interesting aspect of moving around from Region to Region in the mid 1970s was seeing the difference in management styles and realising that the railways had been nationalised only in name and a few superficial details in 1948. On the Southern the managers were loud, sharp and forceful, swearing a lot, their sleeves rolled up, not thinking themselves to be any different from anyone else. The London Midland managers seemed to have been selected from the officers' mess of a propagandist British war movie, while on the Western they were kindly old boys who probably breezed in for a few hours just to check that the chaps were all right before settling into comfortable armchairs with their pipes and *The Times* in gentlemen's clubs in Piccadilly, oblivious to the fact that the railways had been nationalised. Of course, I am talking here about the Regional Headquarters' offices, where old attitudes could persist, safe from the reality of the railway outside. This said, and in my experience, the HQ management of the Southern was markedly more 'in touch' with reality than the other two I have mentioned and this was possibly a positive legacy from the pre-nationalisation days when the Southern had been led by the innovative and expansionist Sir Herbert Walker. The Southern had always been a working railway and had no delusions of grandeur.

Some managers became almost legendary figures amongst the staff and the force of their characters shaped the way many of us saw the railway. For example, in the 1970s the names Brian Hamment-Arnold and Allan Barter were virtually synonymous with the words 'South Eastern'. Hamment-Arnold, as Divisional Movements Manager, who saw out several Divisional Managers without ever securing the post for himself, kept a tight stranglehold on all aspects of the Division's operations. 'H-A' personally examined all potential Signalmen (and there were a great many more boxes then than now) and was the scourge of all operating staff, turning up unannounced at the most extraordinary places at the most unlikely times. Tales abounded about these visits, many probably exaggerated. One story I liked concerned H-A's having got wind of a rumour that the late evening staff at Faversham were leaving just one person in charge of the station while the rest slipped out to the pub. One night, finding just one person on the station, Hamment-Arnold went across the road to the Railway Hotel, ordered a half, turned to the panicking station staff who were hoping he hadn't seen them, said, 'Good evening, gentlemen,' and calmly sat at their table. Embarrassed and scared beyond measure, the staff, not daring to take the smallest sip from their glasses, shuffled out of the pub while Mr Hamment-Arnold serenely finished his drink. For weeks those staff were sweating, awaiting their Form Ones, but H-A evidently thought the point had been made sufficiently, for there were no repercussions. The Station Manager probably got a rocket, however.

Every morning, except when he was out and about on the Division, H-A would come into the Control to find out how the trains were running. As well as speaking to the Deputy Chief Controller he would walk round the panels, checking the running sheets and listening to what the Controllers were saying to each other and on the phone.

If he saw a late start or a delay on the sheets without an accompanying explanation he would say, 'Why is this?' and if you couldn't answer straight away he would tell you to find out. Frequently he would remember and the next time he saw you he would say, 'What was the reason for the late start on the 0819 Barnehurst the other day?'

You were expected not only to have found out at the time but also to have remembered. And that was on a Division that ran more than 2,000 trains every weekday.

The other 'institution' on the South Eastern in those days was Allan Barter, a Mechanical and Electrical Engineer, who had started out working for Brush at Loughborough and who had gone on to design the Isle of Wight electrification scheme using redundant London Transport stock. He was a leading proponent of electric traction, a subject on which he was an expert, and was Chairman of the Electric Railway Society. I remember his disappointment when the electric Class 71s were put into storage, but more about them later on. In the 1970s and '80s Mr Barter was Divisional Traction Engineer on the South Eastern and could be seen, dressed invariably in a heavyweight three-pieced tweed suit, pockets bulging with pens, screwdrivers and other gadgets, sucking on his pipe on the 'bridge' at Beckenham. His office was in a small wing of the building and from the window of the Control we could look up and across at this wing, which resembled the bridge of a ship. Many times the cry of 'Captain Barter's at the helm' would go up and there he would be, gazing out meditatively into the distance as the trains passed below. He was in charge of rolling stock and traction maintenance, and was another person who cropped up at all sorts of places at all hours. As with Hamment-Arnold, he saw out several management regimes, none of which dared to challenge his position. Well into the 1980s I remember him turning up at a main line freight derailment at Hoo Junction in the dead of night in his capacity as the person in ultimate charge of the rerailing gang. He gave a few instructions from time to time before stepping back to relight his pipe and watch the work.

In the cold night air his bulk and natural air of authority made him resemble the Reverend W. Awdry's Fat Controller and he was evidently aware of this, saying to me as he returned from issuing an instruction to the gang, 'My doctor has ordered me not to push ...'

The fact that these stalwarts stayed in their jobs for years and believed fervently in what they were doing gave the railway a solidity and continuity of purpose that was firmly based at the roots of what the railway is really about, i.e. the running of trains. Now that these men are in retirement, I wonder what they have made of Government ministers, company directors and others who have played around shiftily with the railway, quoting vague ideological concepts that come nowhere near to recognising the realities of running a railway but which have put in jeopardy those realities, simply by means of their oversimplification and ignorance of the facts.

While railway managers of the 1970s and early '80s aspired to the solid kind of experience personified by these true railwaymen, this became unfashionable as the years went by. Whereas in earlier times one might try to imply that one had longer service and greater operating experience than was really the case, the later railway manager would consider that a correct business attitude was infinitely more valuable. The reason for this was clear: the years of hard railway experience meant that you were, or could be perceived to be, part of a reactionary culture that was no longer politically acceptable in an era in which the Government was proposing that the railway be run by record shop proprietors, bus conductors and merchant bankers. The lasting job of actually running the trains was being marginalised and this was a dangerous development in an industry that needed the continuity of learning from its past mistakes and experiences – and I use the word 'dangerous' in its most literal sense.

Along with the great characters, many thousands of railway managers were made redundant as sectorisation and privatisation took place, wiping out a wealth of experience and at the same time eliminating resistance to the emerging naivety about how the railway should be run.

In my own case, which was not at all unusual, having had thousands spent on me as a Management Trainee in 1979–81 and having been made redundant in 1993, a relative said to me, 'What a waste of all that money spent on training you' but she couldn't see that to have been a Trainee from the 1970s was actually an impediment in the 1990s, not an attribute.

It would be like the chief of security at the Berlin Wall emphasising his past when applying for a job at Disneyland Paris.

22

Old Boys, Sherry Parties and Mushy Peas

The Management Training Scheme to which I referred in the last chapter had its own, sometimes sad, story. Having already worked on the railway for six years (1973–79) I was amazed to find that graduate entrants were being plunged into what was essentially the 1950s. Despite what I have said about the Southern being more 'hands on', its training scheme was chronically out of date and even had mechanisms built into it to keep it that way. The freight training, for instance, concentrated on the dying vacuum-braked shunting yards and included little about the emerging Speedlink network or the growing trainload freight market. We learned about trunking and sorting in old-fashioned parcels depots, all of which were to be closed within a couple of years. We barely touched new signalling technology or modern rolling stock design, instead spending our time in Absolute Block boxes and decrepit maintenance sheds. We were frowned upon if we asked about management information systems or if we challenged the unwieldy industrial-relations practices. The emphasis was all on learning how to operate the railway as we found it, not on the development of fresh thinking.

The Southern loved to perpetuate this dated approach to management training. It even had an 'old boys' club of which you automatically became a member if you were a trainee – the Southern Railway Cadets' Association. They held an annual dinner at which Bertie Wooster would have felt at home and they liked to pretend that they were an elite, immune from the passing of time. The Secretary issued a membership list annually and it included the 'year' you belonged to and your latest position on the railway. If you left BR, other than through retirement, you vanished from the list as those who chose to leave were not considered to be of the right calibre to be mentioned any more, even though many went on to do far grander things. The list went back to 1949, when the person who was in charge of our training in 1979 had himself been a Cadet. Hiding in his office at Waterloo, Derrick Willey probably thought things were much the same as they had been in 1949.

The training scheme was carefully designed to make protest (or even constructive criticism and suggestion) difficult and I often wonder whether the Regional management realised how cleverly this was engineered by the training people. Several times a year we appeared before a 'Training Committee' consisting of a panel of senior Regional managers. On other Regions this was the opportunity for them to find out how the training was going, what your thoughts were and what opinions, ideas and needs you had; but not on the Southern. In order that you had no time to state any opinions or get the training altered to suit your own strengths, weaknesses or interests you had to prepare a report for the Committee on a subject decided for you by the training people but which had no bearing on the training itself. The interview then consisted mainly of the panel analysing this report, thus precluding any discussion of the training. This was a shocking abuse of the panel's time and of ours, bearing in mind the amounts being spent on our training and the management time they gave up for these committees. Basically it sheltered them from finding out how their successors were being trained and kept us from any discussion of the wider issues we were interested in tackling these senior managers about.

In between spells of practical training in depots, stations, yards and signalboxes we had residential sessions, at which all thirty or so of us, from Inverness to Swansea and Plymouth, met up. These were mainly at The Grove, which had at one time been the country seat of the Earl of Clarendon who, we were told, had given it to the old London, Midland & Scottish Railway, of which he was a Director. This splendid house, with its landscaped gardens, stood in an estate that straddled the Grand Union Canal just north of Watford, the drive crossing the canal by means of an ornate stone bridge. The Grove was for many years the Board's Management Training Centre. Here we studied signalling theory; indulged in problem-solving courses; took part in management games, interviews and mock negotiations; listened to visiting speakers who came from engineering, marketing and financial disciplines; and treated ourselves to heavy drinking in the evenings and partying at night in order to compensate for the rigours of the day. To add a touch of gentility to the proceedings, and to compensate for the debauchery of our late-night behaviour, some of us formed a sherry club and would congregate in the library before lunch to take our aperitifs in the relative grandeur of the recently restored room.

At other times we stayed at the more austere Webb House at Crewe, a former London & North Western Railway orphanage where you were awoken each morning by a man walking along the corridors ringing a loud handbell. The catering at Webb House was more basic and homely than at The Grove and the ladies who cooked and served it always called you 'love'. The contrast between The Grove and Webb House was as if someone had decided to caricature the stereotypes of North and South. At Webb House we learned about computerised operational management systems and in the evenings we slipped out along the road behind the massive railway works in order to drink Boddingtons and Robinsons at street corner locals or to get fish, chips and mushy peas from shops set in the middle of endless red brick terraces. Several relationships were struck up during these residential courses and at least two marriages ensued within our group. After each week at either The Grove or Webb House there were invariably new sources of gossip and scandal.

As a lover of old signalboxes I didn't mind the outdated training we received in the practical signalling part of our training. Being let loose with the quaint and potentially dangerous Tyer's two-position lock and block system between Horsham and Christ's Hospital, for instance, was a real treat and I was lucky to have had the opportunity of working with it. The telegraphic block instruments consisted of miniature signal semaphore arms in little glass-fronted boxes and these went up and down as you gave 'Line Clear' or 'Line Blocked'. They dated from 1874. Another delight was operating the mechanical monstrosity that constituted Redhill 'B' box's Down Platform Starter. This had a contraption next to the signal that looked like the bottom of a dustbin and, depending upon which route you pulled, different metal discs would move to reveal either the letter M for main, T for Tonbridge or R for Reigate. Sheer mechanical genius, as was so much of the signalling. Redhill was altogether an amazing place from the signalling point of view, not least because of the short distances between Earlswood, Redhill 'B' and Redhill 'A' boxes that had resulted in dispensation being given from the need to exchange the 'Call Attention' bell-code before offering a train to the next box. 'Call Attention' was one of the most rigorously enforced bell-codes in most boxes. As with so many things we were trained on, the signalling at Redhill and at Horsham was shortly afterwards replaced, coming under the Three Bridges Signalling Centre.

Most of the Signalmen I learned with were real 'old-timers'. They were unrelentingly meticulous about the use of dusters with which to hold the levers and about not standing on the frame (you never touched a lever with your bare hand and you never allowed your shoe to touch the frame). All instruments and levers were polished each time they were used by the duster that was perpetually in your hand. These men were the kings of their boxes and even the Station Managers would knock before coming into the signalboxes, making sure they wiped their feet carefully on the doormat. One man at Redhill 'B', Vic Gander, was the scourge of the local management and I was warned to be very careful about what I said and did during my time with him – but my admiration for his skill, timing and detailed operating knowledge overwhelmed any fear of him that people had tried to put into me. We got on well and he taught me a lot.

Sometimes you had to find things out for yourself, though. Whilst working Barnham box one afternoon, the Signalman left me to deal with a train coming up from the Bognor Regis branch. Having received 'Line Clear' from Arundel Junction box I was in a position to be able to pull off all the relevant stop signals and therefore also the associated distant signal, which, in effect, indicates to the Driver that he has a clear run. Try as I might, though, I could not get the distant to pull, even with one foot up on the adjoining plate provided for the purpose. The Signalman, who had been watching me with a wry smile on his face, put down his cup of tea and let me know that no one in living memory had been known to pull off the Up Bognor Distant.

The train was still in rear of the signal, so we decided to make a joint effort of it. Together we just did it and a couple of minutes later the Bognor Regis to Victoria came by with the Driver hooting and waving, having never seen the distant signal off before and no doubt having seen it shaking up and down as we tried to pull it off. The pull was something in the order of 1,200 yards of wire, going round a sharp curve and therefore having even more resistance than the distance would have you believe. All over the railway in the old boxes there were long mechanical pulls and you recognised them not only from the box diagram that gave distances but mainly from the footplate positioned halfway up the adjoining lever. These plates were there in order to reduce the likelihood of Signalmen rupturing themselves as the physical exertion needed to operate them was considerable. Of course, a lot of it was down to skill as well as sheer strength, much as is the coupling and uncoupling of trains. The way to manage a long pull was first to take up the slack and then slam the lever home with a sudden burst of strength, making sure that your foot was pressing firmly on the plate.

I remember saying, naively, to one Signalman that at least it should be easy to put the signal back on one of these long pulls. But it wasn't, because if you simply released the catch to free the lever from the 'out' position on the frame, the tension in the wire would make the lever shoot back into the frame, catapulting you headfirst into the instrument shelf. So you had to gather all your strength and restrain the lever on its way back into the frame, again, if necessary, using the footplate to give you the leverage with which to slow it down.

One afternoon I was working Chichester box, which was a nightmare because in addition to the normal bell-codes you had to send the special code 'train approaching' to the boxes either side as well as operating two closed-circuit TV level crossings. The train register had to be completed for each train as well. At that time the Drayton to Lavant stone trains were running and so we had a lot of locomotive movements. On the day in question I had pulled off the 'dummy' signal in the yard for a light Class 73 engine to come out on to the running line and was so busy sorting out the bell-codes and level crossings that I was slow in replacing the dummy at danger. Just as I was about to do this a second light engine 'took the road' and came out on to the running line, which was highly irregular. The Driver should have waited for the signal to be replaced and then cleared again as his was an entirely separate move. However, the Signalman said he wouldn't report it as the root cause of the error had been the fact that I was so slow.

As I had been working as an Assistant Station Manager on an Absolute Block line before the management training began I had already had some signalling experiences. There was one man at Maidstone West box who was willing to let me work the box while he sat back, although he always kept an eye on me. With well over 100 levers, the box was so long that two sets of diagrams and instruments were provided so that you didn't waste time walking backwards and forwards all the time. As well as having highly polished instruments and levers, the brass catches of the sash windows and the brass door handles were constantly gleaming. Unfortunately, by the time I came along a lot of the signalling was redundant, having related to the yard, bay platforms and the former line to Tovil. Maidstone West box still stands, the frame perched high above the track over its complicated interlocking mechanism.

As well as a band of highly skilled Signalmen there was also a dying breed of mechanical-locking technicians. Modern boxes have solid-state interlocking to prevent the setting up of conflicting moves and to ensure that the setting up of routes is done in the prescribed safe order. Before solid state there were relays and before that, mechanical interlocking. Network Rail signalling nowadays incorporates all three systems in varying degrees. While relays and, particularly, solid state take up very little space, the hardware in mechanical boxes can be very extensive. Each box has a locking chart that shows, to use the Barnham story above as a simple example, that a distant signal cannot be pulled off unless all associated stop signals are already off. This has to be translated into a mechanical means of preventing the distant from being pulled before the others. As the interlocking also applies to the telegraphic block instruments (so that the section signal cannot be pulled unless the box in advance has accepted the train) and to points (so that signals cannot be pulled for a route that is not set), the combinations of locking bars beneath the signalling frame can be extremely complicated and bulky, which is one reason why most boxes are raised. In some old boxes the interlocking can become worn, making the job of the locking technician even more difficult if he is to ensure that the integrity of the locking chart is maintained. Locking technicians are another example of a 'one-off' railway job: theirs is a specialism peculiar to the railway and vital for its safety. No other transport system separates the movements of its vehicles with such stringency as the railway industry.

As is inevitable in a large industry, not all the people I met in signalboxes were 'professionals'. I visited the box at Gomshall in Surrey with the Assistant Station Manager from Redhill one day during my management training. She explained to me that the young Signalman had only recently been reinstated after having been disciplined for loosening the bolts on one of the track fishplates outside the box. Apparently he was a railway enthusiast and liked there to be a lot of railway noise as trains went over the joints. I mentioned earlier the anomaly by which young Signalmen were left to work unsupervised in country boxes and things like this were the inevitable consequences.

That same day Gillian Fisher and I visited a remote crossing keeper's cottage at the foot of the North Downs, which was still tied to the railway and was, to say the least, somewhat primitive. So that they could each have some time off, the husband and wife took turns opening the gates for the occasional road user, the normal position of the gates being closed to the road (as, strictly, all level crossing gates and barriers were until recently). There are still a few of these tied crossing houses today, a relic from another era. After sampling the delights of the rural North Downs line, we went for afternoon tea at the watermill at Abinger Hammer, eating sandwiches made with the famous locally grown watercress as we sat by the mill race. A day of contrasts, as so many were on the railway.

One of the most important aspects of the formal operations management training was Single Line Working, or, as the older Rule Books long-windedly called it 'Working Traffic of a Double Line over a Single Line of Rails during Repairs or Obstruction'. In the hierarchy of operational procedures this was near the top and we would be expected to be able to implement it safely if the need arose. So we were trained in the duties of the 'Responsible Officer' and 'Pilotman', either or both of which posts we would have to assume in an emergency. We had to know which signals you could use when running in the wrong direction and which points had to be secured, amongst other things. 'Single Line Working' forms had to be correctly completed and issued to the right people, too. There were special procedures for level crossings, especially where they were normally worked by treadles as these would be activated in the reverse order by a train running 'wrong line'. The Pilotman had to decide the order in which trains were to run on the single line and had to ride on the last train of each flight, acting as a line token. Single Line Working was, and still is, a gem of railway operating procedure whose safety relies mainly on people being properly trained to carry it out. As with many of the old procedures, its use has declined over the years as more and more lines become reversibly signalled and as the expertise is lost.

Not so long after we had finished our training a friend of mine from the training, Nick Mulhall, who worked in the same Area as I did, had to implement Single Line Working on the Maidstone West line while a signalling failure at Snodland was rectified. This failure, incidentally, was caused by the notoriously worn-out state of the interlocking at that box. I was out in the Area car, conveying our new Area Manager on a tour of various freight terminals and we happened to drop in at Snodland signalbox just as Nick was assuming the role of Responsible Officer and working out exactly what preparations needed to be made and who was available to make them. He decided to double as Pilotman, which was then permissible and later became the norm, but he needed someone to clip the points on the up line at Holborough Sidings as these would become facing for a train running in the wrong direction. He told us to do this and off we went with the new Area Manager driving the car.

As we shot by Holborough Cement Works I said, 'That's the turning we need.'

He had been going to take us to Halling Cement Works and clip the points there, which are on the down line.

This episode highlighted two important aspects of safety management. First, that once a person is appointed to a responsible position in emergency, other people, no matter how senior, must act on that person's instructions and, secondly, that it is vital that everyone knows precisely what they are doing and where everything is. This is why aspiring railway managers until the 1980s had such intense and detailed training in operating procedures. Incidentally, if we had have clipped the wrong points there would have been safeguards because the Rule Book stipulated that a green lamp or flag was to be clearly displayed at facing points that had been secured, that the Pilotman was to remind all Drivers of the locations of such points, and that Drivers were then not to exceed 10mph over them. So, in practice, a train running wrong line would have (or should have) stopped short of Holborough Sidings until the points had been properly secured. As with all well thought-out safety procedures, Single Line Working had no total reliance on just one person but had its own inbuilt checks.

The management training, despite its shortcomings, gave us some good days out. The ships, hovercraft and hotels were still owned by BR at that time so we had a spell with those organisations. On a hovercraft trip we went up, one at a time, to the pilot's cabin, while on an overnight Harwich to Hook of Holland crossing we spent some time in the engine room and on the bridge. We were shown how to operate the computer-based navigational forecasting system that plotted the course of all vessels in the vicinity and would draw attention to potential convergences. We were met in Holland by a chap from the Dutch Railways, who took us to several of the town's bars. On another occasion, our planned ride on the train ferry from Dover to Dunkerque had to be cancelled because of a French seamen's strike, so we used the free tickets we'd been given for a day out in Calais, catching up with the train ferry later. While we were training with Freightliner we went aboard a freight vessel that had been converted from passenger use and still had a marvellous wood-panelled dining room.

The culmination of the management training, which was heavily biased towards operating procedures for the reasons I have said, was a mock incident. In our year, we went to the sidings at Letchworth where communications had been set up as if we were at various locations spread over several miles. Different groups were given different responsibilities and messages went to and fro about ordinary train running events until, without notice, one was received saying that there had been a passenger train collision. Depending upon our allocated responsibilities we all had different things to do and, of course, were expected to know how to do them. One important aspect was communication: the need for it, the difficulties in establishing it and the problems of maintaining it. In this respect the mock incident was realistic in that when there is a real incident, communication immediately seizes up as everyone tries simultaneously to find out what is going on. In other ways, though, the mock incident was fairly meaningless, as no two incidents are ever the same and so you can never hope to achieve a blueprint. The person in charge of dealing with the incident in our group was Julian Worth, who, it was obvious to us all even then, was going to be the high flier of our year and who eventually became Managing Director of Transrail before their takeover by EWS. My more lowly position was that of co-ordinating the emergency buses, which I apparently forgot to cancel when 'normal working' resumed. For this I was criticised, whereas, of course, in real life there would have been real buses and their drivers there to remind me.

Because aspiring railway managers at that time were all expected to have a firm operating background to their experience, all trainees were appointed, after training, to junior operations management posts, which in fact meant a Supervisory rather than Management grade. Until the early 1980s there was no choice in this as the more specialist Finance, Personnel and Marketing training schemes had not at that time been introduced. Many trainees, however, had joined the railway in the hope of getting into these areas, in which they already had degrees, and had hung on to the hope of getting out of a dirty shift-working operations job, even as a first appointment. Hence it was that many trainees left as the training drew to a close or else shortly afterwards and a lot of useful expertise was lost.

Different Regions had different ideas about the kinds of jobs trainees should be slotted into and there were many problems to be overcome, not least of which was the fact that every time a trainee was inserted into a vacancy, someone else's promotional hopes were dashed. Thus trainees had to deal not only with their own lack of direct experience but also in many cases with a lot of ill-feeling from people around them. Because some staff were perceived to be being 'disadvantaged' by trainees, the Transport & Salaried Staffs' Association (which was the Clerical and Supervisory trade union and of which I was a member) had a policy of non-co-operation with management trainees, who were deemed to be graduates abusing privilege. In practice there was hardly any non-co-operation but where I did come across it I always pointed out that the training scheme was not just for graduate entrants but also for existing staff. The selection process had not appeared to me to favour one group over the other, although staff entrants were in a decided minority.

Female trainees in operating jobs were still subject in some cases to unreasonable prejudice and one of my 'fellows' had to endure Drivers at Newcastle refusing to have any dealings with her. This sort of nonsense should have elicited the strongest possible management action and also condemnation by ASLEF but the attitude taken seemed to be that Noreen probably wouldn't be in the job long anyway, so what did it matter for a while? Noreen left and has since become a Schools Inspector, another loss of talent from the railway.

The Eastern Region in the early 1980s appointed trainees to station Supervisory positions on its large stations or to Station Managerships on small branch lines, such as Malton. Some Western trainees went straight into freight management and did very well out of it, as well as avoiding platform loads of angry passengers in the rush hour. The London Midland and Scottish Regions put their trainees into Supervisory jobs in busy places, freight or passenger, while the Southern seemed to seek out the least popular Assistant Station Manager posts to put its trainees into, although some went straight into very junior Station Manager posts. I had high hopes of being appointed to the post of Station Manager, Romsey, but the job was abolished just before we qualified. Had my ambition been fulfilled I would have been on duty, bowler-hatted, when the Royal Train bearing the newly married Prince and Princess of Wales arrived – but it was not to be. I was destined for the London suburbs.

With typical rivalry, the Central Divisional management called Susan Carey and me in to tell us that they were preparing to appoint us to certain posts within the Division, while the Region had already said that appointments were to be made by the Training Committee. So we were caught between them and, to some extent, fell out with both parties as we tried to disentangle ourselves. As it turned out, she went to the South Western and I went to the South Eastern, so we both left the Central Division.

All six of us on the Southern were thrust into busy suburban areas with booking offices dealing in millions each year, lots of staffing problems, lots of train cancellations, a high incidence of vandalism and a feeling that we were being tested to see if we would break. Some graduates had, perhaps, a brilliant business aptitude, but if they failed to hold their heads above water in their first appointments, they were deemed to be no good. Of the six of us, four still work in the railway industry, which I think is probably above the average after twenty years.*

* 2018 update: Thirty-five years after the training ended, three of us are still doing railway work. Also, as from the thirtieth anniversary of starting the training, we now have an annual reunion for all the 1979 trainees. So in a much changed world we maintain contact.

23

'Line-Cred'

There were certain incidents you were expected to have got 'under your belt' as an Assistant Station Manager or Station Manager on the Southern in the 1980s and true credibility amongst your peers could only be achieved by having dealt with these. People who had come up through the ranks usually had a head start here, but trainees were watched to see how they would shape up under pressure. Experience of abuse from passengers was vital, but an assault by a passenger or a member of staff really showed that you were getting stuck in. Catching someone out defrauding the railway did you a lot of credit, as did dealing with a derailment. Getting someone dismissed for drinking or fighting was a good move in the credibility stakes, too. Proving early on that you could take point-winding, hook-switch operating, signal flagging and manual operation of level crossings in your stride all helped, but above all else there was one thing on the Southern that you had to have dealt with in order to prove to your colleagues that you'd really arrived as an operating manager and that was a death on the line. Not a very pleasant subject, but one that all railway operating staff have to get involved in from time to time and so just as much a part of railway activity as anything else.

Fatalities (as opposed to the famous railway announcing malapropism 'trains are delayed due to a fertility on the line') tested you not only as a railway manager but also as a person as they obviously touched you in a way far deeper than any other railway event. Hence the tacit recognition that you had made it once you had dealt with your first fatality. Some managers would discreetly look at the evidence to see whether you had taken an undue time getting to the site or other signs of 'chickening out'. The railway instruction was that you were to try to get there before the Police arrived, the aim being that the remains should be moved, by you, clear of the line so that trains could start running again. We were told that merely noting the original position was sufficient. The Police, of course, thought differently and wanted the body left in its original position for as long as it took for them to make their inquiries, the question of running trains being of no interest to them. Sometimes, perhaps needless to say, there was no recognisable body as such, just bits and pieces strewn along the line and on the front and underside of the train. Ones like that always took a long time to deal with as the Police wanted to be able to account for at least the main parts of the body. Occasionally this was not possible – one night near Haywards Heath the Police and railway staff could not account for one of the victim's arms and had to conclude that it had been taken by a fox or other predator.

Similarly, but more gruesomely, a train had hit a man on an accommodation crossing near West Malling in Kent one dark evening and the line had been blocked for about two hours while the body was accounted for and the evidence assessed. In the end, the man's head could not be found and the train was sent forward out of service to Ashford station, from where it was to go to Chart Leacon depot for forensic examination under proper lighting. Now the people on site realised that the front of the train had blood and other remains on it, but passengers and staff at Ashford were horrified to see it drawing into the brightly lit station with a head tucked behind one of the buffers. The Station Supervisor quickly evacuated the platform and reported that it appeared to be the head of a young boy. In fact the man was at least 70 years of age, but in death all the years had been wiped away.

My involvement in that incident was simply as the Controller who took the calls. My own real initiation was with a mentally disturbed man at Maze Hill near Greenwich. A lot of railway suicides are mentally ill people. This one was known to have been a risk to himself and one day he jumped off the parapet of a bridge in front of an up train. It took a long time to clear up and for days afterwards there were still little bits along the lineside until nature's scavengers dealt with the things that humans couldn't or didn't want to have to deal with.

Drivers, of course, are often in shock after such events and have to be relieved from duty. After dark, there may be no warning of the incident, just a thump, but in daylight it is different. One afternoon in 1973 I was on board the 1640 Victoria to Ramsgate, standing with some colleagues in an intermediate brakevan as there were no seats available. As we approached

Rainham the Driver suddenly made a full emergency brake application, which we could not only feel and hear but also see on the brake gauge. He was also leaning on the horn and pressing the Guard's communication bell continuously. The train eventually shuddered to a halt with both bell and horn still sounding. The Driver was found by the Guard simply sitting in his cab, head bowed and unable to say anything. It turned out that a man had stood in front of the approaching train in full view of the Driver, deliberately ignoring the sounding horn and eventually going under as the Driver watched in horror. This was a young Driver who had only qualified a few months earlier. A much more experienced Driver told me that he reckoned a Driver on the South Eastern suburban lines would average one death every ten years, that being his own tally in thirty years of driving.

The Rainham incident I described was without doubt a deliberate act – the man had been told that very day that he was terminally ill, it transpired – while the West Malling one may have been due to confusion on the part of the victim or to poor sight or hearing. Other tragedies occur as a result of trespassing on the line and this mainly affects children. There are notorious black spots where holes are made in fences in order to make short cuts, through which children then venture. One such was near the Dutch House bridge on the Sidcup line where Drivers would often stop to report children playing on or near the line, which is electrified on the third-rail system. One afternoon in 1986 I had to drive the Traffic Manager for that line from Dartford to the Dutch House to deal with a small girl who had been found electrocuted on the line. The railway was often blamed for allowing gaps to remain in fences but there was a strong moral onus on the public too, not only to report such gaps but not to make them in the first place.

Sometimes it is difficult for coroners to come to a satisfactory conclusion in railway fatality cases. One night in 1989, as I was speaking to the Sleeping Car Attendants on the 2325 Euston to Edinburgh, the train came to an abrupt halt somewhere near Stafford. The Driver had heard a bump on the front of the locomotive and it turned out that we had hit someone. In the circumstances there were no witnesses; not even the Driver could say whether the person was trying to get out of the way or not. The bloodstained, brand new Class 90 'Skoda' had to be detached and replaced at Crewe, where the front of the engine was not a pretty sight in the station lights.

Years earlier, when I was Assistant Traction Controller on the Western, there had been a 'bump in the night' incident that was more conclusive. Drivers of a couple of freight trains had reported something dragging along the tops of their cabs as they went under a bridge near Slough. As daylight dawned, a body was found hanging from the bridge. At around the same time we had a spate of decapitations in South Wales, in which people quite deliberately knelt with their heads across the nearside rail as trains approached. A lot of railway people wondered whether media reporting of the first such incident had given the others the idea and that the subsequent ones were therefore 'copycat' incidents. Most staff believed to some extent in the superstition that suicides came in threes and this could have had some basis of truth if media reporting did in fact have some influence.

Numerous incidents concern animals on the line, from the squirrel running ahead of the train along the top of the offside rail as I rode in the cab of a Class 33 from Exeter St Davids to Waterloo in 1975 (it jumped aside just in time) to horses on the line near Slade Green in 1983, which caused damage to the brake gear of two trains as well as electrocution and other injury to the horses, all thanks to some thoughtless person leaving an accommodation crossing gate open. Of much greater note, there was the Scotrail Express that was derailed after hitting a cow, leading to questions about the lack of weight of the driving trailer vehicles that were in use there at the time and that are still in use elsewhere.* Had the train been travelling locomotive first it probably would not have come off the track.

One Saturday morning at Woolwich Arsenal in 1983 an Alsatian dog slipped as it was boarding a train with its owners and fell down between the train and the platform near where I was standing. The dog panicked under the train, leaping up and hitting itself repeatedly on the underside of the train before touching the juice rail and dying through electrocution. The distraught owners waited on the platform while we dispatched the train, the body fortunately being clear of the wheels. We then had to obtain clearance from the Signalman at Dartford to go down and lift the body onto the platform. The owners asked if the dog could be buried by the lineside and our local Permanent Way gang did this for them. Subsequently the owners

* 2018 update: 'Lightweight' driving trailers are no longer in use.

made a donation to the Woking Homes, the Southern's children's home, so they evidently did not put any blame on the railway for what had happened.

Another day, in 1979, when I was at Maidstone West, a swan was electrocuted near New Hythe. Remembering something about swans having a special royal status, I reported the incident to the Police but I could not elicit much interest from them. Perhaps I should have written directly to the Queen.

Some railway staff put themselves at risk by taking short cuts with safety, usually to save time. In the early days of our management training in 1979 we were all taken aside to be told of the death of a recently qualified trainee who had got himself crushed between two sets of Freightliner wagons, there being strict guidelines concerning the distance to be allowed between vehicles before it is considered safe to cross the line. Then one day in 1984 I remember being horrified to see one Guard's method of indicating to the Driver of a stone train that he could set back into the siding at Allington, near Maidstone. Instead of walking up the lineside until he was in view of the Driver and then giving the correct handsignal to set back, he had arranged with the Driver that he would give him a 'splash' on the brake gauge by opening and then closing the brake valve on the rearmost wagon. This involved standing in the four-foot directly behind the train. As well as causing a whiplash effect on the loose brake jumper that could have knocked him over, there were many other reasons why he could have tripped and fallen over in the path of the reversing train.

Most at risk have always been Permanent Way and other staff working on the line 'between trains' and over the years the railway has had to tighten up considerably on their means of protection with better warning systems and greater use of line possessions. Riding in the front of what was then known as an AM10 unit on a Euston–Bletchley service near Carpenders Park one day in the mid 1970s, I heard the Driver sounding the horn more and more urgently. I peered up through the glass screen that divided the passenger saloon from the cab and saw a permanent way worker standing next to our line, bending over some equipment on the adjoining line and with his back to the train. He was simply not responding to the Driver's warning. As the train swept by, the Driver looked back out of his side window. At the very least the slipstream must have been pulling at the man's clothing.

Part of the training we all had to go through, even before the advent of the formal Personal Track Safety courses, was about how to make ourselves safe if we were caught out by an approaching train, the last resort being to lie down on your front between the rails. Whether anyone actually ever had to do that and whether they survived unscathed I do not know. A point that was continually emphasised also was not to step from one line to another to avoid one train only to be killed by a train on the second line, and yet this kept on happening. Every so often the BRB would produce a new, and usually quite grisly, safety film to emphasise the need for personal safety.

One important BR development in railway safety in the early 1990s was the requirement to report all near-misses in exactly the same way as actual accidents were reportable. They could then be investigated with a view to stopping a repeat from developing further. Under those rules, the incident with the trackman at Carpenders Park would have been reportable, would have been investigated and, maybe, a real incident would have been avoided later.

Some suicide attempts were near-misses as well, sometimes because the person involved was making a gesture or a cry for help but at other times because they did not understand railway operations. As the up line approaches Tonbridge it goes under a road bridge, but just before that there are points leading off the through line and into the up platform loops. One day a woman, seeing a train approaching, stood on the parapet of the bridge and, as the train drew near, jumped, failing to realise that the points were set for the diverging move towards the platform. As she fell, the train swung off to the left around her, leaving her injured on the adjoining line. On another occasion someone jumped off the platform at Orpington as a train came in. Fortunately the train was only a four-car, while the person was somewhere near the eight-car stop. So the train came to a stand way ahead of where they were standing on the track. One has to hope that these people received the help they obviously needed, but not guidance in railway operations.

Of course, these failed attempts were tragic in the cases of the individuals concerned and should not be made fun of, but in the context of some of the more gruesome events on the railway it has to be said, however tastelessly, that they provided us with some light relief, possibly because they fell short of the real thing.

24

Hoses, Holes and Harrowing Times

Others who may be on the line from time to time are emergency services personnel, some of whom have frequently exhibited a lack of understanding of safety procedures, despite close liaison with railway authorities.

One evening in 1982 I was dismayed to see Police officers swarming over the electrified line between Woolwich Arsenal and Plumstead stations. No permission had been sought from the signalbox Regulator at Dartford and the conductor rails were still live. None wore any high-visibility clothing. Having arranged for trains to be stopped and for the current to be discharged, I went off down the line to find out what was going on. Apparently they were searching for the proceeds of a robbery that had been committed several days before and therefore could hardly be described as an emergency. What was an emergency, however, was their irresponsible disregard for their own safety.

On another occasion when I was a Controller at Beckenham, the Fire Brigade contacted us to say that they were attending a fire on land adjoining the railway near the south portal of Polhill Tunnel, near Sevenoaks. As a precaution they asked for the current to be discharged, which was duly done. A Charing Cross to Hastings diesel train then shot out of the tunnel, severing hoses and making firemen who were next to the track scatter. The Fire Brigade Officer in charge came back on the phone in angry terms saying that he'd asked for trains to be stopped – which he hadn't. He hadn't even said that his men would be working on the line or that hoses would cross it. Both procedures (current discharge and stopping of trains) were clearly identified and laid down in agreements with the Fire Brigade, but he had initiated the wrong procedure, thus putting the lives of his firemen in danger.

I mentioned in the previous chapter that the Police liked to take sole charge of incidents involving bodies on the line and, having done so, would then take as long as they felt they needed to before allowing trains to run again. The same applied with the other emergency services, it sometimes being part of their mentality to make 'a meal of things'. A member of the public had made a 999 call to report smoke rising from the cutting side along the North Kent line at Angerstein Junction one Saturday morning when I was on duty at Woolwich Arsenal. The Fire Brigade went through their Control to ours to get trains stopped and the current discharged as they would need to gain access to the cutting. The signalbox Regulator at London Bridge asked me to attend the site while he arranged for trains to be diverted via Greenwich.

Having been driven to Charlton in the Senior Railman's Morris Minor I then walked along the track to Angerstein Junction and made myself known to the nearest fireman, who told me that smoke was coming from a hole in the cutting side. These holes were well known by railway staff as they were made by children as hide-outs and were continually having to be refilled by the P. Way staff. If one had collapsed with a child inside, the railway would have been to blame, of course. The fireman I spoke to said that they were concerned that the smoke appeared to be coming from some possibly toxic substance and they needed to identify this substance before they could deal with it. The Officer in charge wanted to speak to me about this, apparently, so I asked where he was.

'He's up there, in his car, mate,' was the reply as the fireman pointed to the top of the almost sheer cutting side, about 40ft above us.

'And how am I supposed to get up there?' I asked.

The message from the 'Chief' on the radio was that that was my problem and that until I'd sorted things out with him face to face no trains would run. Luckily, his men were more co-operative and they lowered a rope down. The one on the track tied it round my waist and I was hoisted up the cutting side. The much-braided Chief was sitting in the back of his car and, as far I could ascertain, did not move from that position during the entire two hours or so of the incident. Several times he demanded to see me and each time I was pulled up the cliff-like cutting side and then lowered again. I became quite an expert at running up a nearly vertical surface but resented being so entirely in the hands of someone who was the Chief of another organisation and who was holding me to ransom.

It turned out that the Permanent Way staff had packed the hole with polystyrene waste for some reason and we found this out by going through the on-call procedure to trace the section Supervisor, who then had to call several other people in order to find out whether anyone knew why there were 'toxic' fumes coming from the hole. All calls and instructions were relayed through the Signalman at London Bridge, with whom I was in contact by means of the signalpost telephone at Angerstein Junction. Every time I had any information that I wanted to get to the Chief I had to indicate that I wanted to be hoisted up again, of course.

Once the material had been identified, the Fire Brigade Chief then authorised his crews to deal with the fire and they lowered themselves, in the manner they had provided for me, on to the ledge leading to the hole. In a matter of minutes the fire was out and the remaining material had been dragged from the hole. Even then, though, we had to wait at least half an hour before the Chief gave us the all-clear to start running trains again along the North Kent line, by which time we had lost all the Saturday shopping traffic to and from Woolwich and Lewisham.

It is tempting to say that the putting on of a uniform, especially one with lots of braid, gives some people an inflated opinion of themselves and into that category must go the Fire Brigade Chief that day. Many railway Supervisors and Managers were similarly pompous and dictatorial when in uniform and were completely different people if you met them socially, unless they had spent so long in uniformed posts that their personalities had been distorted by their work. Uniforms gave many staff a means of hiding themselves behind a mask of assumed authority that they might not have possessed naturally and this has been a mixed blessing.

Some characters were dodgy out of uniform, too. There was a series of inner-city disturbances in the early 1980s, with full-blown riots in Brixton, London's Broadwater Farm Estate and Bristol, amongst other places. Some malcontents decided to cash in on the wave of looting and violence and there were rumours of trouble brewing in and around London. For a couple of days we heard stories of an impending street riot in Woolwich town centre and these stories came to a head one day when I was on duty. The streets became strangely quiet during the afternoon as ordinary people decided to steer clear and some shops were boarded up. The Metropolitan Police had drafted in a lot of officers, horses and dogs. They came to Woolwich Arsenal station to warn us, as if we hadn't already heard what was going on, and to say that they had tipped off the British Transport Police. Their recommendation was that we should secure our premises, but how can you do this if you are operating a public transport service?

Sure enough, as afternoon turned to evening, groups of people started hanging around on the street corners, waiting for something to spark things off. We took the precaution of closing the booking office and securing it as we would at night, and of taking staff off the street level ticket barrier, where they might have been vulnerable to attack.

Having made sure that things were as secure as we reasonably could make them, I was returning along the platform to my office when a couple of men in jeans, sweatshirts and with large beer bellies approached me with a swaggering gait. My instant reaction was that if you were going to start a riot you would probably look just like these two and I was worried that they might be on the lookout for places at which to provoke trouble and to which other rioters might be led. The larger of the two came right up to me. The Senior Railman, possibly sharing my doubts about them, came out on to the platform and stood watching, in case trouble started. This was a recognised, if unspoken, procedure on our stations in which we would assist each other or get help, never leaving anyone unattended if trouble looked possible.

'Transport,' said the man.

What did he mean by that bald statement? Was he asking for transport, in which case a station was probably a fair enough place to be? There were so many possibilities, including the new worry that he might not be quite right in the head.

'Transport,' he repeated, this time impatiently.

The Senior Railman, hearing this, came to my rescue.

'I think they're BT Police, Guv,' he offered, tentatively.

'That's what I've been telling him,' said the man, at last finding that he could say more than one word at a go. 'We've got a few men around in case anything happens. Just telling you, OK?'

Of course, it turned out that the single word 'Transport' in Police circles meant 'British Transport Police' but this officer was not capable of realising the wider possibilities of meaning suggested by the word, from which his intended meaning was but one small derivation.

None of the BTP officers spoke to us after that, not even to find out how many people were going to be on duty or what precautions we had taken or could take. They just slouched around the station looking tough and causing innocent passengers to have doubts about their safety. In fact, nothing happened on the station, although there was some trouble outside with gangs running along the streets, smashing windows and looting a few shops. I stayed on all night just in case the station was attacked but the British Transport Police disappeared without notice around 9.30 p.m.

I witnessed the more sympathetic and professional side of the British Transport Police during the night of 21 July 1989 at Harrow and Wealdstone station. The 1400 Glasgow Central to Euston had become split and partially derailed as it approached Harrow at a speed of 100mph when a motor-alternator carried under the fifth coach had fallen off. After banging around under the carriage floors as the train went over it, it eventually caused the restaurant/buffet/kitchen car to derail. This tore the coach from the first-class coach in front of it, the severed automatic braking system bringing both portions to a halt, but with the rear part left quite along way behind as, being derailed, it had come to a stop much sooner than the front portion. The Chief Steward, Euston-based Zila Attal, had been serving at a table in the first-class open coach next to the break at the time. Zila, seeing that the train was coming apart, grabbed a passenger's mobile telephone, dialled 999 and altered the emergency services before the train had even come to a stop and certainly before the Signalman had been told by the Driver to block the line and put into place the emergency procedures. I recommended Zila for an award and this eventually took place after much pressure, the senior management of ICOBS seemingly not appreciating how important his action had been. I think they sometimes forgot that their restaurants were on board moving trains and that therefore their staff might have to get involved from time to time in things other than catering.

As the only ICOBS manager on duty at Euston that evening (it was sleeper departure time) I stayed on and went to the site in the early hours to retrieve the valuable catering stock from the derailed vehicle. The train was a sorry sight, made even more poignant by the fact that Harrow is an evocative name in railway history because of the disaster there on 8 October 1952 when 112 people were killed. Several oblique references were made to this during the night, which was marked also by Peter Rayner's attendance at his second passenger train derailment that day.

After obtaining clearance to board the damaged restaurant car, I clambered about removing items of catering value, stacking them on the ground in the shadows at the end of the station car park and hoping that nobody would pilfer them while I went back for the next lot. I then rang for a taxi, into which I loaded the catering stores for the journey back to Euston, much to the amusement of the taxi driver. How many other people, I wondered, were riding through the London suburbs in a taxi at two in the morning with several hundred miniatures and beer cans for company?

The BTP set up an incident room at the station and helped passengers off the train. They gave tea to people and arranged hospital treatment for those who needed it. Injuries were very slight, which says a lot for the construction of the Mk III coaches. The most striking thing I noticed about the people who were still lingering at the station when I arrived was that they were covered in heavy dust, presumably thrown up and sucked in from the track. The Police were taking names and addresses of everyone on the train when I got there, taking particular delight in questioning two young people who had been found in a toilet together.

Police officers then scoured the train in order to take out every item of personal property, which they also meticulously logged. Where ownership was not in doubt they restored the items to their owners straightaway, either at the station or by going to their homes or the hospitals to which they had been taken. Other items were restored as they were claimed over the ensuing days. This was the BT Police at their best, drawing upon officers of different ages and both sexes to provide a mix of sympathetic, efficient and reassuring service. They had a call-out procedure so that officers on and off duty from all over London could be drafted in to deal with major incidents. I remember well the sudden exodus of Police from Euston, for instance, on that terrible morning in December 1988 when it became apparent that a major disaster had happened at Clapham Junction. They went across London by the vanload and their departure left a strangely empty feeling of helpless dread in us all at Euston as the gravity of the situation began to dawn on us.

With all four main lines blocked at Harrow the entire sleeper service had to be cancelled that night and before I went on site I had to arrange for the

Sleeping Car Attendants to remain on the trains, which were used as hotels for the night for any passengers wishing to stay. Others went by taxi to Heathrow Airport or simply gave up and went home. It meant that all the out-based SCAs and many passengers were twelve or so hours late getting to Scotland and elsewhere. In the morning all the southbound sleepers had to terminate at Watford Junction, with the passengers, including the Secretary of State for Defence, Malcolm Rifkind, MP being transferred to coaches. Later that day it was decided to run certain InterCity trains, including that night's sleepers, on the DC lines, which are the third-rail electrified suburban lines from Euston to Watford Junction. A fleet of diesels was commandeered and at Watford Junction AC locomotives took over. I rode home the evening after the derailment on the 2325 Euston to Edinburgh service and was alarmed to see the limited platform clearance of the Mk III sleepers at some of the stations as we trundled along the DC lines behind a Class 47. In particular, the overhang of the ends and body centres of these long vehicles over the platform edge of the tightly curved Watford High Street station would have been downright dangerous if anyone had been standing there. Had these vehicles ever used the DC lines before, I wondered? The next day I went to see the ASM at Euston, who had been a management trainee with me and who knew that I was from the Southern, over most of which Mk III vehicles did not have clearance.

I asked him about the 'route availability' of Mk III sleepers through Watford High Street, to which his reply was, 'We don't bother too much about that sort of thing on this Region. Nothing happened anyway, did it?'

He was right: nothing had happened and the sleepers had all run. So why was I concerned?

25

Hours and Hours

I mentioned earlier InterCity's somewhat muddled approach towards sleeping-car trains, until the move upmarket was eventually decided upon. A particular example was the way in which InterCity On Board Services were not geared up to take responsibility for sleeper staff in 1987 and this was an object lesson in how not to manage change on a railway that was changing too rapidly for its own good. Doubtless there were countless other examples too as the railway accelerated towards privatisation.

Sleeping Car Attendants (SCAs) had been the responsibility of Area Managers until they were taken over by InterCity. The AMs appointed people to Attendants' jobs from station positions and vice versa. They also had pools of reserve staff, known as 'panel men', who normally did other jobs but who could step in to cover sleeper work in case of shortage. When they lost control of the SCAs to InterCity they also withdrew this back-up facility and so ICOBS, in effect, needed more SCAs to do the same amount of work. Some ICOBS HQ managers seemed to think that the number of SCAs needed was far greater than it actually was and, when I arrived at Euston to take charge of SCAs in 1988, I found that an SCA recruitment drive had been conducted by managers who had no knowledge of the sleeper requirements. The staff recruited were then surplus and had to be got rid of, which was not a good way of treating people or of running a business that found itself under the extreme financial pressure that was being imposed upon InterCity by the Government's requirement to break even.

Under the Area Managers, the SCAs had existed in a sort of 'time warp'. Signing on and off times stayed unchanged except when they needed to be extended for a particular timetable change, but the AMs didn't reduce the times when another timetable came in that might have permitted this. In this way some staff were signing on, and therefore being paid, nearly two hours earlier than was necessary in 1988.

The rostering changes that had been fought for at such cost by the BRB in the early 1980s had still not been implemented for SCAs as the end of the decade approached. Flexible rostering would have given cost savings and better groupings of nights off duty, but not only had the Area Managers failed to implement it but ICOBS management failed to understand it, too. I was ready to introduce it, having worked out and costed the details over several weeks of work, assisted by the sleeping-car Clerical Officer, Steve MacMeeking. Because of the lack of office space that I mentioned earlier, Steve and I accomplished this task by taking a mobile office – we rode to Northampton and back on board off-peak loco-hauled Mk I 'cobblers' trains. Then, when it was all worked out, I gave notice to the Staff Representatives from all the depots of the intention to hold a meeting to discuss implementation. I had already 'primed up' lots of the staff in order to smooth the way but was then told that the Director of ICOBS, David Sumner, had issued an instruction to my boss at Euston to say that we were not to introduce flexible rostering for SCAs as the idea was too controversial and might lead to unrest. I wondered where the hell he had been during the strikes of 1982 and what had been achieved at that time, if, six years later, the idea was still too controversial for ICOBS.

The next problem was that SCAs were, supposedly, examined and 'passed out' by Area Inspectors, who were employed by the Area Managers and were responsible for periodical examination of staff to ensure that their knowledge of safety matters was up to date. This was particularly important on the sleepers in regard to fire precautions. They were also meant to keep records of these checks, as part of the safety audit procedure. In the spring of 1989 it was decided that ICOBS, as the employer, should keep the records although the Area Inspectors would continue to do the checks. We needed to be able to prove for ourselves that all our staff were competent to do the job, but in the case of the Euston Attendants, the Area Inspectors were unable to produce the records. It transpired that while under the stewardship of the AMs, lots of staff had simply been moved to sleeper work from other jobs without proper training. This came to the notice of Terry Worrall, the Board's Director of Operational Standards (and also, notoriously, the coiner of the phrase 'the wrong kind of snow'), who ordered a complete retraining programme for this previously forgotten group of staff. During the summer leave period of 1989 we had to release staff for a residential retraining course at Rutherglen and then for examination and passing out by the Area Inspectors. The same Inspectors who had failed to maintain proper records over a number of years then claimed hundreds of overtime hours to carry out the re-examinations and were laughing all the way to the bank at the way in which ICOBS staff had been caught working without qualifications while in fact those same staff had only recently been inherited from a regime of their own slovenliness. I made this point in a strongly worded letter to the Director of Operational Standards, with a copy to the Regional Operations Manager at Crewe, neither of whom replied.

This sort of administrative muddle, in which the change of a name could mean that you could get away with murder, was and still is one of the dangers of hurried reorganisation without proper consultation. All over the railway, as reorganisation accelerated, details were being lost or deliberately ignored while incompetence and mistakes were being swept under the carpet. Just over a year after the transfer of SCAs to ICOBS, I found that someone in the Regional Operations Manager's office at Crewe was still being paid by the ROM to produce 'diagrams' for the SCAs, even though they were no longer operations staff. These diagrams, although showing the current train times, were based upon signing on and off times that had been agreed over a pint in a smoky pub somewhere in the north London back streets many years previously and which bore no relation to the requirements of 1989. While ICOBS was a struggling new organisation that did not really understand what it was meant to be doing and had very little information and expertise with which to do it, the old operating organisation was being exposed as complacent, inefficient and, at Area level, corrupt. The closing of the ranks, though, from Inspectors deep in the bowels of Euston station, through the 'we know best' smugness of Crewe to the Director of Operational Standards in the airy heights of Paddington, meant that the new name of ICOBS could be used as a convenient scapegoat.

The excessive time allowed for signing on and off meant that some SCA duties were up to seventeen hours long on Sunday nights when trains were timed to take longer to allow for engineering work diversions. Even with trimmed-back booking-on times there were still turns in excess of fourteen hours. The archaic rostering system inherited from the Area Managers meant that the people who least needed all the money that the long hours entailed, and in some cases least wanted the hours, were the ones who got them. This was because of another anachronistic leftover that the AMs had perpetuated – that of 'link' working in which staff progressed up the links purely on the basis of length of service.

At Euston the link system meant that the most elderly staff worked the Inverness train, which was Link 1, simply on the basis that the number of hours involved on this run was the longest. Link 2 was the Glasgow run and so on until you came right down to the Barrow-in-Furness sleeper. This obviously needed rectifying in an age of fair opportunity. Until I abolished the link system in 1989, replacing it with a 'suitability'-based system with the titled trains as the ones to aspire to, regardless of earnings, I think SCAs may have been the only people on the railway who had a purely earnings-based hierarchy within one grade. In most shift jobs, if staff were of the same grade, they rotated round the roster so that everyone did all the duties in turn during the full cycle.

The switch to the new system in which Euston Attendants worked on the Night Aberdonian and Night Scotsman services as the new Link 1 (we retained the word 'link' to make the transition easier), with Link 2 being a mixture of 'slow' Edinburgh, Glasgow, Aberdeen, Inverness, Stranraer and Fort William work, was received with mixed feelings. Many of the more perceptive staff could see that InterCity was moving away from the slow, part-seating services and therefore that the work in my new Link 2 had its days numbered. The titled lounge-car services were the trains to be on for those who wanted any sort of future and these people started desperately demonstrating their suitability for selection. Job security, retention of good earnings and a part in a developing market became more important that an obstinate hanging on to excessive earnings in a dying market.

Of course, SCAs were by no means the only staff working excessive hours and while their duties touched upon safety-critical items such as fire evacuation, other staff working long hours had more direct safety responsibilities. As I have said before, the railway of the 1970s and '80s relied heavily upon overtime working in order to fulfil its basic commitments to the timetable whilst at the same time being able to demonstrate to the Government that it was cutting staff numbers. The extent of this became a matter of increasing concern to those of us who had to try to cover jobs and was eventually highlighted by the Inquiry into the Clapham crash, at which the ludicrous hours of signalling technicians were condemned by Mr Justice Hidden. Nevertheless, for some time after that the standard night week for Signalmen, Regulators, Controllers, depot Supervisors, etc. on a three-week roster (early, late and night weeks in turn) continued to consist of sixty-four hours. This did not even include any overtime, although it may have included a rest day worked.

At either end of the night week, to make things worse, there was a 'double-double-back' for most staff. Having finished the late-turn week at 2200 on Saturday, you came back at 0600 Sunday morning and then again at 2200 the same day, thus working twenty-four out of forty consecutive hours. That was the start of your seven nights. Coming off nights at 0600 the next Sunday, you then doubled back to a 1400 start the same day, followed by an 0600 start the next day. In other words, at the beginning and end of each seven-night week there were two eight-hour turnrounds. Hence it was that during the Monday morning rush hour, when alertness was vital to maintain timekeeping as well as safety, many staff would have been on their eleventh shift in ten consecutive days. Some would have worked overtime on top of this, the standard way of covering a job if no relief staff were available being to ask the two staff either side of the vacant shift to work twelve hours each to cover it. Thus you could do an eighty-four-hour week of nights. Why was this allowed? Simply because, as I have said, the political pressure was on to reduce staff numbers, but also to keep basic rates of pay down. So staff doubled or even trebled their low basic pay, thus earning a decent living, but with little time off – and the railway was able to keep running.

The ethos up until the 1980s was that staff were meant to be grateful for overtime, as indeed most were. At Woolwich we regularly rostered twelve-hour shifts and did not expect to hear staff complaining about the lack of time they could spend with their families or friends. Occasionally, though, things snapped. One of our Crossing Keepers, working successive weeks of twelve-hour shifts on his own at Charlton Lane Crossing Box, allowed a member of the public into the box and this person was seen to be working it. The Crossing Keeper, John Morrison, was prosecuted for endangering the lives of people on the railway. The case reached the national press and John was given a suspended prison sentence in March 1983. During his trial, attention was drawn to the hundreds of railway people who worked twelve-hour shifts without breaks, day after day.

When it came to light that the case was going to court, the Area management closed ranks, the stance taken being that John should get the 'book thrown at him'. I dissented, believing, as I still do, that the Regional management, Area management and myself were just as much to blame for perpetuating a system that required staff to work such long hours. I was warned against going to the committal hearing at Greenwich Magistrates' Court, but went all the same. I was the only BR manager in attendance and it was abundantly plain to me that BR was on trial as much as John was. This, of course, was something the rest of the management did not want to hear. Although John was technically the guilty party, as he readily admitted and with good grace, he was treated as much as a victim as a perpetrator and I was pleased to see this. In order to avoid any further bad publicity it was decided not to sack him but to transfer him to work under supervision as a carriage cleaner at Slade Green.

In my early shift-working days, when I did my first eight-hour double-back off nights, a more experienced Controller, Mike Eagleton, asked me if I felt tired. I had that burning sensation behind the eyes that is familiar to shift workers and which was described at the time as having 'eyes like piss-holes in the snow', so I said yes, I was tired. Mike's reply was that if I had to adjust my sleeping pattern back from day to night I was bound to be tired and I might as well be tired at work and be paid for it as be tired at home, not feeling like doing much. So we were tired in the company's time rather than our own and were grateful for it, earning 'time and three-quarters' for the privilege and then having groups of days off when we weren't so tired. I soon became accustomed to this and on one occasion worked thirty-one consecutive days, on different shifts. Whether this was a sensible system for a responsible employer is another matter and is one that, to some extent, has been inherited by Network Rail and the TOCs to whom the recommendations of the Hidden Report apply just as they did to BR.

26

Nightwork

Shift working creates its own breed of characters who exist largely independently of the rest of the world, at least in social or domestic terms, especially if they are regularly working weeks of sixty-four or more hours. With no ability to make regular commitments to attend meetings, classes, etc., or even to watch every episode of *The Bill* or *EastEnders*, they tend to overdo things or splash out when they do have free time. For many shift workers, rest days come in groups of more than two days and are therefore more of a 'holiday' than is a nine-to-fiver's weekend.

On the railway, nine-to-fivers were usually regarded with some disdain by shiftworkers. They were people who considered things to be of vital importance but which could nevertheless be left from Friday afternoon until Monday morning when they suddenly assumed urgency again. This seems slightly ridiculous to shift workers, which makes the job of their daytime bosses more difficult. The Chief Controller at Beckenham in the 1970s, for instance, had a hell of a time with some Controllers. Ron Crittell was the person who first appointed me to the railway. His full title, in true archaic railway terminology, was Chief Trains Clerk and Chief Controller, which, coupled with his initials at the bottom of a memo would read C.R.C., C.T.C. & C.C. The Deputy Chief Controllers, who were in charge of each shift and were answerable to Ron, were a law unto themselves. Bob Higgins, otherwise known as 'The Commodore', would rant and rave at all hours of the day and night, but especially at the Chief Controller if he dared to show his face. The Commodore's was the shift with the highest standards, though, and while you had your bit of fun when he was on duty you were expected to take the job of running the railway seriously. The other two 'resident' DCCs were pretty lax and the only direction offered on their shifts was towards the pub, which, incredibly, was downstairs in the same building. Approaching the 1979 General Election, some of us invented spoof political parties to take the mickey out of certain of our colleagues and I invented the Saturday Late Turn Party as a dig at the antics that sometimes took place on that shift.

At night, if things were quiet, the 'old boys' would tell you about scrapes they had in the steam days or in the days of the old Orpington Control, which had been in a Nissen hut with the track diagrams for each panel suspended from the curved ceiling above their heads. One of them, who incidentally had the distinction of being the only Labour Councillor at the time on Tunbridge Wells Council, had been a Driver before becoming a Controller at Orpington. One night there was a fire in the rolling stock shed next door and Ivan went through the smoke to drive out one of the trains, thus saving it from possible destruction. He was simultaneously reprimanded for driving a train without authority and praised for saving the stock. In a heavily regulated railway there were many people who could tell of 'bollockings' that consisted of their being told off for doing something and then, after the formal interview, thanked for doing it.

Another Controller had been a steam Driver at Ashford and used to tell me about the recovery trains that lifted the track along closed lines such as the Kent & East Sussex. The Relief DCC, Bill Duke, who had dared to break ranks by going to work at Paddington for a while before returning to the South Eastern, and was therefore seen as a bit of an outsider, just as I was, had started his career as a Booking Clerk at Goudhurst on the long-closed Hawkhurst branch – a line about which there were few memories. Another DCC, Ron Perkins, had been the person to take the call saying that there had been a crash at Lewisham in December 1957, in which eighty-nine died. Meanwhile, Basil Grant, a Controller on the horrendously busy and complicated Area 4, would tell stories of his days as a Relief Signalman. One evening the young Basil had been on late turn at the Weald box, which was in the middle of nowhere just south of Sevenoaks Tunnel. The Hastings diesel trains had just been introduced and as Basil lived at Wadhurst he arranged for the Driver of the down Hastings to pick him up at the Weald. As the train was nearly at a stand he climbed up on to the wooden step by the leading brakevan door, just behind the cab.

'Right away, then, Driver!' he shouted and the Driver, who had been looking back, shut his window and accelerated away.

It was then that Basil found that the brakevan door was locked. He was hanging on to the handrails on the outside of a train that was rapidly gaining speed on a downhill gradient. Because of the vibration and movement of the Hastings unit (they were notoriously 'rough-riding') he daren't let go with even one hand in order to find his carriage key and so he had to cling on for his life until the train eventually drew into Tonbridge station, where the exhausted and terrified Basil fell off gratefully on to the platform.

Before the advent of Train Crew Supervisors, signalbox Regulators, TOPS and Information Technology, the role of Divisional Controllers was much greater than now. Controllers decided which trains were to run and when, making regulation decisions for junctions and passing these to the Signalmen concerned. They controlled Guards' duties, 'manipulating' these to fit all types of contingency and matching these with Drivers and traction in order to form, or save, the service.

Signalbox staffing was another aspect that was taken care of by the Controls after the roster office people had gone home. On the South Eastern Division in the 1970s, even after the opening of the London Bridge power signalbox, there were still more than seventy boxes to be manned, mostly on a three-shift pattern. Before the opening of the Victoria powerbox, which is actually situated at Clapham Junction, we had boxes every few miles along the Chatham mainline, all manned by Signalmen of the highest grade. Towards the end of this era a lot of the 'resident' Signalmen left the service on early retirement, either not wanting to make the change to the new technology or being surplus to the new, smaller requirement for Signalmen. This meant that the boxes became worked almost exclusively by Relief Signalmen who worked twelve-hour shifts, day in and day out, to keep the service running during the transition. There was a band of Relief Signalmen, many of whom were passed out to work anywhere from Factory Junction in London right down to Richborough Sidings in East Kent. Many of them prided themselves on the number of boxes they were qualified to work and on nights you could join in their own running 'open' conversations on the control circuit lines. In particular, for many months Control Circuit 14, which covered the Loughborough Junction, Blackfriars, Shepherds Lane and Factory Junction area, became a sort of open chat line for the group of men who were paid a fortune to keep these vital boxes running until the new box was ready.

BR was a mixture of old and new. 'Absolute Block' boxes with semaphore signals survived alongside more modern equipment. 33033 and 33113 pass Canterbury East with a Channel Tunnel construction train in March 1992. (Photo: Nick Pullen)

In the 1970s a typical railway Control was one such as at Beckenham, at which I was a Relief Controller from 1976 to 1979.There was a step up from the corridor into the Control and the door was marked 'Private', both of which deliberate features gave us added status over the rest of the Divisional offices in the building. On entering the room you first passed the Controllers' lockers, in which we kept our personal effects and also our own copies of the operating publications, etc. Next was a door to our private 'galley'. And then into the main part of the room. At the back of the room, in the centre of an elevated platform, sat the Deputy Chief Controller. From where he sat he could see all the panels. At the far side of the room by the window was his typing desk where he would keep up to date his log of events. In a row in front of the DCC sat the Guards' Controller, the Locomotive Controller and the Power Controller (a misnomer for Rolling Stock Controller). The Power Controller had an Assistant, who also doubled as teleprinter operator for the whole office. In front of this lot there was a step down to a larger part of the room and around the outside walls were the Area panels, facing outwards. On the South Eastern we had four Area Controllers, two each side of the room with an Assistant Controller between each pair. These Assistants had to collate train-running information and pass messages to and from the Controllers, serving the two Controllers either side of them. Some Assistants did more controlling and decision-making than their Controllers, in practice. At the end of the room there was a desk for the retired Controller who had come back as a part-time Roster Clerk, while in the middle of the room there was a large table upon which various record books were kept and where items to be signed for were displayed.

Each Controller and Assistant had a communications console built on to the desk, consisting of a slanting panel with rows of switches for selecting telephone lines (BR internal, Control Circuit or, at that time, GPO) and these could be used to hold calls while others were dealt with and to create 'conference' lines in order that Controllers could make three or four-way discussions available, which was very useful and time-saving when things were 'up the wall'. Assistant Controllers' consoles were equipped with the numbers necessary to conduct the business of both their Controllers and so nobody needed to reach across anyone else or use their console in order to make or receive calls. Every person had their own personal handset or headset that we kept in our lockers and then plugged into a socket in the front of our desks, which led to the frequently heard expression, if you lost your temper under pressure, 'That's it, I'm pulling out now.' All inwards calls were indicated by flashing lights next to the appropriate switch on the consoles and there was a central buzzer that sounded if an incoming call to anybody in the room remained unanswered. At busy times the buzzer would be sounding continuously, of course.

At one side of the room was the TOPS Inquiry machine for use in determining freight loadings, for obtaining statistics and for finding out about the running of freights coming towards the Division. It was also used to provide information upon which to base the distribution of coal empties to the three Kent pits of Tilmanstone, Betteshanger and Snowdown as well as to assess the resource requirements for Dover train ferry traffic.

On the wall behind the TOPS machine there was a framed 1in Ordnance Survey map of the entire Division and next to the machine were the teleprinters. The South Eastern had been at the forefront in the development of communication chains based upon a network of teleprinters, having set the system up in October 1970. The telex operator sent out train-running information, stock alterations and all sorts of other information to a network of stations where staff relayed the messages by telephone to other locations as specified by pre-determined communications flowcharts. At times of disruption there could be very long messages, sometimes even complete service revisions, and these would be recorded on ticker tape as they were typed on a second machine. The tape, when ready, could then be run through the main machine to transmit the message at high speed, several times if copies were needed for distribution at large locations.

Each night there was similarly a long 'stock' telex with all the altered train formations and stock movements needed to get units to where they were required for the forthcoming day or to provide rolling stock information needed during the day. This would take account of units needed at particular depots for various types of maintenance – we had maintenance depots at Stewarts Lane, Slade Green, Chart Leacon, Gillingham, St Leonards West Marina and Ramsgate, as well as having to work units to Selhurst and elsewhere occasionally. The stock telex would also show where during the day trains were to be split, joined or swapped over in order to redress imbalances from the previous day, to put the correct formations back into workings or to meet special needs. All these moves would be worked out by the night-turn Power Controller and the Area Controllers, each of whom would first circulate a 'slip' upon which the revised working was worked out. When everyone was satisfied that all the various requirements had been met and that none conflicted, the stock telex could be put together, typed on to tape on the reserve machine and then transmitted at speed on the main teleprinter.

Sometimes the stock telex ran into well over 100 items, many of which could easily be of ten or more lines (our passenger fleet consisted of more than 2,000 vehicles) and if you had been 'on the telex' on such a night, you staggered back dazed upon finishing it, but with a sense of satisfaction as you saw the tape chattering through the machine afterwards. Every night it was vital to get all the moves sorted out and transmitted before the day's passenger service really got going because everyone's attention would be needed elsewhere during the rush hour and some of the moves specified might be needed early on. It was also a question of unspoken honour between shifts – you tried never to leave anything undone that would normally be done on your shift, no matter how pressed or tired you were.

Because of the volume of messages, their length, complexity and frequency, the railway had developed telegraphic code words and abbreviations that all senders and recipients of messages were expected to understand. Thus '1714VA-SRA CAPE' meant that the 1714 from Victoria to Sheerness was cancelled, while '15†52 GPS-CS, 8VEP 4CEP vice 12VEP' would have meant that the empty stock leaving Grove Park Shed for Cannon Street at 1552 had a CEP unit instead of one of its booked VEP units, thus reducing seating capacity. 'WARNPASS, DERAILMENT, WELLINGBOROUGH' would mean that stations should display boards warning passengers. Some of the words were rather strange, as with the engineers' wagon names I mentioned earlier. 'GOOSE, SCUNTHORPE', for instance, meant stop loading wagons for Scunthorpe while 'GOSLING, DOVER' meant stop forwarding wagons to Dover. Many of these applied throughout BR but the Southern's internal station codes had some peculiarities, too. So while Charing Cross was a predictable CX and Dartford a reasonable DT, Bromley South was BP, Sandwich was SAD, Clapham Junction was PA and Brighton IG. I don't know who dreamt these up, but I do know that it was a matter of pride not to have to look up a code.

Sometimes, when the service had really been knocked about, stock would end up all over the place and to get it sorted out in the space of one night would not be possible. Empty trains would fly about all across the Division, attaching, detaching and re-forming at various depots in order to sort the stock out for the morning, making the maximum number of moves possible for each crew. If there was a gap in the programme worked out by the Power Controller, the crew would take a 'taxi' unit with them as well as any other stock needed so that they could get to the next leg of the working, eventually returning the taxi unit to the depot of origin where it would be put back into its proper working. When things had been particularly bad and units had been sent to lots of places other than where they were booked to end up, some units would be 'lost'. Every night, whether or not this was the case, a 100 per cent physical check was made of 'painted numbers' at all berthing points and this was then phoned through to the Power Assistant. Sometimes people would misread a number when out checking the units and so the same number could be reported at two locations or not reported at all. The Power Assistant then had to send someone out again to check the numbers. After a while you got to know which individuals were likely to be wrong and therefore who to send out again into the cold at four in the morning for a recheck.

Eventually the fleet list would be completed and it was extremely rare for a unit still to be outstanding by the end of the night turn. If this did happen, an item would be included on the stock telex asking all points to look out for it and, just as it was usually the same people who gave inaccurate information in the first place, it was normally the same few sharp-eyed staff on stations or in depots and signalboxes who would spot the missing unit going by. It was, of course, vital to efficient fleet maintenance as well as to correct allocation of different types of stock that the exact whereabouts of each unit should be known at all times. Systems such as MTS (Master Timetable System), which was linked into the signalling system at London Bridge powerbox and which could not only run the platforming at Charing Cross without intervention by the Signalman but also follow the unit numbers involved, were only at a developmental stage in the mid 1970s. In the meantime, we had to rely on telephone messages and form-filling, made all the more difficult by the fact that the fleet was so large, and the depot capacity so limited, that lots of stock had to be 'out-berthed' overnight and between the rush hours at unstaffed sidings such as Bickley, Swanley, Minster and Blackfriars Carriage Roads. At these locations we had to rely on late-turn staff taking the numbers in the evening and then reporting them accurately before they went home. Similarly, someone from Cannon Street had to walk each night to Southwark Depot (the former Ewer Street/Grande Vitesse Goods station), which was unstaffed on all shifts, to check the unit numbers there. In fact, taking into account the depots, staffed berthing points and unstaffed berthing points, there were more than thirty places on the South Eastern Division that held passenger rolling stock each night, many of them susceptible to vandalism and only the main ones having any carriage-cleaning facilities.

As well as the three Divisional Controls and the Regional Control at Waterloo, which were all manned by 'operations' staff, the Southern Region had a Maintenance Control at the former Southern House, Croydon. This Control, known as Maintrol, was run by the Chief Mechanical & Electrical Engineer and the Controllers there allocated rolling stock work between depots and made decisions regarding the programming of work, taking into consideration stock availability, locations of depots, the whereabouts of particular units and workshop capacity. The Power Controller at each Division obviously had to work closely with Maintrol in order to balance the sometimes conflicting needs for rolling stock maintenance, maximum efficiency at the workshops and the operational and commercial needs of the Divisions.

At the same time as the Power Controller was sorting out all the rolling stock requirements, the Area Controllers might well be making stock and crew alterations of their own to take account of crew shortages, overrunning engineering work or other disruptions. Thus there was plenty of scope for conflicting arrangements to be made and 'slips' would be traded briskly about the room in order to keep everyone informed and to try to avoid mistakes.

Area Controllers would aim to work out the consequences of delays and cancellations in terms of crew and stock displacement in order to make arrangements to minimise the continuing effect of disruption. On the South Eastern this could rapidly spread as, say, a down Chatham side train might well form an up South Eastern side train upon arrival at Ramsgate while an up Sidcup line train, upon arrival at Charing Cross, could well form a down Mid-Kent line service, while its crew could be diagrammed for a down Orpington service. So disruption on one route could very easily spread to other routes and frequently did so, despite the interventions of Controllers. When things went badly wrong the service would degenerate into a series of 'specials', with stock and crews simply being sent out and back along the various routes in order to provide some sort of service. When possible, Controllers would always try to keep each train's proper identity (e.g. 2B02 0744 Slade Green – Charing Cross) because in that way they could identify the resources used in working it from the rolling stock and crew diagrams. If trains started to run as specials you knew you were fighting a losing battle in expecting any crews and stock to be at the right place at the right time to form their next booked workings. Bearing in mind, for example, that the

Area 1 Controller had more than 110 trains running in his Area between 1630 and 1730 each weekday, so it was obviously important that booked workings were adhered to wherever possible. Things could quickly turn into chaos if identities were lost.

Of course, there had to be a basic plan that we always tried to get back to and this was the Working Timetable in conjunction with the Drivers', Guards' and rolling-stock diagrams. Against each train in the rolling stock working book we would write, in different colours, the booked Driver's and Guard's duty numbers so that, if the train was delayed or cancelled, we could quickly work out the implications in terms of the crews' next duties, as well as that of the rolling stock. Each day we updated this information to take account of special notices and other altered workings.

On a railway as complex as the South Eastern the process of matching resources to the timetable took months of planning each time. The planners

The South Eastern Division's Control at Beckenham oversaw the running of more than 2,000 trains per day – passenger, freight, parcels, news, Motorail, boat trains, the Night Ferry and engineering trains. Controllers Dick Lee and Wally Hammond are seen here in the early 1970s. (Photo: Brian Garvin)

had to seek to use each crew member and each piece of rolling stock economically, taking into account the route and traction knowledge of the crews at each depot, the need to give them their breaks within the agreed timescales on each shift and to do so at recognised 'PNB' (Physical Needs Breaks) points, as well as the need to provide things such as maximum seating capacity for the busiest trains. Inevitably there was a lot of toing and froing between diagrammers, train timers and the commercial people who specified the overall plan in order to sort out a host of detailed problems, such as connectional times, before the timetable could be 'put to bed'. Each time a new timetable came out, which was twice yearly in order to take into account changes in demand and other circumstances, there was always a debate about to what extent it should be resource-led or business-led.

The most easily worked timetables, and therefore the ones most likely to run to time, have generally been resource-led. Basically this means that you sit down and see how much rolling stock and how many crews there are (and where), then you calculate how many trains the infrastructure can cope with and within these limits you build up a service. A purely business-led timetable, however, begins by saying that in an ideal world we would like to run, say, a service every twenty minutes along one route with additional trains calling at main stations every ten minutes. You then see how closely that can be matched within existing resources, with any surplus resources then being disposed of, if possible, or any additional resources being funded by the business, again if possible. Either way, it takes a long time for the aspirations and the possibilities to be matched and on a system such as was BR I don't think anyone would claim to have devised a perfect timetable or to claim that to do so was possible. With so many constraints and ambitions pulling in so many directions and with changing travel needs emerging, any 'perfect' timetable would soon start to falter in any case and would eventually need revision.

When all the timings and resource allocations had been agreed, the timetable would be published, with the whole country's deliberations being collated to form the Great Britain Passenger Train Timetable, or the 'All Systems Timetable' as it was known within BR during its early years. This is the book that is sold in bookshops and is available in reference libraries.

The mammoth task of co-ordinating all the services into one book was first achieved in 1974 and has been continued ever since. Despite the sell-off of the passenger services to numerous franchisees, with the inherent possibility of dissent between them, the timetable has so far continued to be published in much the same form as by BR, thanks to the influence of the Association of Train Operating Companies.

Another nightly activity at the Divisional Control was the compilation of train-running statistics. Staff at every station at which trains terminated, whether it be two trains or 200, had to record the arrival times and to sort these into RT (right time), 1'–5' late, 5'–10' late and so on. There were more than forty such places on the South Eastern Division. On the night turn this information was rung through to the Assistant Controllers, who then compiled the Divisional timekeeping statistics route by route. Cancellations were also totalled up and shown under different headings such as Driver shortage or signalling failure. As a Relief Controller Grade 'B' I was sometimes called upon to cover these more junior positions, some of whose occupants had a tendency to call in sick on Saturday nights. On most 'gangs' it was the unofficial custom to let the Assistants go home after they had done the figures on Saturday night, so I would be paid the equivalent of seventeen and a half hours for a rest day Saturday night worked at 'B' rate, but would be back home by 2 a.m..

Many timekeeping statistics were, and still are, fairly meaningless in terms of how late the bulk of passengers have been at their destinations for the reason that it is only the arrival time at the train's destination that is recorded rather than an intermediate point where the train may well have been busier. This applies particularly to a rush-hour dominated system such as the South Eastern but also applies to long-distance trains and the distortion is made greater if 'recovery' time is built into the timetable towards the end of a train's journey.

Take, for example, a twelve-coach evening rush-hour service from Cannon Street to Ramsgate via Chatham. Approaching the 'Bermuda triangle' of the Medway Towns (otherwise referred to as the 'Medway timewarp'), the train might well suffer a delay because of congestion and conflicting moves at Rochester Bridge Junction. Around 300 people alighting at Chatham could then each be five minutes late home, 100 at Gillingham also five minutes late, 200 at Rainham four minutes late each as the train starts to get a clearer run again and 50 people at Sittingbourne three minutes late home. Along the uncongested run between Faversham and Ramsgate there might well be some recovery time built into the timing as well as less likelihood of delay and so twenty people alighting at Ramsgate might well end up right time. So a tick goes in the RT box on the form even though the vast majority of passengers using the service were late home. To add to this, we were told in the 1970s to cancel trains rather than run them late, if possible, so 1,000 people could be thirty minutes late home after having to be crammed into a later train and yet the statistics would show excellent timekeeping.

Now in the days when these figures were largely a tool for railway management decision-making only, these distortions may not have been all that important in that they were no doubt recognised by the decision-makers, or so I should hope. Recovery time, after all, was not devised as a means of contriving to show that the railway was better at running to time than was really the case. Quite the reverse in fact: it was a recognition that late running was frequent and could adversely affect the next workings of crews and rolling stock. So a couple of minutes leeway built into timings would give a cushion against these effects and limit the spread of late running to other services. As from the early 1990s, however, the train-running statistics, still compiled in basically the same way I have described, formed part of the Passengers' Charter initiative and were used to trigger fare refunds. All that unscrupulous Train Operating Companies would need to do is to ensure that a lot of make-up or recovery time is built in towards the end of each running in order to make this triggering substantially less likely.

What else did we get up to at the dead of night? Sometimes things would be very quiet and we would take turns to have a snoop around the rest of the building, seeing what we could discover. At Waterloo we found a room containing hundreds of old ledgers and maps, including the surveyors' instructions regarding the construction of the London, Chatham & Dover Railway. A colleague of mine claimed one night to have seen a letter in which it was arranged that the Permanent Way Supervisor at Hastings would, on a specified day, suddenly declare that Ore Tunnel had become unsafe for use and thus precipitate the closure of the Ashford to Hastings line. At Beckenham we examined our own staff files and could even look through the correspondence in the Divisional Manager's Secretary's in tray. Security was lamentable among people who thought that work finished at five o'clock.

27

The Press Gang and the Ferry Man

At the time I was working in the Divisional Control at Beckenham we still had newspaper trains and also the Night Ferry, both of which were railway 'institutions'.

The paper trains ran from Victoria to the Kent coast and to Hastings. Other trains, of course, ran from other London termini as well as from Manchester and Glasgow. Until the early 1980s around 1,500 tonnes of papers were moved nightly by rail. All the London papers were still printed in Fleet Street at the time and it was the move to Wapping by News International in January 1986 that fragmented the delivery system to the London stations and contributed to the complete loss of the traffic from rail to road, other than as parcels traffic. News International switched to its own road delivery, in breach of a contract with BR that still had four years to run, and in 1987 they were followed by the Mirror Group, who negotiated their way out of their contract.

Every night, delivery vans from all the papers raced across London to get the bundles to the stations on time. If a paper was running late, which could be because they had been holding back for an 'exclusive' or because of print problems, they could ask for a delay on a particular train or on all trains. Such requests were normally for five minutes, sometimes ten and in extreme circumstances fifteen. The fact that it could be run this close shows how fine the papers cut things in order to print as late as they dare. This touch-and-go brinkmanship between printing and delivery was a precursor of what was later known as JIT, Just In Time distribution.

Each year one paper took on the task of representing the Newspaper Publishers' Association (NPA) on nights and all requests for trains to be held went through this representative, who would then contact the appropriate railway Control to arrange the delay. The papers had a sort of code of honour between them which meant that no paper took undue advantage of the arrangement and also that the year's representative would act impartially. There was a different representative on Saturday nights because of the different titles published, so you could be dealing with a *Financial Times* person all week and then someone from the *News of the World* on Saturday night.

The paper trains were composed mainly of vans but some also carried a brake compartment passenger vehicle, usually inhabited by people who had missed the last ordinary train home and were the worse for wear, but also by nightclub workers of various persuasions. There was a very popular young lady called Jane who was a regular on the 0310.

On Saturday nights the running of the paper trains was a nightmare, with services being diverted, split, cancelled, retimed and supplemented in order to get the papers around the various engineering sites. Every night a high priority was placed on getting these trains to run to time, NPA delays notwithstanding, but on Saturday nights this was a thankless task. They were usually retimed to leave Victoria earlier than on other nights and this in itself was not popular with the publishers, the more so as the actual departure times would be different nearly every week as the effect of engineering works was different. It is probably fair to say that this messing about with the timings was another contribution to the demise of the paper trains. The amount of handling was one more factor, with loaders, drivers and vans being employed at the printrooms, further loaders at the London stations and then unloaders and more vans at the destination stations. Some trains carried travelling sorters as well.

One perk from the paper trains was that staff at the loading stations could get free copies, which were all stamped 'VOUCHER'. As an Assistant Controller at Waterloo in 1974 it was one of my jobs to liaise with the NPA, passing on to the various stations the requests for the holding of trains, and it was also one of my 'duties' to go down to the station at about four o'clock to fetch our free copies. When I moved to Paddington I found that one of the Traction Controllers had made this his job, taking an undue time about it each night while he chatted to the Station Supervisor about his days as a Signalman in the 1950s and so on. Such was the nightly routine.

As well as the paper trains we also despatched the Night Ferry each evening from Victoria. This was the *Wagon-Lit* train from London to Paris and Brussels but which sometimes conveyed cars for places as far as Switzerland. The cars had been built between 1935 and 1952 and were operated, largely unchanged, by the *Wagon-Lit* Company until October 1976. From that time the SNCF took over the maintenance of the vehicles while BR looked after the staffing and laundry requirements. The *Wagon-Lit* Conductors were replaced by BR Sleeping Car Attendants. On the other side of the Channel the SNCF and SNCB provided haulage and train crews.

By the late 1970s it was apparent that the *Wagons-Lit* and their accompanying *fourgons* (luggage vans) would need refurbishing, but the SNCF were baulking at the cost of doing this. The use of BR Mk I sleepers was discussed but was made inappropriate by the Taunton sleeper fire, which also meant that attention to the Night Ferry became more urgent. Twelve people had died in a Mk I sleeper at Taunton in July 1978, the incident

BR ran a nightly *Wagon-Lit* train from London Victoria to Paris and Brussels, using the Dover to Dunkerque train ferry. Here the 'Agatha Christie' style sleeping cars and accompanying luggage *fourgons* are being shunted into the shed at Victoria. To the left is one of the Motor Luggage Vans that were formed into the fourteen-car trains that met every daytime sailing at Dover and Folkestone. (Photo: Kevin Lane)

raising questions over the safety of these vehicles. The cause of the fire had been laundry items stacked against an electric heater, but some of the Ferry vehicles had open-fire kitchen ranges.

Eventually the SNCF and SNCB wanted to pull out of the operation financially, simply providing traction and crews under contract their side of the Channel, and so it was that BR briefly became the principal, operating antiquated French-built dark blue coaches with open kitchen ranges and the appearance of being props for *Murder on the Orient Express*. The fires, which were in the Attendants' lobbies, were a source of concern on many occasions. The Attendants had to stoke them to provide hot water and heating, also raking out the ashes when necessary. Many times station staff and Signalmen would report that smoke and flames had been seen coming from the Night Ferry as it passed and the train would have to be stopped for examination. As the train was customs-cleared at Victoria, Paris and Brussels it was not supposed to be brought to a stand at a place where anyone could easily leave or join it, which in practice meant that we were not supposed to stop it at a station. If the Ferry (or 'doss house' as it was disrespectfully called) was stopped in a station or if we knew that it would be standing somewhere else for some time, we were supposed to tell the local Police on behalf of the Customs & Excise, but if you actually did this, no one remotely understood what you were talking about.

Trying to explain to the Station Officer in the local nick at Staplehurst that a customs-cleared ferry train was at a stand down the road invariably led to a reply along the lines of, 'So, what do you want me to do about it?'

When the train got down to Dover it was shunted over the linkspan on to the ferry, no doubt with much jolting and groaning. Lots of freight wagons, potentially earning far more for the railways, had to be left behind most nights while the vessel set sail underutilised. This particularly applied when there were certain categories of dangerous goods awaiting shipping as these could not go on alongside the Night Ferry.

In the morning the inwards Night Ferry rumbled its way up to Victoria, cutting a swathe through the morning rush hour, a splendid sight amongst the drab suburban 'EPB' trains. I recall one morning when there had been a freight train derailment near Tonbridge and the up Ferry had to run round at Paddock Wood and go via Maidstone West and Dartford. Having arranged all this, we wondered what on earth the commuters on the Dartford lines must have made of it when a *Wagon-Lit* train came along in place of the expected EPB in the middle of the rush hour. The Night Ferry was usually hauled by a Class 71 electric locomotive with a one-tone chime whistle, which made its approach even more distinctive. One winter's morning as we were waiting for a train at Bromley South, some of the more boisterous commuters started throwing snowballs from one platform to another and the Night Ferry, with its whistle chiming continuously as it rattled through, was pelted with snowballs from both sides. *Bienvenue en Angleterre*!

The Night Ferry was a railway institution and, as with most things that reached that rare status, it could not last. It was reported to have lost £120,000 in its last year of operation, which, in the context of present day cross-Channel operations, was not a lot. The sleeping cars were severely outdated in terms of comfort and safety, however, while the staff numbers needed to deal with the train were out of all proportion to the revenue. In addition, it was jeopardising efforts to attract more of the new Speedlink freight traffic to the train ferry. Perhaps it was odd, though, that the Continental railways pulled out first, as BR had more of a reputation for pruning loss-making services. It was a sad night when, in October 1980, the last Night Ferry pulled out of Victoria and the illuminated 'NIGHT FERRY' sign with stars and the moon against a dark blue background had to come down from the position it had held for so long above Platform 2.

So over the years Victoria became more and more standardised. The Brighton Belle had last run in April 1972, the Golden Arrow in October of the same year, the Night Ferry in October 1980 and the paper trains in July 1988. The 'classic' passenger traffic to and from the Continent was in decline following the sale of Sealink and the remaining passengers were increasingly being encouraged to travel on ordinary service trains rather than on the fourteen-car boat trains that had connected with every sailing until the early 1980s. Some of the later boat trains were formed of four cars only while the hourly Network Express to and from Dover Western Docks was advertised as the train for Continental connections. Despite these moves to remove the unusual, the Victoria of the late 1970s and early '80s clung on to a calculated and exclusive mystique, which worked to the advantage of the management and staff alike, but in very different ways.

At that time Victoria was its own administrative Area, with strong connections in the local business community. It frequently saw the Royal

Train and so the Area Manager had 'contacts at the Palace' as well as with other London institutions. He was often to be seen in evening dress, preparing to go to a function of some sort. While he cultivated and enjoyed this air of exclusivity that made the comparatively dull Divisional management at Croydon keep their distance, there was another layer of mystery being carefully maintained downstairs. The station at that time was effectively run, not by the management, but by a 'Mafia' consisting of the Station Supervisors and certain long-serving henchmen. In particular there was one Supervisor who, it was alleged, kept a tight rein on all the nefarious activities as well as running the station sufficiently well to avoid attention.

Sources connected with Victoria told me about some of the alleged operations. Unofficial portering, which could earn large tips, was organised by this Supervisor for a pay-off, while the jobs these porters should have been covering were done under duress by staff who had not yet earned their privileges with him. Similarly, staff paid for the right to work on the ticket barriers, which were the most lucrative in terms of excess fare fiddles. There were also rumoured to be arrangements by which preference was given to particular cabbies, again for a fee. Then there were fiddles with the timekeeper who clocked staff on and off duty and one such timekeeper was actually dismissed for accepting money in return for making out that certain staff had been at work at night when in fact they were either moonlighting elsewhere or were at home. At that time there were a lot of staff on nights as the railway provided loaders for the paper trains, some of whom were casual and so might not be missed by anyone in authority.

In 1980 I was asked by the Divisional Manager at Croydon to investigate the losses of self-help luggage trolleys at Victoria. Of course, self-help luggage trolleys were a direct threat to porters' tips and had been introduced specifically in order to rid the railway of the corruption and extortion that had developed with tipping and also with unofficial portering and touting. To assess the scale of the problem I first went to see the Terminals Inspector in the Divisional offices, who confirmed that several hundred pounds worth of trolleys were disappearing every week – they cost about £100 apiece at the time. He also doubted whether I or any other 'outsider' would be able to trace the bulk of them. Sure enough, upon my preliminary investigation, I could find the odd one at the Coach Station down the road or being used by a tramp, but that was all.

I went to Victoria with the Terminals Inspector one morning. The Supervisor had a tight reporting system in operation that meant that he got to know very quickly if any of the Divisional management or Inspectors were on his 'patch', even though there might well be 1,000 or more other people milling about as well. Sure enough, as we walked across the Central side concourse, he came up to us, saying that he'd heard we were on the station and was there anything he could do to help us. We were then entirely in his hands. He guided us around the labyrinth of cellars and arches underneath the station, having volunteered the suggestion that a complete delivery of trolleys might have been put down there and forgotten about. Pretty soon we had lost track of which doors we had actually gone through, so whether or not we had really seen every possible hiding place was never known, except to the Supervisor. Similarly there were places up on the roof and around the Grosvenor Hotel but I don't know whether we saw all of them, despite clambering up narrow stairs and along catwalks. Having given us what was described as a complete tour of all the possible places where trolleys might 'inadvertently' have been left, but which in reality left us more confused than when we had started, he then offered the suggestion that the trolleys were being taken by local children who then dumped them in the River Thames. Doubtless many of them were indeed in the river, but at whose instigation? Or were they being sold wholesale for scrap? For someone who knew within a couple of minutes if there was anyone prying on his station, he was surprisingly lax when it came to spotting these 'children' who were running off with railway property.

In fairness to the Supervisor and his colleagues, it must be said that there is a great and perhaps natural temptation to create an air of mystery, exclusivity and even notoriety around your job, especially if you are one of the few who are thoroughly familiar with a place as operationally and architecturally complex as Victoria, with a wealth of varied activities both day and night. In that way you come to be depended upon and thus create your own job security, as well as enjoying a spot of infamy.

Not only self-help luggage trolleys were going missing from the London stations. In 1980 (and indeed for several years more) the Central Division was still using 4-SUB units for its suburban services. These very basic electric units dated from before nationalisation and so were some of the few remaining vehicles to carry both prefix and suffix 'S' on their carriage numbers, signifying that they were both Southern Region and Southern Railway vehicles. The SUBs needed oil tail lamps as they were not fitted with either electric tail lights or illuminated roller blinds. These lamps had to be removed or attached each time units were combined or separated from each other, also being transferred from end to end at terminal stations. As well as pilferage and damage, there was an inherent imbalance in the workings of that year's timetable, which meant that some stations accumulated lamps while others ran a deficit. Victoria was a nett loser, as were several other stations, whilst London Bridge was among the nett gainers. I was commissioned to come up with a programme for rectifying this imbalance. At the same time, as a management trainee, I was following the progress of the resignalling work going on in south London. The contrast summed up so much of what I saw on the railway over the years and my report on the tail lamps began with the words, 'At the same time as implementing the most advanced signalling system in the world to control its lines from Victoria, the Central Division is operating a suburban passenger service largely based on rolling stock designed before the Second World War.' It was one of many examples of the old having to work alongside the new, with varying degrees of compatibility in an industry that could only ever update itself piece by piece. Examples still abound, such as the Class 365 units that come to Canterbury, to be signalled by semaphores and an Absolute Block System invented in the century before last or, conversely, the remaining 1950s slam-door multiple units that ran for a while alongside Eurostar trains through the solid-state interlocking Ashford signalling area.

After a while the somewhat tarnished romance of the Night Ferry was replaced by the recreated glamour of the Venice–Simplon–Orient Express (VSOE) that still runs to and from Victoria and elsewhere with its glorious Pullman cars. The first VSOE left Victoria on 25 May 1982 and guests included the BRB Chairman, Sir Peter Parker, and showbiz celebrities such as Liza Minelli. The idea was conceived by James Sherwood, Chairman of Sea Containers (the firm that had bought Sealink from the railway and that was later the parent company of the Great North Eastern Railway franchise). He had hoped to run the VSOE through to the Continent on the train ferry but, as BR had found with the Night Ferry, the costs of doing this were prohibitive and so the VSOE ran with one train in Britain and another on the Continent.

Of course, the VSOE was not a service train in the way that the Night Ferry was. While the Ferry was supposedly in competition with the airlines for day-to-day traffic between the capitals, the VSOE was a 'travel experience' much in the same way as were InterCity's (and later Regency's) Land Cruises. For this reason it did not run every day and the British train was used for excursion purposes in between runs to Folkestone Harbour. Thus the VSOE can still be seen on trips to Canterbury West or Bath, for example. A Class 73 electro-diesel locomotive was painted in Pullman livery by BR but as, perversely, this engine was allocated to the Civil Engineer at the time, it was usually to be seen hauling ballast trains while Gatwick Express Class 73s or RES 47s pulled the VSOE. The Pullman cars were maintained originally by BR under contract at Stewarts Lane and there, as anywhere else you saw and continue to see them, they provided an inspiring sight. And so they should do, bearing in mind the £11 million bill footed by Sea Containers to buy and restore them.

At the same time as the VSOE was reviving the old Pullman Car spirit, InterCity was expanding its own Pullman services on its main routes to and from London. The word 'Pullman' could now legally be used for services other than those operated by the former Pullman Car Company and the prestige associated with the name was valuable to InterCity. So heavy was the custom in the late 1980s (when I was working for ICOBS) on some InterCity Pullmans, such as the morning Manchester Pullman, that two catering vehicles had to be formed into the sets. ICOBS staff working on these trains were supplied with Pullman badges and were required to stand by each door to greet passengers as they boarded, much as the old Pullman Conductors had done. On the morning services the majority of coaches on InterCity Pullmans were first class and most passengers had the famous Great British Breakfast, served 'at seat' throughout the first class. On later trains, many had lunch, afternoon tea, high tea or dinner and the catering revenue was very considerable indeed. So too were the problems associated with the logistics of supplying such volumes of meals at the same time as running buffet counters on trains that could be running at up to 125mph.

Turning now from revival to the theme of demise once more: the insecure future of the paper trains and of the Night Ferry contributed to the end of the DC electric Class 71 locomotives, which were perhaps the Southern's equivalent of the Western's diesel-hydraulic Class 52 fleet, mentioned by me much earlier in the context of assertion of Regional independence. This small fleet, with its distinctive body design and combination of third-rail collector shoes and overhead pantograph, was designed for the Night Ferry, the Golden Arrow, the paper trains and Continental freight traffic on its way from the train ferry to Hither Green Continental Freight Depot.

Introduced in 1958, they demonstrated that at that time the Southern presumed that these internal South Eastern peculiarities had a secure future. Because they were DC, the locos could not work under the wires of the AC LMR or, of course, on non-electrified lines, so they were effectively prisoners on the electrified parts of the Southern. Lacking the versatility of the electro-diesel Class 73, which could go on to diesel power to pick up trains from non-electrified sidings, the Class 71 necessitated the construction of overhead gantries with DC catenary at Dover, Hither Green, Hoo Junction and Shephersdwell in order to be of any use on freight services, although some gantries dated from an earlier Southern Railway experiment with DC overhead power. The investment was a great statement of faith in the future of DC traction, but the limited scope available for these unusual locomotives meant that the money was largely wasted. Nevertheless, some of the gantries stood for many years as a memorial to Southern electric independence. Several 71s had been converted in 1967 to the electro-diesel Class 74 to provide more versatility but all were 'mothballed', or so we were told at the time, in December 1977. They never emerged, however, although 71001 has since been restored and is used for special workings.

One of the assumptions made by the Southern when the Class 71 fleet was commissioned was that Hither Green Continental Freight Depot (CFD) had a long-term future and that therefore there would be a lot of internal South Eastern freight trips to be made to and from the train ferry. But the patterns of freight distribution were changing and the fruit and vegetable business that formed such a large proportion of the Continental train ferry market of the 1960s was revolutionised first by the transfer of Covent Garden market to Nine Elms and secondly by the establishment by Transfesa of its own import depot at Paddock Wood, both these events taking place in 1974.

Having concentrated its south London freight handling at Hither Green, thus closing the depots at Ewer Street (Southwark) and Bricklayers Arms and having invested in overhead DC yard electrification and a dedicated fleet of Continental traffic locomotives, the Southern Region found itself caught

71001 using overhead DC supply at Hither Green Yard in 1976. The Class 71s were a Southern Region electric peculiarity, using third rail on the running line and overhead in yards. (Photo: Brian Garvin)

in the wind of change. The 71s could not work the non-electrified sidings at Paddock Wood, while Hither Green CFD was badly placed for the new market requirements. Equally, though, Paddock Wood was badly placed from the point of view of rail revenue. While the BRB Chairman, Richard (later Lord) Marsh, described it at the opening ceremony as a great opportunity for the railway, the harsh reality was that the train ferry vessels were filling up with traffic that earned the SNCF, in particular, some good, long-haul revenue, but which gave BR a haul of just 41 miles. At Paddock Wood the traffic, mainly from Spain, was transhipped to lorries, some of which then performed trunk hauls in the UK.

At times in the 1970s the Paddock Wood Transfesa traffic was very heavy and we would run anything up to four specials a day in addition to the booked service of about the same number. Nowadays the depot is used for other purposes and the fruit and veg trains no longer run, the market having

The Dover–Dunkerque train ferry carried more freight than goes through the Channel Tunnel today, as well as conveying the Night Ferry train from London to Paris and Brussels. 33205 and 33211 are seen loading the *Nord Pas de Calais* vessel in 1991, propelling side-by-side in order to keep the link span level. (Photo: Nick Pullen)

changed again and it having been the policy of Railfreight International in the 1980s to aim for ferry traffic that entailed a rail haul this side of the Channel at least to London and preferably far beyond. So the unmistakable smell of onions wafting through the wooden and steel-mesh sides of the old Transfesa wagons and into the open window of your rush-hour train as you passed is consigned to memory. Hither Green CFD was handed over to a firm of Japanese car importers and for a while trainloads of cars ran there, but the site then became part of the new Kent Link Networker rolling-stock berthing point.

28

Games of Monopoly

Over the years railway managers had to become increasingly aware that they were existing in an ever more competitive market. To some extent the competition was always recognised within the railway but it was 'fashionable' in political and media circles to portray the nationalised railway as either being immune to outside commercial pressures or, at least, thinking that it was. In fact, the deregulation and opening up of competition in the 1980s resulted in a considerable sharpening up of the railway's finances, marketing strategy, public relations and resource management. While the freight railway had always been susceptible to changing industrial practices, with whole markets opening and closing for it, the passenger railway market had traditionally changed more slowly.

Deregulation of road haulage took place as early as 1974, while bus services were deregulated in 1986. Both had the effect of making railway management reassess operating needs, finances and, most visibly, marketing strategy. By means of the 1980 Transport Act, the Government deregulated the long-distance coach business and for a while there were scare stories circulating to the effect that our basic passenger business was under threat. Tacky coach operations started up, such as the pot-holed open-air 'coach station' that occupied what is now the British Library site at St Pancras, at which a whole variety of coaches would ply for long-distance trade, their customers having little recourse to information regarding the operators. Bizarrely, the site was on railway land. In November 1980 I (along with Susan Carey) produced a report entitled *Coach Deregulation – The End of the Line for Railways?* in which we assessed, in particular, the impact of deregulation on the Central Division's Gatwick Airport traffic. This traffic was so important to the Division that it was sometimes mockingly called the 'Gatwick Division'. The only new operation we could find was one marketed as Gatwick Skylink and which supposedly ran from Leeds and Northampton, although only a couple of sightings of it were ever made. We concluded at the time that the amount of traffic lost was minimal. Later on, however, by the time I was working in the Dartford Area, one of Britain's busiest commuter areas, we had to take coach competition more seriously.

The main problem for us that could have arisen was that if an appreciable number of regular commuters left us, the revenue loss could not have been matched by a reduction in costs. We would still need the same infrastructure, fleet size and crew numbers to run trains with 80 per cent occupancy as we would for 90 per cent. So where would the balance come from? Either from fare increases, which would accelerate the transfer to road, or from the Public Service Obligation grant from the Government – a highly unlikely source given the political climate. In fact, as it transpired, the abstraction of traffic was nothing in comparison with the reduction in commuting caused by the later economic recession. In 1982 it was estimated that season-ticket revenue was down by 3 per cent because of coach competition, while it was down in the same year by 15 per cent because of strike action. The loss was accelerating, though, as more firms dabbled in the market and by mid 1983 the decline in revenue caused by coach competition was as much as 10 per cent in some places.

Coach firms were openly canvassing our passengers, handing out leaflets to them and offering inducements. This was fair enough in principle, but not when they came on to our premises to do it. A firm at Erith set up a coach service to London and sent someone right into the booking hall of our station to drum up support. He seemed somewhat taken aback when I told him to leave. While the railway at the time was definitely an operations-dominated business, I think many coach firms, passengers, politicians and media people would have been surprised by the extent to which we were interested in protecting our revenue and the extent to which we realised (and always had) that we were in competition with coaches, buses and cars. In the Dartford Area we countered the competition by introducing specially discounted early morning season tickets from Gravesend and Dartford to London in a revival of the old workmen's tickets. There was also a new fast service to London from these towns each morning, with a matching return service in the evening.

Some coach services were set up quite successfully but they all relied upon people whose travelling patterns were the same, day in and day out. Lots of commuters worked late occasionally or would go out in London after work and for them our regular and late evening services were essential in preference to a coach that ran once a day. The coach firms made great play of the fact that their fares were cheaper than ours, but so they should have been. They had no specific infrastructure costs to meet, fewer safety systems, no stations, no passenger information systems and they only offered services at times when they knew they could fill their vehicles. In London they would drop off and pick up passengers at the roadside regardless of the yellow lines. At one stage the City of London Police grew fed up with this and had a purge on coaches that were snarling up the traffic opposite Cannon Street station. As passengers waited on the pavement the Police simply waved the coaches on and the passengers had to troop over the road to the station and buy single tickets home by train, much to the amusement of the Booking Clerks. Politically inspired deregulation may have meant an opening up of new choices, but with it came fewer guarantees, less protection against unscrupulous operators and less accountability. Yet, oddly, the same Government, only a few years later, was introducing Passengers' Charters.

Connected with all this was the strange myth that BR was a monopoly, which, under contemporary political thinking therefore had to be broken up. This was rather like saying that Lever Bros was a monopoly because you could only buy Persil made by them, whereas, of course, you didn't have to buy Persil at all if you didn't want to. Similarly, no one had to travel by train and certainly no one had to send their parcels or freight by rail. Presumably commuters chose to travel by train because they considered it safer and quicker than driving, while business people chose to go by train from, say, London to Manchester because rail gave them a city centre to city centre service while air involved traipsing to and from the suburbs. If the alternatives were less desirable that was hardly the railway's fault. At least the choice was there, in a way that it wasn't at the time when it came to water or gas supply, for example. There was and is no railway journey for which no choice of another mode of transport exists in Britain, except possibly if you're going to Rannoch Moor. This point was made by the National Council on Inland Transport in their Memorandum to the Select Committee on Nationalised

Industries as far back as 1977 with the words, 'Railways no longer operate in monopoly or partial monopoly conditions. They are in direct competition with (a) cars, (b) lorries, (c) buses, (d) aeroplanes and (e) to a small extent, coastal shipping and waterways.'

Competition could also be very keen. When InterCity extended its discounted APEX fares to all journeys over 150 miles in September 1992, coach operators complained that the railway was offering 'unfairly' cheap special fares on the Anglo–Scottish routes, but these were the same coach operators who had earlier welcomed deregulation. InterCity's Managing Director Chris Green responded with the words, 'From today, InterCity is going on the offensive ...' But for years before that the railway had been making special offers and attracting repeat business through, for example, the marketing of Railcards, which were probably the single most successful ploy in taking people off the coaches and out of their cars.

The ability of the railway to compete in particular markets was enhanced by the creation of distinct brand names and brand products, with their own marketing strategies and target audiences. The first brand name was InterCity (1966) but for many years this operated in name only, with the Regions actually controlling the traction and rolling stock fleets as well as train running arrangements. Later, when InterCity had its own distinctive 'swallow' livery along with separate management and resources it became a more marketable product. Similarly, Network SouthEast and Regional Railways were visibly different products. The success in creating these brands, which undoubtedly increased public awareness and sales, also meant, though, that they could be more easily split up under privatisation, so the very success of the railway's marketing strategy helped towards its demise, as did its financial success, to which I alluded earlier.

Railcards were targeted specifically at certain sections of the community. They were the precursors of today's supermarket loyalty cards as they encouraged repeat business and brand loyalty. Sometimes we had promotions to launch or relaunch these cards and the most memorable of these was the relaunch of the Senior Citizens Railcard in the 1970s, when it was decided to allow all cardholders a free day's travel one Saturday. I recall that we had to 'strengthen' many trains because of demand and also that we had to hire a bus to take some of the people from Ashford to Rye, so inundated were the service trains.

At 'local' level, on stations, we were encouraged by the marketing people to promote the sales of Railcards and of other offers, both through poster advertising and by getting Booking Clerks to mention them to customers. However, because until the late 1980s all station management was operations biased, this sort of activity was regarded as being in some way superficial and not proper railway work. In the early 1980s there was one Relief Station Manager on the South Eastern who would inspect all the poster boards to ensure that the correct posters were being displayed and he was regarded with wry amusement for doing so, as if, to use the parlance of the next decade, he had 'lost the plot'. Similarly, when in 1982 I decided to launch a 'blanket' poster campaign on the Woolwich line to monitor the success, or otherwise, of poster advertising at stations, my efforts were dismissed as irrelevant by the Area management. Nevertheless, by saturating Charlton station for a month with posters for Seaside Savers and Belvedere station with posters for Family Railcards I was able to demonstrate increased sales of the 'plugged' products at each station whilst maintaining sales of other products at the same levels as before. Railway poster sites on stations were not just there to make the place look pretty, as most local managers thought – they could be used to sell and were surely meant for just that.

Despite the national efforts of the adverting agencies and image makers, the management of brand and promotional names was lamentable in some cases. The Selective Pricing Policy had been introduced in 1969, followed in 1973 by the National Reduced Fares Plan with brand names such as Awayday, which were heavily advertised in the media. But, right up to the day the last BR passenger train ran, what did it say on your ticket when you bought an Awayday? 'CHEAP DAY RETURN'. It was as if the railway was ashamed of its own branding. Similarly, Network SouthEast was set up as a new organisation to run all the Home Counties railways and was promoted by branding trains and stations. But was the name ever in the telephone directory? No. Under 'British Rail' the entry told you which number to ring for information on services – 'local' and 'national'. So why invent the names Network SouthEast and InterCity if you then describe them as 'local' and 'national'? Only Red Star had sufficient self-confidence to have its name correctly listed.

As it became clear that the railway was to be split up, so the problems of brand mismanagement became worse. NSE routes had individual brand names and symbols, such as Kent Coast and Great Northern, which, while an attractive idea in itself, led to the ludicrous branding muddle seen on stations – the BR symbol, the NSE symbol and the route symbol, each detracting from the integrity of the others. The Divisions of NSE (which in themselves were an organisational convenience and formed no part of the marketing strategy) failed to adhere strictly to the brand names within their own jurisdictions. For example, in the Kent Coast brand area, there were frequently to be seen posters referring to 'South Eastern' services rather than Kent Coast, perhaps in anticipation of NSE's demise in 1994, when responsibility passed temporarily to the South Eastern Train Company, but more likely because railway people lacked brand discipline.

At Victoria, years after NSE had been established, you could still hear announcements concerning 'suburban' or 'local' services, when the brand name was 'South London Lines'. Trains were advertised as 'the mainline service to ...' or 'the fast train to ...', when the timetable had them branded as 'Network Express'. As things spiralled out of control, some trains were even given two brand names, neither of which was enforced. Thus some Kent Coast Network Expresses were also, for a while, branded as 'Kent Clipper' while some Sussex Coast Network Expresses became also 'Capital Coast Express'. This was branding gone wild and showed that NSE had descended into an anarchy of local whims. Chris Green's 1986 vision of Network SouthEast as 'one railway for Londoners', itself a mere thirty-eight years after nationalisation, could have been expected to have delivered just that, but turned out to be short-lived as his successors lost sight of his aim. But as NSE was about to be disbanded in any case, did it matter if its Divisions strayed into their own flights of fancy?

What a far cry this all was from the days of the old BR *Corporate Image Manual*, that dullest of books that dictated, amongst other things, that stations should all be painted black and white and that posters should all be of the same basic format. Liveries, station signs and lettering styles were all controlled by the Design Research Unit in the interests of a standardised approach throughout BR. Uniforms were to be black, grey or dark blue, depending upon grade, and new station premises could be selected from a catalogue of cheap prefabricated buildings. Hence the proliferation of the tacky 'clasp' style buildings, first built in 1966 at Fleet in Hampshire (from where I travelled to school at the time, behind steam traction) and since built and, thankfully, demolished elsewhere. What a contrast there is between these dreary 'utility' buildings and the later generation of rebuilt stations such as Rainham (Kent), East Croydon and the Victoria Island complex. Her Majesty the Queen opened the new Euston station on 14 October 1968: built to the basic design of W.R. Headley, who was also responsible for the gloomy Birmingham New Street, it was a black and white memorial to an age of blandness and destruction. But on 5 December 1991 she opened the restored and redeveloped Liverpool Street station, a brilliant combination of the old and the new. In his book *British Society since 1945*, Arthur Marwick comments that (in the 1960s), 'At last technology was allowed to influence artistic form,' but railway architects learnt over the ensuing years that they didn't necessarily have to destroy the old in order to update facilities and the new Liverpool Street must be one of Britain's most stunning displays of how technology can accommodate a combination of artistic forms through architectural skill, sensitivity and imagination. Whilst Euston and Birmingham New Street stand in lasting memory of the Corporate Identity era, Liverpool Street stands for an architectural individuality that enhances its business objectives far more than the Corporate Image ever did.*

Nicholas Ind (in *The Corporate Image*), appears to regret the passing of BR's Corporate Identity, quoting Frederique Huygen's 1989 comment that 'over the years ... the corporate identity and equipment have fallen victim to the ravages of time'. But both Ind and Huygen seem not to have realised that by 1989 there was, in effect, no longer any one body to have a coherent corporate identity. Furthermore, the very words 'Corporate Image', as in the title of Ind's book, had become an anathema in an era in which it was important not to appear to be part of a large organisation. Hence Fremlin's beer and Beefeater restaurants appeared not to be owned by Whitbread while Habitat and Mothercare seemed to be unrelated to each other.

Somewhere between the dictatorial imposition of a standardised corporate mediocrity and the unchecked diversity of BR's last years there may be a happy medium, but it will presumably never be found now. The cohesive InterCity image of around 1990 was probably the closest and best we shall

* 2018 update: London King's Cross and its neighbour St Pancras each now boldly demonstrate the idea of the old and the new complementing each other.

The redeveloped Liverpool Street, with its inspired juxtaposition of old and new, is a stark contrast to the redevelopments of Euston and Birmingham New Street in the 1960s, when the vogue was for destruction of the old at all costs. (Photo: Nick Derbyshire Architects)

see, with its dreamy sepia TV adverts and solid, reassuring train decor. As long-term investment, such as is needed for station projects and rolling-stock development, dries up in some of the short-term franchising areas, we may be left with decaying buildings and trains with a proliferation of sometimes tacky and transient franchise liveries, house colours and symbols as Britain continues (for the time being) as the only country in the European Community without a national train-running organisation.

Conclusion

The 'immortal' Regions, those bastions of pre-nationalisation railway heritage, were finally laid to rest more than forty years after the system went into state ownership. Divisions too were abolished and for a while the very word 'Division' was taboo; that is, until the emerging business sectors adopted the word again, in true cyclical fashion. Areas went also, but I am sure that word will emerge again at some time in the future as new organisations to run the railway come and go. Perhaps the slightly bizarre word 'Territory' might even be resurrected. One thing that is certain is that the organisational roundabout will never stop as new Governments, owners and operators seek that elusive goal of the ideal way to manage a railway. While in the 1970s that roundabout was an overloaded, groaning fairground carousel struggling to turn, it became in the space of twenty or so years more like a centrifuge with railway people hanging on for dear life. And as the centrifuge was made to spin ever faster, so it shook itself apart: Sir Peter Parker's 'crumbling edge' of the 1970s became a crumbling whole of the '90s.

The years covered by this book saw a process of management and political change that developed from a quicksand of lethargy through an era of imposition to one of implementation of 'kneejerk' and rather vague ideological dogma that had little place for skill, expertise or the lessons of experience. It had been decided that Britain's nationalised railways, once advertised as 'the backbone of the nation', were to be run by people who knew little about the subject and who appeared to think that all industry was, or should be, as simple as that of a street-trader selling one product for a few hours a day. All that can be hoped for is that the tighter regulatory regime of the 1997 Labour Government with its Strategic Rail Authority will curb the excesses of those who entered the industry with the sole aim of making a fast buck and that the true long-term interests of the industry and its users will prevail.* The very fact that the Government gives the private sector operators more subsidy than it gave to BR in its last years should mean, one would hope, that they should be held accountable to the Government and the taxpayer as well as to their shareholders.

But whichever ideological brand it becomes accountable to and however it may be organised, Britain's railway remains a vital part of the country's infrastructure. And increasingly so as the true costs (financial, environmental and social) of road dependency become clearer. Behind all the arguments, though, and behind all the political and media hype, thousands of people who really do know how to run a railway – ordinary, everyday people who have seen, done and will recognise many of the things I have described in this book – have been getting on with their jobs and carry on doing so, day in, day out, night in, night out in one of Britain's most important, lasting and diverse industries. Long may they continue to do so.

* 2018 update: Since I wrote this in 2002 there has been very little progress in this direction by the Labour Government or its successors. The inherent weaknesses of the franchising system are as evident now as they were then.

Bibliography

Most of the text is anecdotal, but the following were consulted for verification of dates, figures, etc:

Modern Railways, various issues, 1970–99.

Railway World, various issues, 1973–93.

Rail, various issues, 1994–99.

Railnews, various dates 1980–99.

The Times, various dates, 1973–94.

The Journal of Transport History, March 1993.

BR operating and industrial relations publications, various, 1956–91.

BRB Annual Report & Accounts, various years.

National Freight Corporation, Annual Report, 1969.

House of Commons Papers, various.

New Opportunities for the Railways, HM Government White Paper, 1992.

The Birth of British Rail, Michael R. Bonavia, George Allen & Unwin, 1979.

British Railways Today & Tomorrow, G. Freeman Allen, Ian Allan, 1959.

British Rail after Beeching, G. Freeman Allen, Ian Allan, 1965.

Man of the Rail, A.J. Pearson, George Allen & Unwin, 1967.

Sir Herbert Walker's Southern Railway, Charles F. Klapper, Ian Allan, 1973.

The Great Railway Conspiracy, David Henshaw, Leading Edge, 1991.

New Directions for British Railways?, Glaister & Travers, Institute of Economic Affairs, 1993.

British Marshalling Yards, Michael Rhodes, OPC, 1988.

Night Ferry, George Behrend and Gary Buchanan, Jersey Artists Ltd, 1985.

The Corporate Image, Nicholas Ind, Kogan Page, 1990.

Transport Planning for Greater London, Buchanan/Bursey/Lewis/ Mullen, Saxon House, 1980.

British Society since 1945, Arthur Marwick, Penguin, 1982.

The author.